Vulnerable Witnesses within Family and Criminal Proceedings: Protections, Safeguards and Sanctions

Vulnerable Witnesses within Family and Criminal Proceedings: Protections, Safeguards and Sanctions

Frank Feehan QC, 1KBW
Caroline Harris, Barrister, 1KBW

Contributors
Andrew Baughan, Barrister, 1KBW
Martha Holmes, Barrister, 1KBW
Anna Sutcliffe, Barrister, 1KBW
Max Turnell, Barrister, 1KBW

Bloomsbury Professional
LONDON • DUBLIN • EDINBURGH • NEW YORK • NEW DELHI • SYDNEY

BLOOMSBURY PROFESSIONAL
Bloomsbury Publishing Plc
41–43 Boltro Road, Haywards Heath, RH16 1BJ, UK

BLOOMSBURY and the Diana logo are trademarks of Bloomsbury Publishing Plc

British Library Cataloguing-in-Publication Data

A catalogue record for this book is available from the British Library.

ISBN: PB: 978 1 52650 723 5
ePDF: 978 1 52650 725 9
ePub: 978 1 52650 724 2

Typeset by Compuscript Ltd, Shannon
Printed and bound by CPI Group (UK) Ltd, Croydon, CR0 4YY

To find out more about our authors and books visit www.bloomsburyprofessional.com. Here you will find extracts, author information, details of forthcoming events and the option to sign up for our newsletters

Contents

Abbreviations and acronyms

ABE	Achieving Best Evidence
AJA 1970	Administration of Justice Act 1970
A-G	Attorney General
A-G's ref	Attorney General's reference
CDA 1998	Crime and Disorder Act 1998
CAJA 2009	Coroners and Justice Act 2009
CCA 2013	Crime and Courts Act 2013
CJA 2003	Criminal Justice Act 2003
CJPOA 1994	Criminal Justice and Public Order Act 1994
CJIA 2008	Criminal Justice and Immigration Act 2008
CJPA 2001	Criminal Justice and Police Act 2001
CrimPD	Consolidated Criminal Practice Directions
CPR 2015	Criminal Procedure Rules 2015, SI 2015/1490
FPR 2010	Family Procedure Rules 2019, SI 2010/2955
LAA	Legal Aid Agency
LASPO	Legal Aid and Sentencing and Punishment of Offenders Act 2012
NFG	Notes for Further Guidance (for the PACE codes)
PACE 1984	Police and Criminal Evidence Act 1984
PCC(S)A 2000	Powers of Criminal Courts (Sentencing) Act 2000
PoCA 2002	Proceeds of Crime Act 2002
SOA	Sexual Offences Act 2003
SOPO	Sexual Offences Prevention Order
YJCEA 1999	Youth Justice and Criminal Evidence Act 1999

Table of Cases

[*All references are to paragraph numbers.*]

S

Table of Statutes

[*All references are to paragraph numbers.*]

Table of Statutory Instruments

[*All references are to paragraph numbers.*]

Table of Codes of Practice and Conventions

[*All references are to paragraph numbers.*]

Chapter 1

SUMMARY OF THE PURPOSE OF THE HANDBOOK

1.1 The area of law relating to vulnerable people and how they can be assisted in order for them to be able to fairly participate within family and criminal proceedings is one that has developed considerably over the last decade and one that it is hoped by the authors of this book will continue to positively develop in the future to ensure that the most vulnerable can be protected and assisted to engage fairly in these proceedings whatever their role within them may be.

The progress made in the area of criminal law was noted by Lady Justice Hallett who recently stated:

> 'In recent years the criminal justice system has made huge strides in its efforts to ensure that vulnerable witnesses are treated fairly and appropriately during the trial process. This court has strived to ensure that a proper balance is maintained between the interests of a witness and the rights of a defendant.'[1]

Lady Justice Hallett also reminded those acting in such proceeding that 'we should add that every advocate (and trial judge) is expected to ensure that they are up to date with current best practice in the treatment of vulnerable witnesses.'

Within family law there has been progress with the Family Procedure Rules 2010[2] being amended to include Part 3A Vulnerable persons participation in proceedings and giving evidence and Practice Direction (PD) 3AA Vulnerable persons: participation in proceedings and giving evidence. In the recent case of *PS v BP*[3] with respect to vulnerable witnesses giving evidence in family proceedings Hayden J provides a number of helpful observations.[4] Hayden J states that his 'observations' are intended to be a 'life belt until a rescue craft arrives as there is real need for there to be a legal structure.' Therefore, we will need to wait to see whether there will be further developments in the near future.

1 *Regina v YGM* [2018] EWCA Crim 2458.
2 SI 2010/2955.
3 [2018] EWHC 1987 (Fam) (27 July 2018).
4 Ibid, at [34].

1.2 *Summary of the Purpose of the Handbook*

The aim of this text is to provide a stage by stage guide for practitioners in both family and criminal cases with respect to vulnerable people who are connected/party to those proceedings. The criminal jurisdiction has a much more codified approach to the giving of evidence by those now seen as vulnerable which has been in place and been developing for a considerably longer period than in the family law jurisdiction. A subsidiary aim of this book is to allow both jurisdictions to be aware of how different and how similar the approaches are. Family law may have much to learn from criminal law (for instance in the use of a central register of intermediaries by the NCA[5]) whereas criminal law may gain some insight into the more tailored approach to the taking of evidence seen in the wide variation of special measures employed in family cases.

1.2 There are parts of this book that all should read. In many serious fact-finding cases in the family law jurisdiction the rules concerning the initial stages of investigation by the police will be of vital importance in ensuring that procedures aimed at securing best evidence both before and during Achieving Best Evidence interviews are followed. Similarly, the section concerning joint hearings (still rare in the experience of the authors of this book, largely perhaps because of ignorance as to what may be achieved by them and how they are conducted) may be of use.

1.3 It is imperative that those who are involved in proceedings are able to fairly participate in them; this is the case in criminal proceedings whether they are witnesses or defendants and in family proceedings whether they are witnesses or parties. As anyone who has experience with court proceedings and the preceding period will understand, both pre-proceedings and the proceedings themselves can be highly stressful for those not familiar with them and can be a minefield of the unknown. If the person involved is also a vulnerable person this can make the experience all the more stressful and their ability to fairly and fully participate hampered. It is imperative therefore that practitioners are aware of the need to consider vulnerable people connected with proceedings and how they can be assisted at all stages throughout proceedings and also prior to proceedings.

1.4 With respect to criminal proceedings this handbook involves a consideration of all the stages from both a defence and prosecution perspective. This text addresses cases from the pre- to post-proceeding stages, setting out a step-by-step list of considerations at each stage as well as providing a detailed analysis of the key considerations, including interviews of vulnerable suspects, achieving best evidence interviews and complainants in proceedings involving allegations of sexual abuse.

1.5 With respect to family proceedings there is a consideration of all stages of family proceedings including the pre-issuing of proceedings and post final order.

1.6 The handbook has divided the chapters primarily into a stage-by-stage approach as well as there being a more detailed analysis of key topics; for example the court's approach to child witnesses, intermediaries and the official solicitor.

---

5 Registered intermediaries are only available for witnesses and not defendants.

1.7 As it is not unusual for there to be interconnecting family and criminal proceedings and it is of great assistance for practitioners to have a clear understanding of the rules and considerations in both sets of proceedings, there is consideration of the overlap between the sets of proceedings as well as a consideration of the possibility of a joint hearing and how those joint hearings should normally be conducted.

1.8 This handbook looks at not only the legal considerations with respect to vulnerable people being able to provide evidence in proceedings but also at the protections and special measures available not only while proceedings are ongoing but also both pre- and post-proceedings, including anonymity and protective orders.

1.9 The text cites the relevant legislation, case law and also the key legal resources that are available to practitioners, including the Advocate's Gateway.

Chapter 2

GENERAL PRINCIPLES AS TO THE EXAMINATION OF WITNESSES

INTRODUCTION

2.1 This handbook is intended as a guide to the ever-developing law in relation to vulnerable witnesses. It is necessary however to give some basic guidance to the law in relation to witnesses in general and the relevant rules relating to the examination of witnesses in court. It is not within the scope of this handbook to address every detail of the general law and users should consult more widely in the literature where an issue arises which is not dealt with here.

CRIMINAL CASES

Examination-in-chief

2.2 In criminal cases examination-in-chief is conducted orally with the witness present in court except where permission is given by the court either to adduce that evidence by: (a) live video link;[1] (b) a pre-recorded interview;[2] or (c) a written statement.[3] Vulnerable witnesses who give evidence in the circumstances considered in this handbook will often fall into one of those exceptions; however the general principles of examination-in-chief will apply subject only to those changes necessary in the circumstances.

Leading questions

2.3 Leading questions may not usually be asked in examination-in-chief or re-examination.[4] However, leading questions may be permitted by a court where

1 Criminal Procedure Rules 2015, SI 2015/1490.
2 Dealt with in detail later in this book.
3 CJA 2003, s 120.
4 For a recent example of authority for this trite proposition see *Pop v R* [2003] UKPC 40.

such is agreed in relation to uncontroversial matters, where a witness is classed as 'hostile' (but not merely 'unresponsive');[5] or where in the interests of justice it is necessary to allow leading questions where a witness suffers from intellectual or communication problems.[6] In such circumstances the court must enable vulnerable witnesses to give their best evidence.[7]

2.4 In a pre-recorded Achieving Best Evidence (ABE) interview[8] the rule against leading questions still applies and where such is to be tendered as the evidence in chief of that witness the interview may be excluded as unreliable and/or inadmissible if pressure has been applied by the use of leading questions to obtain evidence.[9] Paragraphs from the Ministry of Justice guidance entitled Achieving Best Evidence in Criminal Proceedings Guidance on interviewing victims and witnesses, and guidance on using special measures the that may assist Practitioners when apply to excluding ABE interviews which contain leading questions are found at paras 3.61 and 3.62 which state as follows:

> 'Leading Questions
>
> 3.61 A leading question is one that implies the answer or assumes facts that are likely to be in dispute. For a question to be construed as leading will depend not only on the nature of the question but also on what the witness has already said in the interview. When a leading question is put improperly to a witness giving evidence at court, opposing counsel can make an objection before the witness replies. This, of course, does not apply during recorded interviews, but it is likely that, should the interview be submitted as evidence in court proceedings, portions might be edited out or, in the worst case, the whole recording ruled inadmissible.
>
> 3.62 In addition to legal objections, research indicates that witnesses' responses to leading questions tend to be determined more by the manner of questioning than by valid remembering. Leading questions can serve not merely to influence the answer given, but may also significantly distort the witness's memory in the direction implied by the leading question. For these reasons, leading questions should only be used as a last resort, where all other questioning strategies have failed to elicit any kind of response. On occasion, a leading question can produce relevant information which has not been led by the question. If this does occur, interviewers should take care not to follow up this question with further leading questions. Rather, they should revert to open-ended questions in the first instance or specific-closed questions.'

---

5 Eg, *R v Manning* [1968] Crim LR 675.

6 Eg, *R v H* [2003] EWCA Crim 1208.

7 *Criminal Practice Direction 2015* [2015] EWCA Crim 1567.

8 Ie, an interview conducted under the 'Achieving Best Evidence' Guidelines.

9 See *Re N (A Minor) (Sexual Abuse: Video Evidence)* [1997] 1 WLR 153; *TW v A City Council* [2011] 1 FLR 1597; *Re W v Re F (Children)* [2015] EWCA Civ 1300; *Re E (A Child) (Evidence)* [2016] EWCA Civ 473, [2017] 1 FLR 1675.

Hostile and unhelpful witnesses

2.5 A witness who is found on application to the court to be adverse to the party calling them may be treated as 'hostile' and cross-examined by that party. A hostile witness is not one who is merely forgetful or disappointing, but one who is unwilling to tell the truth or is patently adverse to the case they were called to support.[10]

2.6 Where a witness is merely unhelpful through lack of memory, or in other respects (such as by reason of any intellectual deficit or lack of understanding) fails to 'come up to proof' that witness is not hostile and may not be cross-examined. A party may however call other witnesses to make good the evidential deficit even if that evidence contradicts the unhelpful witness or proves that their evidence is wrong or mistaken.[11] Where a witness seems confused or merely fails to remember the contents of a statement of evidence they may be allowed to refresh their memory by reading a copy of the statement.[12] This may regularly apply to witnesses who are vulnerable in a general intellectual sense rather than the particular sense dealt with later in this handbook.

Refreshing memory generally

2.7 A witness who is to give evidence in a criminal trial will often have waited many weeks or even months between having made their statement and giving their evidence. It is therefore understandable that a witness may be assisted by rereading their statement prior to giving evidence in order to refresh their memory. It is standard practice for a witness on attending court to be given their statement to reread prior to going into court to give evidence. Further, once a witness is giving evidence it is not uncommon for a witness to wish to refresh their memory from their previous statement. Therefore the court may permit the witness to refresh their memory during their evidence. The general provisions are contained in the Criminal Justice Act 2003, s 139: a witness giving oral evidence in criminal proceedings about any matter may at any stage in the course of doing so refresh his memory of it from a document made or verified by him at an earlier time if: (1) he states in his oral evidence that the document records his recollection of the matter at that earlier time; and (2) his recollection of the matter is likely to have been significantly better at that time than it is at the time of his oral evidence.[13]

2.8 Where a witness has an intellectual deficit causing difficulties with reading it is sufficient that the statement was read to them.[14] It is likely that such would have to be the procedure on refreshing the witness's memory from the document and the circumstances of that would be a matter for the trial judge.

---

10 See *R v Manning* (above); and Criminal Procedure Act 1865, s 3.

11 Eg, *R v Osborne and Virtue* [1973] QB 678.

12 *R v Maw* [1994] Crim LR 841; see also CJA 2003, s 139.

13 CJA 2003, s 139(1)(a) and (b).

14 See *R v Gordon* [2002] EWCA Crim 412.

2.9 The trial judge will decide whether the criteria of the Criminal Justice Act 2003, s 139(1)(a) and (b) are met and has a residual discretion to refuse to permit memory to be refreshed in this manner.[15]

The Criminal Justice Act 2003, s 120 contains provisions as to evidential value of previous statements of a witness when they are admitted in evidence during their oral evidence including when a statement is used to refresh the witness's memory.

Credibility affected by vulnerability

2.10 When considering the admissibility of either positive 'good' character evidence or negative 'bad' character evidence of a non-defendant these are the general principles. With respect to bad character evidence the provisions of admissibility are set out in the Criminal Justice Act 2003, s 100 which states that:

> 'in criminal proceedings evidence of the bad character of a person other than the defendant is admissible if and only if:
>
> (a) it is important explanatory evidence;
>
> (b) it has substantial probative value in relation to a matter which:
>
> (i) is a matter in issue in the proceedings; and
>
> (ii) is of substantial importance in the context of the case as a whole; or
>
> (c) all parties to the proceedings agree to the evidence being admissible.'

With respect to good character evidence, the general rule is that such evidence is not admissible as a party is not permitted to bolster the credibility of a witness called on their behalf by calling other evidence that solely goes to credibility. This is only permitted where there has been an attempt to attack credibility and such evidence may then be permitted in rebuttal. Such evidence, when in relation merely to general allegations of untruthfulness, is restricted to a general rebuttal as to reputation.[16] Where such an attack is based upon an intellectual deficit then it will usually consist of expert evidence and therefore expert evidence may be called to rebut,[17] or even as part of the prosecution case where it is possible to anticipate the evidence being called on the part of the defence.[18]

Cross-examination

2.11 Cross-examination of prosecution and defence witnesses is subject to the same principles. There are few specific restrictions on the questions put in cross-examination save that there are certain statutory restrictions on

15 *R v McAfee* [2006] EWCA Crim 2914.
16 Eg, *R v Lodge* [2013] EWCA Crim 987.
17 See *R v Robinson* [1994] 98 Cr App Rep 370.
18 Ibid.

cross-examination by defendants in person[19] and that cross-examination is subject to any reasonable restriction as to time that the court may impose under the overriding objective in the Criminal Procedure Rules 2015 (CPR 2015).[20] Subject to that discretion to maintain proper progress, cross-examination may be conducted for numerous reasons, but usually to challenge or undermine a witness's evidence in chief or to use a 'friendly' witness to assist the defence case.[21]

2.12 It is well established that where a prosecution witness is unable to undergo cross-examination or becomes too ill or too distressed to continue the judge has a discretion to halt the trial but they can also let it continue and address any potential unfairness to the defendant by careful warnings and directions to the jury.[22]

2.13 Advocates are subject to professional rules as to the matters which may be put to witnesses in questioning – in particular the questions must be relevant.

Failure to cross-examine

2.14 The normal rule[23] is that where a party does not cross-examine a witness on any matter that party is taken to accept the truth of the witness on that issue and is not thereafter permitted to contradict it, call evidence to the contrary or address the jury to the effect that it cannot rely on the evidence.[24]

Restrictions on cross-examination by defendant in person

2.15 A defendant is ordinarily entitled to cross-examine on his own behalf.[25] However, there are now statutory restrictions on this right. The Youth Justice and Criminal Evidence Act 1999 (YJCEA 1999), s 34 provides in relation to adult complainants in sexual offence cases:

> 'No person charged with a sexual offence may in any criminal proceedings cross-examine in person a witness who is the complainant, either—
>
> (a) in connection with that offence, or
>
> (b) in connection with any other offence (of whatever nature) with which that person is charged in the proceedings.[26]

---

19 See paras **2.15–2.18**.

20 SI 2015/1490. Under r 3.2(e) there is a requirement of active case management on the part of the court and this includes ensuring that all evidence (including disputed evidence) is presented in the shortest and clearest way.

21 Sometimes also the prosecution case: see *R v Ross* [2007] EWCA Crim 1457.

22 *R v Pipe* [2014] EWCA Crim 2570; *R v Stretton* [1986] 86 Cr App Rep 7.

23 This rule has been held not to apply in magistrates' courts – *O'Connell v Adams* [1973] Crim LR 313 and *Wilkinson v DPP* (2003) 167 JP 229. However, in the experience of the authors of this book this rule is abided by in the magistrates' court.

24 *R v Hart* [1932] Cr App Rep 202; *R v Wood Green Crown Ct ex p Taylor* [1995] Crim LR 879.

25 *R v Brown* [1998] 2 Cr App Rep 364.

26 YJCEA 1999, s 34.

In relation to child complainants and child witnesses to the commission of the offence there is similar provision but in relation to a wider range of offences:

> (1) No person charged with an offence to which this section applies may in any criminal proceedings cross-examine in person a protected witness, either—
>
> (a) in connection with that offence, or
>
> (b) in connection with any other offence (of whatever nature) with which that person is charged in the proceedings.
>
> (2) For the purposes of subsection (1) a 'protected witness' is a witness who—
>
> (a) either is the complainant or is alleged to have been a witness to the commission of the offence to which this section applies, and
>
> (b) either is a child or falls to be cross-examined after giving evidence in chief (whether wholly or in part)—
>
> (i) by means of a video recording made (for the purposes of section 27) at a time when the witness was a child, or
>
> (ii) in any other way at any such time.'

2.16 The offences to which that section applies are: (a) sexual offences against children, in relation to which protection is given to all persons under 17 years; and (b) kidnapping, false imprisonment, abduction and offences of assault in relation to which protection is given to persons under 14 years.[27]

2.17 In a provision also likely to be invoked in cases where a witness is vulnerable, a residual provision in YJCEA 1999, s 36 permits the prosecution to apply for similar protection for any witness in any case[28] to which ss 34 and 35 do not apply. Thus, the trial judge may prohibit any defendant from cross-examining a witness (not restricted to complainants or eye-witnesses) if it appears that the quality of the evidence would be diminished by the cross-examination being conducted in person or improved by it not being conducted in person.[29] A range of non-exhaustive considerations apply to the determination, including the relationship (if any) between the witness and accused, the nature of the issues and likely questions and the views of the witness.[30]

2.18 Where a prohibition is made, the court must invite the defendant to procure representation and give him a set time to do so or, in default, and after due consideration, may appoint representation on his behalf.[31]

---

27 YJCEA 1999, s 35(3), (4) and (5).
28 Except a co-accused: YJCEA 1999, s 36(4)(a).
29 YJCEA 1999, s 36(2).
30 YJCEA 1999, s 36(3).
31 YJCEA 1999, s 38.

Further protection of complainants in sex cases

2.19 In addition to protection from cross-examination by their alleged assailants, those witnesses in criminal cases who are also complainants in allegations of sexual offences are protected either from questions being asked or evidence being adduced in relation to their sexual conduct save where the court gives permission on application from a defendant. The court must not give permission unless the question relates to a relevant issue and that issue is not mere consent, unless: (1) the issue of consent is in relation to conduct at or about the time of the offence in question; or (2) the issue relates to conduct that is so similar to the conduct complained of, or other conduct that occurred at or about the time of the alleged offence, that it cannot reasonably be explained as a coincidence.[32]

2.20 The prosecution may adduce evidence of sexual conduct but only to the extent necessary to allow the evidence to be rebutted or explained by the defendant.[33]

2.21 There is an enormous body of law in relation to this protection which is beyond the scope of this chapter.

Vulnerable witnesses

2.22 The developing law on the matter of vulnerable witnesses is the subject matter of the rest of this handbook but in summary the court in the criminal jurisdiction has a duty to take every reasonable step to encourage and facilitate the attendance of witnesses and to facilitate the participation of any person in the proceedings.[34] This includes giving directions for the appropriate treatment and questioning of a witness (including the defendant) especially where the questioning takes place via an intermediary.[35]

Vulnerable witness – limitations on cross examination

2.23 CPR 2015, r 3.9(7) requires that where directions for addressing the appropriate treatment and questioning of vulnerable witnesses are required first to invite representations by the parties and by any intermediary; and then subsequently set ground rules for the conduct of the questioning, often referred to there being a ground rules hearing. The ground rules may include:

'(i) a direction relieving a party of any duty to put that party's case to a witness or a defendant in its entirety,

(ii) directions about the manner of questioning;

(iii) directions about the duration of questioning;

32 YJCEA 1999, s 41(1)–(3).
33 YJCEA 1999, s 41(5).
34 CPR 2015, r 3.9(3).
35 CPR 2015, r 3.9(6).

(iv) if necessary, directions about the questions that may or may not be asked;

(v) where there is more than one defendant, the allocation among them of the topics about which a witness may be asked; and

(vi) directions about the use of models, plans, body maps or similar aids to help communicate a question or an answer.'

FAMILY CASES

2.24 The general provisions as to the examination of witnesses in family cases are significantly different from the approach in criminal cases in that, in common with the ordinary civil jurisdiction, the family court has a wide discretionary power to control the evidence in each case by giving directions on the issues to be tried, those on which evidence is required, the nature of the evidence and the manner in which it is provided. The family court must give effect to the overriding objective of dealing with cases 'justly'.[36] Dealing with cases justly includes: (1) setting timetables; (2) deciding upon the issues to be investigated and those where such in not necessary; and (3) deciding the procedure to be followed. This broad discretion means that each case is more likely to be managed according to its particular facts and that the competing interests of the parties are more likely to require specifically tailored solutions.

Examination-in-chief

2.25 As with any civil court the conduct of examination-in-chief in the family court is significantly restricted. This is the result of the general power to control the evidence.

2.26 In the family court the court may control the evidence by giving directions as to: (a) the issues on which it requires evidence; (b) the nature of the evidence which it requires to decide those issues; and (c) the way in which the evidence is to be placed before the court.[37]

2.27 The court may use its power under the Family Procedure Rules 2010 (FPR 2010) to exclude evidence that would otherwise be admissible and may permit a party to adduce evidence, or to seek to rely on a document, in respect of which that party has failed to comply with the requirements of the rules.[38]

2.28 The general rule is that evidence is given in writing for the purposes of interim hearings[39] and orally at final hearings. Video link evidence may

36 FPR 2010, SI 2010/2955, r 1.1.

37 FPR 2010, r 21.1(1).

38 FPR 2010, r 21.1(2) and (3).

39 This does not however apply to hearings for secure accommodation orders, interim care orders or interim supervision orders – FPR 2010, r 22.2(2).

be permitted.[40] Any party called to give evidence at a final hearing will ordinarily have been ordered to file a witness statement.[41] The witness statement of any party or witness stands as their evidence in chief[42] and questions may only be asked of that person with the permission of the court to amplify the statement and to give evidence on new matters that have arisen since the statement was served.[43] Permission will only be granted if there is good reason not to confine the evidence to the statement.[44]

Evidence as to credibility

2.29 Where a person has been cross-examined as to credibility it is permissible to adduce evidence to re-establish credit. This is so under very old authority.[45] Where it is to be said that an intellectual or communication difficulty gives rise to problems of credibility, expert evidence may be permitted to rebut that suggestion prior to cross-examination on the point just as is permitted in the criminal jurisdiction.[46]

Hostile and unhelpful witnesses

2.30 Given the provision of written statements this is less likely than in the criminal court; nevertheless the same principles apply. Notably, however, where a witness is merely unfavourable rather than hostile other evidence may be called which corrects or contradicts that witness including evidence of a statement made by that witness on a previous occasion.[47] Calling such corrective evidence does not impugn all of that witness's evidence. The truth of the matter is then for the judge.

Cross-examination

Limitations on cross examination

2.31 As part of its power to control evidence the family court may limit cross-examination, both as to issues and duration.[48] However, in practice most courts will allow cross-examination which can be shown to be relevant and necessary. There is no statutory bar on examination as to any matter; however it is likely that intrusive and unnecessary questions as to sexual conduct will be subject to judicial intervention and it is submitted that the statutory bar which applies in

40 FPR 2010, r 22.3.
41 Different considerations will apply to some vulnerable and child witnesses – FPR 2010, PD3AA.
42 FPR 2010, r 22.6(2).
43 FPR 2010, r 22.6(3).
44 FPR 2010, r 22.6(4).
45 *Annesley v Earl of Anglesea* [1743] 17 State Tr 1139.
46 See para **1.6**.
47 See Civil Evidence Act 1965, ss 1–4, 6(3).
48 FPR 2010, r 22.1(1)–(4).

the criminal court will be seen as a proper guideline to be taken into account in practice in the family courts.[49]

2.32 At present there is no regulation to prevent cross-examination of a complainant by an accused, a matter which has been the subject of significant concern by the President of the Family Division.[50]

Purpose of cross-examination

2.33 As in the criminal court, the purpose of cross-examination is to undermine the evidence-in-chief of the witness, to impugn credibility, to draw attention to facts to which a witness has not referred but which are relevant. Where a court is to be asked to disbelieve or criticise a witness that witness should be cross examined; a failure to cross-examine a witness as to a relevant point will be treated as acceptance of the evidence unless otherwise contradicted.[51]

2.34 In particular the importance of allowing a witness in family proceedings to respond to the allegations against them has been emphasised in a number of authorities. In *Re B (Children),*[52] Ward LJ held at paragraph 33:

> 'Those findings amount to a finding that the mother knew that she had shaken the child and was lying to protect herself. Mr Braithwaite for the local authority concedes very fairly that he did not suggest to her that she had fabricated this evidence. He did not challenge her honesty; neither did the judge. It is, in my judgment, wrong that serious findings of this kind could be made without the witness having had the opportunity to deal with them. It is unfair and it amounts to a serious procedural irregularity, which would compel this court, in my judgment, to send the matter back for further hearing, so that the family have a fair opportunity to defend themselves.'[53]

Recent authority from the Court of Appeal[54] has cast doubt on the need always, and specifically, to 'put the case' to respondent parties where the nature and substance of the case against them is well-known. However the court was clear that such circumstances are case-specific and it is suggested that it remains good practice to put specific allegations so that a response can be made.

Vulnerable witnesses

2.35 In November 2017 the FPR 2010 were amended to include Part 3A which sets out the court's duties and powers in relation to vulnerable witnesses

49 See para **1.17**.
50 *Re J (Children)* [2018] EWCA Civ 115 per McFarlane LJ at paras 65–75.
51 *Brown v Dunn* (3 March 1989, unreported), CA.
52 [2006] EWCA Civ 1186.
53 See also *Lancashire County Council v D & E* [2008] EWHC 832 (Fam) paras 217–222.
54 *Re B (A Child)* [2019] 1 FCR 120.

whether children, adults or protected parties.[55] Vulnerability is to be assessed with reference to a non-exhaustive list of considerations.[56] The duty of legal representatives to raise the issue of vulnerability is imposed by the requirement to work co-operatively with the court and each other to allow participation without diminishing the quality of evidence.[57]

2.36 In the case of adults who are not protected parties the court will consider whether, by reason of any relevant consideration, the quality of that person's evidence is likely to be diminished so that a participation direction is needed.[58] In the case of children and protected parties the court will consider the position in every case, since the requirement to consider whether the quality of their evidence is diminished prior to making participation directions is inapplicable in those cases.[59]

2.37 Participation directions include matters such as whether to allow questioning via an intermediary[60] and whether to set ground rules for questioning including: (1) directing that questions asked by one advocate should not be repeated by another; (2) questions or topics to be put in cross-examination should be agreed prior to the hearing; (3) the use of a single advocate or the judge to put questions;[61] and (4) whether cross-examination should take place before the hearing in a pre-recorded session.[62] The court may also consider whether the relevant person has already given evidence and been cross-examined under the vulnerable witness provisions in the criminal jurisdiction and therefore whether those recordings stand as evidence in the family proceedings.[63]

2.38 The rest of this book is concerned with the specific provisions and subsequent case law which alters and amends the approach to the examination of witnesses who are assessed as vulnerable in accordance with the statutory and regulatory criteria.

DUTIES OF ADVOCATES

2.39 Both solicitor advocates and counsel have duties to witnesses when asking questions in court as part of their general and overriding duty to the court in the administration of justice. The summaries below relate only to the examination of witnesses and should not be taken as a complete guide to professional behaviour.

55 In summary a protected party is a person (adult or child) who lacks litigation capacity and acts by a litigation friend. Such persons may nevertheless give evidence; see FPR 2010, Pt 15 and PD15A.
56 FPR 2010, r 3A.7.
57 FPR 2010, PD3AA para 1.4.
58 FPR 2010, r 3A.4.
59 FPR 2010, r 3A.2.
60 FPR 2010, r 3A.8.
61 FPR 2010, PD3AA para 5.5.
62 FPR 2010, PD3AA para 5.4.
63 FPR 2010, PD3AA para 5.6.

Practitioners are advised to have regard to their relevant professional regulations and guidelines in full.

Counsel

2.40 The general duty to the court is set out in the Bar Standards Board handbook. The duties require counsel to act with independence in the interests of justice. This duty overrides any inconsistent obligations (other than obligations under the criminal law). It includes the following specific obligations: not knowingly or recklessly to mislead or attempt to mislead the court; not to abuse the role of advocate; to take reasonable steps to avoid wasting the court's time; to take reasonable steps to ensure that the court has before it all relevant decisions and legislative provisions; and to ensure that the ability to act independently is not compromised.[64]

2.41 The duty to avoid abusing the role of an advocate includes the following requirements: not to make statements or ask questions merely to insult, humiliate or annoy a witness or any other person; not to make a serious allegation against a witness who was available to be cross-examined unless that witness had a chance to answer the allegation in cross-examination; not to make a serious allegation against any person, or suggest that a person is guilty of a crime with which the client is charged unless: (a) there are reasonable grounds for the allegation; (b) the allegation is relevant to the client's case or the credibility of a witness; or (c) where the allegation relates to a third party, to avoid naming them in open court unless this is reasonably necessary.[65]

Solicitor advocates

2.42 Solicitor advocates must achieve the following outcomes:[66] not to attempt to deceive or knowingly or recklessly mislead the court; not to be complicit in another person deceiving or misleading the court; to comply with court orders; not to place oneself in contempt of court; to inform the client of the circumstances in which advocates' duties to the court outweigh their obligations to the client; to comply with advocates' duties to the court; to ensure that evidence relating to sensitive issues is not misused; and not to make or offer to make payments to witnesses dependent upon their evidence or the outcome of the case.

2.43 Indicative behaviours which will tend to support compliance with the outcomes sought are also set out in the Solicitors Regulation Authority handbook.[67] They include: drawing the court's attention to relevant cases and statutory provisions, and any material procedural irregularity; immediately informing the

64 BSB Handbook February 2018 r C.3.
65 BSB Handbook February 2018 r C.6.
66 SRA Handbook version 19 October 2017 Chapter 5.
67 Ibid Chapter 5.

court, with the client's consent, if during the course of proceedings the advocate becomes aware that they have inadvertently misled the court, or ceasing to act if the client does not consent to informing the court; and refusing to continue to act for a client if the advocate becomes aware they have committed perjury or misled the court, or attempted to mislead the court, in any material matter unless the client agrees to disclose the truth to the court;

Indicative behaviours are also set out which will tend to support a finding of non-compliance:

(1) constructing facts supporting the client's case or drafting any documents relating to any proceedings containing:
   - (a) any contention which is not considered to be properly arguable; or
   - (b) any allegation of fraud, unless instructed to do so and there is material which reasonably shows, on the face of it, a case of fraud;

(2) suggesting that any person is guilty of a crime, fraud or misconduct unless such allegations:
   - (a) go to a matter in issue which is material to your own client's case; and
   - (b) appear to you to be supported by reasonable grounds;

(3) calling a witness whose evidence is known to be untrue;

(4) attempting to influence a witness, when taking a statement from that witness, with regard to the contents of their statement;

(5) tampering with evidence or seeking to persuade a witness to change their evidence;

(6) when acting as an advocate, naming in open court any third party whose character would thereby be called into question, unless it is necessary for the proper conduct of the case;

(7) when acting as an advocate, calling into question the character of a witness you has been cross-examined unless the witness has had the opportunity to answer the allegations during cross-examination.

Chapter 3

VULNERABLE PEOPLE: PRE-PROCEEDINGS/ INVESTIGATION STAGE

PRE-PROCEEDINGS IN CRIMINAL LAW: THE INVESTIGATION STAGE

An overview of key principles

Introduction

3.1 In the early stages of an investigation, before any court proceedings have commenced, it is important that all the professionals involved are aware of any vulnerable people or potentially vulnerable people who are connected to that investigation and the need to ensure that they are properly protected. Further, it is imperative that the evidence that they may be able to contribute to future proceedings is preserved and it should be noted that this is as much the case for suspects as for complainants and other witnesses. The authors of the book are aware of occasions when accounts from vulnerable witnesses and defendants have not been taken quickly enough; and due to their limited cognitive functions the delay has meant that the experts have agreed that any account now taken would unlikely to be reliable. Therefore care is obviously required but also expediency is also often required. This can be a real difficulty for the defence when it is often necessary to obtain prior authority before an expert can be instructed.

3.2 This principle of the need for awareness of vulnerable people is true in relation both to potential criminal and family proceedings; for example, where there is the involvement of social services and a child has been made subject to a child in need plan, care needs to be taken when speaking to children and vulnerable adults and the appropriate training needs to have been given so that those involved know how to proceed if allegations are made and also how to accurately record relevant or potentially relevant information.

3.3 This section primarily addresses the considerations professionals should have prior to charge/commencement of legal proceedings when the matters are being investigated by the police although divided into specific sections for ease of reference there is overlap between the sections.

3.4 The police and the investigation that has been conducted by the police often have a fundamental role within both family and criminal proceedings and an understanding of the police powers and duties when conducting that investigation is essential for those involved in these proceedings.

3.5 Police powers, duties and responsibilities are predominately governed by the Police and Criminal Evidence Act (PACE) 1984 and the associated PACE codes of practice. In addition, the PACE codes have notes providing additional guidance (NFG). This legal framework is intended to regulate police powers and intend to protect public rights. To some extent this statutory framework does provide clear guidance as to what is expected at each stage of the investigation. Case law also provides further explanation of how the rules have been interpreted.[1] It is of interest that persons other than police officers who are 'charged' with the duty of investigating offences or charging offenders are required by PACE 1984, s 67(9) when discharging that duty to 'have regard to any relevant provisions of the code'. It is clearly foreseeable that there could be times when social workers for example are obtaining evidence to establish whether misconduct has occurred and therefore arguably there should be regard to these codes, the relevant word in this section is 'charged' with the duty of investigating and whether the LA can be said be charged with investigating or not.

Key definitions:

3.6 When seeking to identify potentially vulnerable people two key areas are children and those suffering from a mental disorder.

A child is a person under 18 unless stated otherwise: PACE 1984, s 37(15); this is also how a child is defined under the UN Convention on the Rights of the Child (see para **7.4**). In PACE and the Codes children are referred to as juveniles. With respect to the Codes, the test for the police is whether a person 'appears to be' under the age of 18 rather than it being confirmed that they are. Therefore, the police should err on the side of caution with respect to young people.

3.7 Mental disorder is defined under the Mental Health Act 1983, s 1(2) as 'any disorder or disability of the mind'.

The Codes

3.8 The PACE Codes of Practice are divided into specific sections A to H and these are set out in the box below. The link to access the full codes of practice online is: https://www.gov.uk/guidance/police-and-criminal-evidence-act-1984-pace-codes-of-practice#pace-codes-of-practice:

- Code A: Code of Practice for statutory powers of stop and search and the need for a police officer to make a record of a stop or encounter
- Code B: Code of Practice for searches of premises by police officers and the seizure of property found by police on persons or premises

1 *R v Fulling* [1987] 2 ALL ER 65.

- Code C: Code of Practice for the detention, treatment and questioning of persons by Police Officers
- Code D: Code of Practice for the identification of persons by Police Officers
- Code E: Code of Practice for the audio recording of suspects in the police station
- Code F: Code of Practice on visual recording with sound of interviews with suspects
- Code G: Code of Practice for the statutory power of arrest by police officers
- Code H: Code of Practice in connection with: The detention, treatment and questioning by Police Officers of persons in police detention under section 41 of, and Schedule 8 to, the Terrorism Act 2000 The treatment and questioning by Police Officers of detained persons in respect of whom an authorisation to question after charge has been given under section 22 of the Counter-Terrorism Act 2008

3.9 It is essential that all practitioners are aware of the basic duties and procedural requirements of the police during an investigation; this includes those practitioners who only normally become involved once the case has come to court. Having such an understanding will help practitioners identify key areas including:

- knowing what rights/procedures should have been in place and also looking at records to see which were provided to protect/assist a vulnerable witnesses/ defendants – this can help to identify what assistance a witness/defendant my require at future hearings;
- being able to identifying what evidence should be available;
- knowing in what form evidence should be recorded;
- knowing what, if any, breaches there have been of the procedural requirements and the impact this may have on the proceedings; and
- knowing what further investigations and/or disclosure should be requested.

3.10 The PACE codes, if relevant, are admissible in evidence in criminal or civil proceedings: PACE 1984, s 67(11).

3.11 In addition to the PACE codes, the Code of Practice for Victims of Crime (Office for Criminal Justice Reform 2005) places a further obligation on the police to identify vulnerable or intimidated victims and to provide them with an enhanced service.

3.12 There is a helpful police guidance document entitled: Vulnerable and Intimidated Witnesses – A Police Service Guide 2011 which sets out and identifies key considerations for the police when dealing with vulnerable people and compliments the Achieving Best Evidence in Criminal Proceedings: Guidance on Interviewing Victims and Witnesses, and Guidance on Using Special Measures (Ministry of Justice 2011) – see more detail below.

3.13 *Vulnerable People: Pre-Proceedings/Investigation Stage*

3.13 The Vulnerable and Intimidated Witnesses – A Police Service Guide 2011 states:

> 'All victims and witnesses are entitled to receive a high-quality service from the police, from their initial contact with the first officer or member of police staff that they meet, throughout the investigation and beyond to the pre-trial and trial processes'.

3.14 *Early identification*: A key feature of the codes and the guidance is that children and vulnerable adult witnesses must be identified as early as possible in the process and police officers/police staff have a crucial role to play in identifying the relevant people. The police are generally the first point of contact a person involved in an investigation will have and the police often have the benefit of face-to-face contact with that person.

Sanctions for failure to comply with the codes

3.15 *Criminal liability*: When considering the sanctions for failure by the police to follow PACE codes of conduct it is not correct that a failure by an officer to follow the PACE code is a criminal offence in itself; however, that does not mean that it could not result in a criminal prosecution against an officer, for example a purposeful and wilful breach of the codes could be perverting the course of justice, but a breach does is not in itself establish criminal liability. However, a breach may lead to internal police disciplinary proceedings.

3.16 *Exclusion of the material obtained at trial*: A breach of codes may be relevant in criminal proceedings for a number of reasons and the fact that the codes are admissible when relevant may lead to it being adduced at a criminal trial that there was failure by the police to act in a certain manner, for example breaches are also often relied upon to support an application exclude evidence under PACE 1984, ss 76 and 78.

3.17 Another key piece of the legislation governing the treatment of vulnerable suspects is Article 6 of the European Convention on Human Rights (ECHR) this provision is often relied upon when making applications for the exclusion of material under PACE 1984, ss 76 and 78.

3.18 In addition to the ECHR when considering how police officers should act in their dealing with children the police must also have regard to the UN Convention of the Rights of the Child and in particular the following two Articles are of relevance:

3.19 Article 3:

> 'In all actions concerning children, whether undertaken by public or private social welfare institutions, courts of law, administrative authorities or legislative bodies, the best interests of the child shall be a primary consideration.'

3.20 Article 37:

'Parties shall ensure that:

(a) No child shall be subjected to torture or other cruel, inhuman or degrading treatment or punishment. Neither capital punishment nor life imprisonment without possibility of release shall be imposed for offences committed by persons below eighteen years of age;

(b) No child shall be deprived of his or her liberty unlawfully or arbitrarily. The arrest, detention or imprisonment of a child shall be in conformity with the law and shall be used only as a measure of last resort and for the shortest appropriate period of time;

(c) Every child deprived of liberty shall be treated with humanity and respect for the inherent dignity of the human person, and in a manner which takes into account the needs of persons of his or her age.

In particular, every child deprived of liberty shall be separated from adults unless it is considered in the child's best interest not to do so and shall have the right to maintain contact with his or her family through correspondence and visits, save in exceptional circumstances;

(d) Every child deprived of his or her liberty shall have the right to prompt access to legal and other appropriate assistance, as well as the right to challenge the legality of the deprivation of his or her liberty before a court or other competent, independent and impartial authority, and to a prompt decision on any such action.'

3.21 Further, in relation to those vulnerable due to a disability there is the UN Convention on the Rights of the Person with Disabilities. In the preamble it states:

'(e) Recognizing that disability is an evolving concept and that disability results from the interaction between persons with impairments and attitudinal and environmental barriers that hinders their full and effective participation in society on an equal basis with others,'

The idea of an evolving concept is very helpful and it is correct that is often apparent during an investigation and proceedings. There is a need for all those involved in considering vulnerable people to be alive to this idea. Article 12 addresses equal recognition before the law and article 13 addresses access to justice.

Police – an overview of their duties and codes re vulnerable people

Police duties/responsibilities

3.22 What follows focuses on specific parts of the PACE codes relating to vulnerable witnesses and vulnerable suspects and is not a full overview of the PACE codes.

3.23 Police forces have their own force safeguarding policies which are usually available online and these conform to the Authorised Professional Practice (APP) guidance. The APP website is an invaluable source of information for practitioners assessing the powers that the police have/should have used see https://www.app.college.police.uk/detention-and-custody-index/. With respect to children and vulnerable people there are separate links:

Children: https://www.app.college.police.uk/app-content/detention-and-custody-2/detainee-care/children-and-young-persons/Vulnerable adults: https://www.app.college.police.uk/app-content/mental-health/

Vulnerable Suspects

3.24 With respect to vulnerable suspects, one key source of information is any interactions the suspect has had with the police including if they have been stopped, arrested and interviewed. This information may provide a basis for submitting that the defendant may need special measures at a first hearing or may be unfit to enter a plea. It is noteworthy that during certain investigations it may not be clear from the outset who is the suspect and who is the potential complainant and so the police should have an open mind when investigating a case and therefore 'suspects' and 'witnesses' should be considered in conjunction with each other. It disappointing in cases to see police officers recording one person as a 'victim' and another as the 'perpetrator' when an investigation has not been completed, although in the experience of the authors of this book, it is not uncommon for the police to use this terminology before there has been a conviction.

Stop and search

3.25 Code A governs the exercise by police officers of their statutory powers to search a person or a vehicle without first making an arrest. In addition, it covers requirements on police officers and police staff to record encounters not governed by statutory powers (Code A 1.03). For practitioners the record of any search can be important and should not be overlooked.

The stop and search of a person in an investigation may be the first encounter the person has with police during the investigation and therefore the police's first opportunity to assess first hand their vulnerability – although it may be that the police will already have information that identifies that the person is, or is likely to be, vulnerable, eg a child or a person under a mental health order. Clearly a stop and/or search can be a difficult experience for a vulnerable person; for example, the person may have difficulties in understanding or may be in fear. How that stop and search is carried out and the behaviour of the person during and after it can be highly relevant in relation to vulnerable people; it may for example provide evidence to support a defence relating to mens rea or explain how a person has behaved subsequently. Therefore, the search records may contain relevant information as may any police officer's body camera footage (if available). When court proceedings have started, practitioners may need to consider, if the material has not already been provided, whether a disclosure application is appropriate for the material relating to any stop and search on the basis that the material may go to a number of matters including assessing vulnerability and/or a defence or in fact a first account.

A defence application for further disclosure is made under the statutory provisions.[2] However, it may be that those acting for a defendant will ask for disclosure under the common law rules of disclosure if the material sought is relevant to a preliminary issue before the statutory provisions have been evoked. The case of *R v DPP, ex parte Lee*[3] sets out the requirement for the Crown to provide disclosure at a preliminary stage prior to the statutory provisions having been evoked.

3.26 It should be noted that Code A does not apply to:

'(a) the powers of stop and search under:

(i) the Aviation Security Act 1982, section 27(2), and

(ii) the Police and Criminal Evidence Act 1984 (PACE), section 6(1) (which relates specifically to powers of constables employed by statutory undertakers on the premises of the statutory undertakers);

(b) searches carried out for the purposes of examination under Schedule 7 to the Terrorism Act 2000 and to which the Code of Practice issued under paragraph 6 of Schedule 14 to the Terrorism Act 2000 applies.

(c) the powers to search persons and vehicles and to stop and search in specified locations to which the Code of Practice issued under section 47AB of the Terrorism Act 2000 applies.'

3.27 The first key consideration and protection for vulnerable people when the police are carrying out a stop and/or a search is that Code A is clear that powers to stop and search must be used 'fairly, responsibly, with respect for people being searched and without unlawful discrimination'. Dealing with vulnerable people 'fairly and responsibly' must place a duty on the officers and how they deal with vulnerable people especially when Code A is read in conjunction with the Equality Act 2010, s 149 (set out below). This duty is also further expanded within the notes to the PACE codes (see Notes 1 and 1A). Where the codes refer to the 'relevant protected characteristics' these are: age, disability, gender reassignment, pregnancy and maternity, race, religion or belief, sex and sexual orientation: Equality Act 2010, s 149. The inclusion of both age and disability make it clear that vulnerability is a key factor and given that the police are under a duty to advance equality it surely must be the case that they should act to allow those who are vulnerable to be able to fairly engage.

---

2 Mainly contained within CPIA 1996.
3 [1999] 1 WLR 1950.

's.149 Public sector equality duty

(1) A public authority must, in the exercise of its functions, have due regard to the need to—

(a) eliminate discrimination, harassment, victimisation and any other conduct that is prohibited by or under this Act;

(b) advance equality of opportunity between persons who share a relevant protected characteristic and persons who do not share it;

(c) foster good relations between persons who share a relevant protected characteristic and persons who do not share it.

(2) A person who is not a public authority but who exercises public functions must, in the exercise of those functions, have due regard to the matters mentioned in subsection (1).

(3) Having due regard to the need to advance equality of opportunity between persons who share a relevant protected characteristic and persons who do not share it involves having due regard, in particular, to the need to—

(a) remove or minimise disadvantages suffered by persons who share a relevant protected characteristic that are connected to that characteristic;

(b) take steps to meet the needs of persons who share a relevant protected characteristic that are different from the needs of persons who do not share it;

(c) encourage persons who share a relevant protected characteristic to participate in public life or in any other activity in which participation by such persons is disproportionately low.

(4) The steps involved in meeting the needs of disabled persons that are different from the needs of persons who are not disabled include, in particular, steps to take account of disabled persons' disabilities.

(5) Having due regard to the need to foster good relations between persons who share a relevant protected characteristic and persons who do not share it involves having due regard, in particular, to the need to—

(a) tackle prejudice, and

(b) promote understanding.

(6) Compliance with the duties in this section may involve treating some persons more favourably than others; but that is not to be taken as permitting conduct that would otherwise be prohibited by or under this Act.

(7) The relevant protected characteristics are— age; disability; gender reassignment; pregnancy and maternity; race; religion or belief; sex; and sexual orientation.'

3.28 With respect to stop and search the PACE Code considers the case of what is referred to as 'innocent possession':

> [in essence this means] 'that the person does not have the guilty knowledge that they are carrying an unlawful item which is required before an arrest on suspicion that the person has committed an offence in respect of the item sought (if arrest is necessary – see PACE Code G) and/or a criminal prosecution) can be considered. Innocent possession can be particularly relevant for vulnerable persons as the Code accepts and considers that 'it is not uncommon for children under the age of criminal responsibility to be used by older children and adults to carry stolen property, drugs and weapons and, in some cases, firearms, for the criminal benefit of others, either:
>
> - in the hope that police may not suspect they are being used for carrying the items; or
> - knowing that if they are suspected of being couriers and are stopped and searched, they cannot be arrested or prosecuted for any criminal offence.'

3.29 The stop and search powers therefore allow the police to intervene when criminal gangs and groups are using young children to further their criminal activities. The Code and notes give guidance that whenever a child under ten is suspected of carrying unlawful items for someone else or is found in circumstances which suggest that their welfare and safety may be at risk, the facts should be reported and actioned in accordance with established force safeguarding procedures. Each force has its own safeguarding procedure but these are in line with the APP.

3.30 This reporting and actioning is in addition to treating children as potentially vulnerable or intimidated witnesses in respect of their status as witnesses to criminal offences committed by those using them as couriers. Safeguarding considerations will also apply to other persons aged under 18 who are stopped and searched under any of the powers to which the Code applies.

3.31 A further safeguard is under the Children Act 2004, s 11 which requires:

> chief police officers and other specified persons and bodies to whom this section applies to make arrangements for ensuring that:
>
> (a) their functions are discharged having regard to the need to safeguard and promote the welfare of children; and
>
> (b) any services provided by another person pursuant to arrangements made by the person or body in the discharge of their functions are provided having regard to that need.[4]

3.32 Therefore, it is a clear principle that when police stop and search vulnerable people they must treat them fairly and take into account their vulnerability.

---

4 CA 2004, s 11(2).

Powers to require removal of face coverings

3.33 The Criminal Justice and Public Order Act 1994, s 60AA also provides a power to demand the removal of disguises.

> 60AA Powers to require removal of disguises
>
> (1) Where—
>
> (a) an authorisation under section 60 is for the time being in force in relation to any locality for any period, or
>
> (b) an authorisation under subsection (3) that the powers conferred by subsection (2) shall be exercisable at any place in a locality is in force for any period,
>
> those powers shall be exercisable at any place in that locality at any time in that period.
>
> (2) This subsection confers power on any constable in uniform—
>
> (a) to require any person to remove any item which the constable reasonably believes that person is wearing wholly or mainly for the purpose of concealing his identity;
>
> (b) to seize any item which the constable reasonably believes any person intends to wear wholly or mainly for that purpose.

3.34 The PACE code considers face coverings, etc and when an officer should exercise their powers. Police officers must reasonably believe that someone is wearing an item *wholly or mainly for the purpose of concealing identity* in order to request that face coverings are removed. There is also a power to seize such items where the officer believes that a person intends to wear them for this purpose.

3.35 NFG12 of the PACE Code A identifies that many people customarily cover their heads or faces for religious reasons – for example, Muslim women, Sikh men or women, Hindu women, or Rastafarian men or women. A police officer cannot order the removal of a head or face covering except where there is reason to believe that the item is being worn by the individual *wholly or mainly for the purpose of disguising identity*, not simply because it disguises identity, so a distinction is made. Where there may be religious sensitivities about ordering the removal of such an item, the officer should permit the item to be removed out of public view. Where practicable, the item should be removed in the presence of an officer of the same sex as the person and out of sight of anyone of the opposite sex.

3.36 An officer may seize any such item which is discovered when exercising a power of search for something else, or which is being carried, and which the officer reasonably believes is intended to be used for concealing anyone's identity.

3.37 This power can only be used if an authorisation given under the Criminal Justice and Public Order Act 1994, s 60 or 60AA, is in force. Authority under PACE 1984, s 60AA for a constable in uniform to require the removal of disguises and to seize them may be given if the authorising officer reasonably believes that activities may take place in any locality in the officer's police area that are likely to involve the commission of offences and it is expedient to use these powers to prevent or control these activities. An authorisation under PACE 1984, s 60AA may only be given by an officer of the rank of inspector or above, in writing, specifying the grounds on which it was given, the locality in which the powers may be exercised and the period of time for which they are in force. The period authorised shall be no longer than appears reasonably necessary to prevent, or seek to prevent, the commission of offences. It may not exceed 24 hours. An inspector who gives an authorisation must, as soon as practicable, inform an officer of or above the rank of superintendent.

3.38 This officer may direct that the authorisation shall be extended for a further 24 hours if crimes have been committed, or are suspected to have been committed, and the continued use of the powers is considered necessary to prevent or deal with such activity. This direction must also be given in writing at the time or as soon as practicable afterwards.

Arrest and initial detention of suspects

3.39 Article 5 of the ECHR addresses a person's right to liberty and security and covers arrest and detention.

3.40 Code G is the Code of Practice for the statutory power of arrest by police officers. It is not always appropriate or necessary to make an arrest in order for a there to be an interview of a suspect and it is common practice for a person to attend a police station voluntarily for the purpose of assisting with an investigation; however such a person is free to leave at will unless they are then arrested. When police respond to an incident/report they should conduct an immediate risk assessment and with respect to a suspect this will include conducting an assessment of that person and their behaviour APP(DC) Response, Arrest and Detention. Vulnerability is a consideration for police when deciding whether and when to arrest a suspect or whether alternative approaches are more appropriate including detention under the Mental Health Act 1983 (MHA 1983) and street bail.

3.41 When deciding whether to make an arrest, police officers are required to consider the age of a child or young person (Code G). Another key consideration with respect to the arrest and detention of children is timing, and officers must be careful not to detain children for longer than is necessary and should where possible not detain children overnight (Code C).

3.42 With respect to the detention of a child, the custody officer should comply with the PACE 1984, s 38(6).This requires that when a custody officer has authorised the police detention of a child they should ensure that the arrested child is moved to local authority accommodation unless: (a) they certify that, by reason of such circumstances as are specified in the certificate, it is impracticable for them to do so; or (b) in the case of an arrested juvenile who has attained the age of 12 years, that no secure accommodation is available and that keeping the child in other local authority accommodation would not be adequate to protect the public from serious harm from the child.

3.43 Police officers do have the power to detain under the MHA 1983, s 136 and where a person appears to an officer to 'to be suffering from mental disorder and to be in immediate need of care or control', the officer may, 'if he thinks it necessary to do so in the interests of that person or for the protection of other person ... remove the person to a place of safety'. A place of safety is widely defined in the MHA 1983, s 135 as meaning residential accommodation provided by a local social services authority, a hospital, a police station, an independent hospital or care home for mentally disordered persons or any other suitable place; however a police station should only be used in exceptional circumstances: MHA 1983 Code of Practice (2015) ss 16.36–16.44.

3.44 It is correct and in line with ECHR that when a person is brought to a police station under arrest they must be brought before the custody officer as soon as practicable after their arrival (Code C2.1A). For each person brought into custody under arrest, a separate custody record must be opened as soon as practicable and all information recorded under the Code must be recorded as soon as practicable in the custody record unless otherwise specified (Code C2.1) – this can therefore be an invaluable document in proceedings to assess how the suspect was treated in custody and may explain the information obtained for example in relation to the interview.

3.45 Code C, paras 3.13–3.17 provide guidance as to how vulnerable suspects should be processed and the steps that should be taken. With respect to children the custody officer must, if it is practicable, ascertain the identity of a person responsible for their welfare. That person may be the parent or guardian or, if the child is in local authority or voluntary organisation care, or is otherwise being looked after under the CA 1989, a person appointed by that authority or organisation to have responsibility for the juvenile's welfare or any other person who has, for the time being, assumed responsibility for the child's welfare. Such an identified person must be informed as soon as practicable that the child has been arrested, why they have been arrested and where they are detained. This right is in addition to the child's right in section 5 not to be held incommunicado.

3.46 Code C, para 3.15 states that, if the detainee is a child, mentally disordered or otherwise mentally vulnerable, the custody officer must, as soon as practicable, inform the appropriate adult, (who in the case of a child may or may not be a person responsible for their welfare) of:

- the grounds for their detention;

- their whereabouts; and
- ask the adult to come to the police station to see the detainee.

3.47 When a vulnerable person is arrested and taken to police custody the APP requires that custody staff prioritise the processing of that person on arrival at the station. Where practicable the officers will have called ahead to inform the custody suite of the imminent arrival of the vulnerable suspect. All suspects, including vulnerable suspects, must be informed of their rights and entitlements by the custody officer. All suspects brought into custody must be assessed and that assessment includes an assessment of their vulnerability and an assessment of their fitness to be detained.

3.48 Code C, para 9.5 requires that the custody officer must make sure a detainee receives appropriate medical attention as soon as reasonably practicable if the person: (a) appears to be suffering from physical illness; (b) is injured; (c) appears to be suffering from a mental disorder; or (d) appears to need medical attention. This applies even if the person makes no request for medical attention and whether or not they have already received medical attention elsewhere.

3.49 With respect to the giving of the police caution and the warning that failure to give relevant information may lead to an inference being drawn when a person fails or refuses to answer a question about one of these matters or to answer it satisfactorily that they later rely upon in evidence, as set out in Code C, para 10.11 the suspect must first be told in ordinary language: (a) what offence is being investigated; (b) what fact they are being asked to account for; (c) this fact may be due to them taking part in the commission of the offence; (d) a court may draw a proper inference if they fail or refuse to account for this fact; and (e) a record is being made of the interview and it may be given in evidence if they are brought to trial. (This information must not be given to a child or persons who are mentally disordered or otherwise mentally vulnerable unless the appropriate adult is present.) If a child or a person who is mentally disordered or otherwise mentally vulnerable is cautioned in the absence of an appropriate adult, the caution must be repeated in the adult's presence.

3.50 There are also guidance and statutory provisions relating to:

Association with adults by children: In summary, children are not to be allowed to associate with adult detainees whilst being detained, conveyed to and from court or waiting to be so conveyed. An exception to this is permitted in accordance with the Children and Young Persons Act 1933, s 31 where the young person is jointly charged with an adult or relative.

3.51 *Intimate searches of children*: In summary, an intimate search of a child may take place only in the presence of an appropriate adult of the same sex, unless the child/young person expressly asks for an appropriate adult of the opposite sex, who is readily available. The search may take place in the absence of the appropriate adult if the juvenile specifically requests this, provided the appropriate adult is present when the request is made and the adult agrees. The decision should be recorded and signed by the appropriate adult.

Police interviews of vulnerable suspects and in particular the use of appropriate adults

3.52 Under the PACE Codes of Practice, before any detained person is interviewed there must be an assessment by the custody officer in conjunction with the officer in charge of the investigation and appropriate healthcare professionals as necessary, shall assess whether the detainee is fit enough to be interviewed (Code C, para 12.3). This means determining and considering the risks to the detainee's physical and mental state if the interview took place and determining what safeguards are needed to allow the interview to take place. The custody officer shall not allow a detainee to be interviewed if the custody officer considers it would cause significant harm to the detainee's physical or mental state. It should be noted that vulnerable suspects listed at Code C, para 11.18 shall be treated as always being at some risk during an interview and these persons may not be interviewed except in accordance with Code C, paras 11.18–11.20. The category of vulnerable suspects includes: a child; a vulnerable adult; anyone who appears unable to appreciate the significance of questions and their answers; and anyone who appears unable to understand what is happening because of the effects of drink or drugs, or an illness or condition.

3.53 Code C, para 11.15 states that a child or person who is mentally disordered or otherwise mentally vulnerable must not be interviewed regarding their involvement or suspected involvement in a criminal offence or offences, or asked to provide or sign a written statement under caution or record of interview, in the absence of the appropriate adult unless Code C, paras 11.1 or 11.18–11.20 apply. These exceptions in summary are when delay would: (a) lead to; interference with, or harm to, evidence connected with an offence; interference with, or physical harm to, other people; or serious loss of, or damage to, property; (b) lead to alerting other people suspected of committing an offence but not yet arrested for it; or (c) hinder the recovery of property obtained in consequence of the commission of an offence. Interviewing in any of these circumstances shall cease once the relevant risk has been averted or the necessary questions have been put in order to attempt to avert that risk.

3.54 It should be noted that a custody officer is not limited to the provision of an appropriate adult to ensure the vulnerable person is safeguarded during an interview and can consider the provision of others, for example health care professionals.

3.55 Failure to have the relevant safeguards/assistance present in an interview as set out in the Code can lead to the exclusion of the interview as evidence at trial under the PACE 1984, ss 76 and 78.There is specific Home Office Guidance with respect to appropriate adults – the link is https://www.gov.uk/government/uploads/system/uploads/attachment_data/file/117625/guidanceappadultscu

3.56 In essence the role of the appropriate adult is to ensure that a mentally disordered/vulnerable person is not disadvantaged during a police interview and when in police custody, as a result of the disorder/vulnerability from which he or she suffers. It should be noted the role is not limited to just during the interview.

3.57 Code C, para 11.17 states that if an appropriate adult is present at an interview, they shall be informed that they are not expected to act simply as an observer; and that the purpose of their presence is to:

- advise the person being interviewed;
- observe whether the interview is being conducted properly and fairly; and
- facilitate communication with the person being interviewed.

3.58 It is of real note and importance for those acting as legal representatives to be aware that appropriate adults do not have legal professional privilege. However, the presence of an appropriate adult during a legal consultation does not remove the legal professional privilege between lawyer and client.[5] Therefore, real consideration needs to be given by representatives as to whether an appropriate adult should be present when legal advice is being given.

3.59 Appropriate adults are not there to give legal advice and appropriate adults should consider whether a detained person should have advice from a legal representative and have the right to ask for a legal representative to attend for the vulnerable person if in their best interests Code C, para 6.5A.

3.60 The appropriate adult's role is a wide one and cover the whole detention and not just the interview; this clear from the requirements in the code which include that the detained person should have their rights explained to them with the presence of an appropriate adult Code C, paras 3.17 and 3.18 and the appropriate adult is entitled to inspect the custody record (Code C, para 2.4). Further, if the Appropriate adult is present at the time when continued detention is being considered they must be given the opportunity to make representations (Code C, para 15.3).

3.61 Code C, para 11.18 prohibits the interview of any person who appears unable to appreciate the significance of questions and their answers; or to understand what is happening because of the effects of drink, drugs or any illness, ailment or condition except when an officer of superintendent rank or above considers delaying the interview will lead to the consequences as with vulnerable witnesses and is satisfied the interview would not significantly harm the person's physical or mental state.

VULNERABLE WITNESSES

Collecting of evidence from vulnerable witnesses

Achieving Best Evidence interviews

3.62 The guidance on the APP website is very helpful with regard to police investigations and vulnerable witnesses see https://www.app.college.police.uk/app-content/investigations/victims-and-witnesses/#approach.

5 *A Local Authority v B* [2008] EWHC 1017 (Fam).

3.63 *Vulnerable People: Pre-Proceedings/Investigation Stage*

3.63 Police officers must as well as the ABE guidance and the Codes also consider Ministry of Justice (2015) Code of Practice for Victims of Crime.

Taking statements

3.64 Taking statement/accounts from vulnerable witnesses including defendants must be done with real care and often can only be done by those who have had the appropriate training. There is a real risk if it is not done properly that the evidence will be unreliable and the risk that a future reliable account cannot be obtained, for example due to a vulnerable person being susceptible to suggestibility such that their true account will then be lost. Further, real psychological harm can be caused to vulnerable people if an account is not taken in the right circumstances and with the right help and support.

3.65 Where possible there should be a pre-contact assessment where it is known or suspected that a witness is vulnerable. There may need to be an initial contact before any formal statement or account is taken. At this initial contact it may be necessary to take a brief account. It should be remembered that a record of this account should be taken (whether at the time or written down contemporaneously) and the police will need to decide whether it is necessary to ask such questions to prevent the loss of evidence or the protection of the witness or others.

Achieving Best Evidence interviews

3.66 The Achieving Best Evidence in Criminal Proceedings Guidance (ABE Guidance) on interviewing victims and witnesses, and guidance on using special measures sets guidance to assist those responsible for conducting video recorded interviews with vulnerable, intimidated and significant witnesses, as well as those tasked with preparing and supporting witnesses during the criminal justice process. The Guidance incorporates best practice from local areas and the expertise of practitioners, charities and voluntary groups who support victims and witnesses at a local level. The Guidance sensibly notes that 'it cannot cater for every possible set of circumstances that might arise. Each witness is unique and the manner in which they are interviewed and subsequently prepared for their court appearance must be tailored to their particular needs and circumstances.' A full analysis of the Guidance is beyond the scope of a practitioners' handbook aimed at day to day issues and so this overview is aimed at pointing out the major issues.

3.67 The ABE Guidance incorporates key matters identified in the Cleveland Report: The Report of the Inquiry into Child Abuse in Cleveland 1987 (hereafter the Cleveland Report) 'contains a plethora of salient and important guidance with respect to cases involving allegations of sexual abuse'.

3.68 The Guidance is divided into stages: the first stage considers the planning and preparation and high-lights the importance of this stage. The purpose of an investigative interview is to ascertain the witness's account of the alleged event(s) and any other information that would assist the investigation and the guidance is clear that a well-conducted interview will only occur if appropriate planning has taken place. It is important that, as far as possible, the case is thoroughly reviewed before an interview is embarked upon to ensure that all issues are covered and key questions asked, since the opportunity to do this will in most cases be lost once the interview(s) have been concluded.

Planning

3.69

(a) The ABE Guidance states [at Para 2.1]:

> 'A well-conducted interview will only occur if appropriate planning has taken place. The importance of planning cannot be overstated. The success of the interview and thus an investigation could hinge on it. Even if the circumstances necessitate an early interview an appropriate planning session that takes account of all the information available about the witness at the time and identifies the key issues and objectives is required.'

(b) Further, planning guidance requires the officers to be aware or previous interventions with a child interviewee [Guidance Para 2.46] and 'other life experiences' relevant to the inquiry [Guidance Paras 2.51 (for children) and 2.111 (for vulnerable adults)]. This may be relevant because another aspect of the guidance is that the interviewer is supposed to inquire into apparent inconsistencies with a witness [Guidance Paras 2.161–2.163]. It is in part those previous life experiences that may give rise to such questioning.

(c) Finally:

> 'A full written record should be kept of the decisions made during the planning process and of the information and rationale underpinning them. This record should be referred to in the body of the Criminal Justice Act 1967 statement subsequently made by the interviewer in relation to the planning, preparation and conduct of the interview ...' [Guidance Para 2.222].

(d) It is also surely trite by now that any initial interaction with a child or vulnerable person prior to ABE interview should be merely to ascertain that there is an allegation, against whom it was made and its general nature. Records should be meticulously kept. Thereafter it may be necessary with a particularly vulnerable, nervous or apparently traumatised witness to complete further conversations as part of the preparation for interview [Guidance Para 2.223ff]. In such cases these familiarisation meetings should be the subject of full recordings at least by way of notes [Guidance Para 2.237] and should completely avoid any mention of the presumed offending.

(e) In family cases the most thorough recent analysis of the requirements is in para 42 of the judgment of McDonald J in the case of *AS v TH, BC, NC, SH (by their Children's Guardian)*.[6]

Interview

3.70 After the planning and preparation stage is conducting the interview and clearly the basic goal of an interview with a witness is to obtain an accurate and reliable account in a way which is fair, is in the witness's interests and is acceptable to the court. The Guidance states that for all witnesses, the interview must take place in four phases: (i) Rapport; (ii) Free Narrative Account; (iii) Questioning; and (iv) Closing. The first three are evidently the most important.

3.71 **Rapport**: It is plain that the rapport stage must be repeated at every interview [see Guidance Para E3.8]. The rapport stage should be part of the recorded interview.[7] The rapport stage should allow the interviewer to gain an understanding of the capacity of the witness and to be able to tailor language and questions to that capacity. It is at the rapport stage that the questioner will ensure that ground rules such as speaking from personal experience and not merely repeating the accounts of or given to others should take place. Similarly the exercise in establishing that the witness understands the difference between truth and lies and the need to tell only the truth occurs here. Readers should refer to Guidance Paras 3.7–3.22 for more detail and advice.

3.72 **Free Narrative Account**: The interviewer should initiate an uninterrupted narrative account of the incident(s) or event(s) that are the subject of the investigation. The invitation should be open ended but should not merely be an attempt to get the witness what they have said to others nor should the interviewer strain to achieve an allegation which it is understood has been made before.[8] Any need for clarification should be in the broadest terms such as 'is there more you can tell me?' or 'can you put it another way to help me understand better?' [see Guidance Para 3.27]. The interviewer should be very careful not to indicate approval or disapproval of the information given [Guidance Para 3.28]. Reticence on the part of a witness can be addressed by asking if there is anything that can be done to make it easier for them but endearments, encouragements, verbal reinforcement and physical contact is not appropriate [Guidance Para 3.33].

3.73 **Questioning**: The interviewer should consider telling the witness that the interview is now going to move on to some questions being asked and that the ground rules about truth, lies and accuracy still apply. In complex cases there may be a break before this begins [Guidance Paras 3.36–3.37]. Questions are used in a hierarchy: (a) open-ended questions ('describe what you saw/felt/what happened'); (b) specific closed questions ('what did it look like?'); (c) forced

6 [2016] EWHC 532 (Fam).

7 See *Re E (A Child) (Evidence)* [2016] EWCA Civ 473; [2017] 1 FLR 1675.

8 See, eg, *TW v A City Council* [2011] 1 FLR 1597.

choice questions ('was it hard or soft'); and (d) leading questions ('where did he put/touch you with it?'). If forced choice questions are used it is all the more important to reinforce the witness's ability to simply say that they do not know or do not remember. Leading questions are a last resort and will rarely if ever give rise to useful evidence [see Guidance Paras 3.35–3.64].

3.74 **Closure**: this consists of recapitulation (if necessary) and the ending of the session in a sensitive and calm way. If recapitulation is done then: (a) the interviewer should try only to use the words used by the witness; and (b) the interviewer should make sure that the witness knows that they can interrupt to correct or to add further details [see Guidance Paras 3.80–3.883].

Bail pre-charge and conditions

3.75 Bail is an extensive topic in its own right and is not fully set out here.

3.76 When representing vulnerable defendants, it will be necessary to make sure that any bail conditions imposed do not put them at a risk of harm or that due to their circumstances they are in effect being set up to fail due to an inability to be able to comply with the conditions.

3.77 Different provisions govern bail pre-charge to bail post charge. Pre-charge bail can be imposed where there is as yet insufficient evidence to charge a suspect and he is released pending further investigation (PACE 1984, ss 37(2), 34(2) and 34(5)). Where it is no longer necessary to detain a suspect to secure or preserve evidence or obtain it by questioning, yet the police are not in a position to charge, the suspect must be released, but it is open to the police to release him on bail where there is a need for further investigation of any matter for which he was detained. It is important to consider under which provisions the suspect is released on bail and whether there is a power to impose conditions. Where the PACE 1984, s 37(2) is cited and the custody officer has authorised the release of the suspect, having determined that there is currently insufficient evidence to charge, he may be released pending the obtaining of further evidence and conditions of bail can be attached where necessary to prevent the suspect from failing to surrender, offending on bail, interfering with prosecution witnesses or otherwise obstructing the course of justice, or for his own protection. Where the PACE 1984, s 34 is cited (for example, where detailed and lengthy investigation is required and no assessment of the evidence can be made), no conditions of bail can be imposed – see *R (on an application by Torres) v Metropolitan Police Commissioner.*[9]

3.78 Where the police consider that there is sufficient evidence to charge, but the matter must be referred to the CPS for a charging decision (PACE 1984, s 37(7)(a)) the police may release a suspect on bail to return to the police station at a future date and may impose conditions.

---

9 [2007] EWHC 3212.

3.79 The legislative structure of pre-charge bail has been significantly amended by the introduction of the PCA 2017, Pt 4, Ch 1 which came into force on 3 April 2107. The then Home Secretary, Amber Rudd stated:

> 'Pre-charge bail is a useful and necessary tool but in many cases it is being imposed on people for many months, or even years, without any judicial oversight – and that cannot be right.'

3.80 These important reforms will mean fewer people are placed on bail and for shorter periods. They will bring about much-needed safeguards – public accountability and independent scrutiny – while ensuring the police can continue to do their vital work.

3.81 Under the new system, the police would make the initial decision to release a suspect on bail. That decision would be reviewed by a superintendent after 28 days, at which point they could authorise further bail, up to a total of three months, in exceptional circumstances. Any application to extend pre-charge bail beyond three months would have to be approved by a magistrate.

The decision to prosecute and alternatives to prosecution

3.82 Those representing and deciding whether to commence proceedings against vulnerable adults and children; should be aware of the considerations with respect to the decision to prosecute and also alternatives to prosecution.

3.83 The full code test set out in the Code for Crown Prosecutors (Director's Guidance on Charging) has a two-stage test; the evidential stage and the public interest stage in the case of vulnerable suspects this is most likely to have relevance with respect to the public interest to prosecute stage. This is further considered in **Chapter 7**.

3.84 The two key alternatives to a prosecution are cautions and fixed penalty notices. Cautions are not criminal convictions (although there are consequences to cautions – which must be considered when advising a client to accept a caution). Cautions can be a sensible alterative to a prosecution for a child or vulnerable adult defendant. There are three categories of caution, the simple caution, the youth caution and the conditional caution. With respect to Youth Cautions there is specific guidance in the Youth Cautions: Guidance for Police and Youth Offending Teams.[10]

PRE-PROCEEDINGS MATTERS IN FAMILY CASES

3.85 In family cases the pre-proceedings stage, where it occurs at all – almost exclusively in public law children cases – is much more fluid than in criminal cases.

10 The APP website gives useful guidance, especially for non-criminal law practitioners with respect to police duties and considerations when charging and links to the relevant statutory provisions and guidelines: see http://www.app-college.police.uk/app-content/prosecution-and-case-management/charging-and-case-preparation/.

Except in cases of urgency a family subject to the attention of the local authority is likely to have been so for a considerable period of time before proceedings are envisaged. The regulations applying to 'child in need investigations' and case conferences is beyond the scope of a book concerned with vulnerable witnesses. Practitioners are directed to the major textbooks on child law practice for the regulations and guidance concerning the duties of social workers and the proper frequency of visits and meetings.

3.86 Put briefly, however, pubic law proceedings begin with a Letter Before Action sent to the parents by the local authority after a legal planning meeting involving the key professionals involved with the family. If the conclusion of that meeting is that the case meets the threshold criteria for public law orders then the letter is sent. Thereafter a pre-proceedings meeting must take place within seven days of the letter. At the meeting the professionals and the parents seek to agree a plan for improvement in the care of the children.

3.87 Following the meeting a 'period of change' is allowed to see if the plan for improvement can be effected. There must be a further meeting – a 'pre-proceedings review' – within six to eight weeks of the pre-proceedings meeting. If sufficient progress is made then the pre-proceedings process ends. If some progress is made then the 'period of change' can be extended and a further review held in six to eight weeks. The whole process should not extend more than 18 weeks in total.

3.88 If after an appropriate amount of time it is felt that no, or insufficient, progress is made then the matter moves to an application to court and the Public Law Outline procedures take effect.[11]

Pre-Proceedings Practice – a reminder in relation to vulnerable persons

3.89 With regard to pre-proceedings meetings and reviews practitioners should all be aware of the way in which learning and communications difficulties can distort a person's responses to social work intervention well before the stage of issuing proceedings. A full understanding of the way in which social workers should adapt their practice to those with evident problems in communication and understanding is often a vital part of representing such a person.

3.90 Established authority[12] has stated very clearly that social workers must be aware of the 'Good Practice Guidance on Working with Parents with a Learning Disability' of 2007.[13] This guidance was updated in 2016 in collaboration between the British Association of Social Workers, Bristol University and the Esmée Fairbairn

11 FPR 2010 PD12A.

12 Eg *A County Council v A Mother and another* [2011] 2 All ER D 33 (Jun); [2011] EWHC 402 Fam.

13 http://webarchive.nationalarchives.gov.uk/20080910224541/dh.gov.uk/en/Publicationsandstatistics/Publications/PublicationsPolicyAndGuidance/DH_075119.

Association.[14] A failure to act in accordance with good practice is just as relevant to the forensic exercise as the need to ensure such good practice in the investigatory and court arenas.[15]

3.91 Where a child (or, it is submitted, a vulnerable adult witness) is to undertake an 'Achieving Best Evidence' interview there should always be consideration of an intermediary being instructed at that stage.[16] Those instructing intermediaries and conducting any assessment of a potential interviewee in the ABE process should be meticulous in the making and preservation of the notes of their interactions with the witness. A failure to keep a careful record may be harmful to the integrity of the process and the final outcome.[17]

3.92 They should usually refer the party to the adult learning disability team (or equivalent) who will then be able to carry out further assessments and complete a report if necessary (see *Re P (A Child) (Care and Placement Order Proceedings: Mental Capacity of Parent)*,[18] per Wall LJ:

> '[175] It is, I think, inevitable that in its pre-proceedings work with a child's family, the local authority will gain information about the capacity of the child's parents. The critical question is what it does with that information, particularly in a case where the social workers form the view that the parent in question may have learning difficulties.
>
> [176] At this point, in many cases, the local authority will be working with the child's parents in an attempt to keep the family together. In my judgment, the practical answer in these circumstances is likely to be that the parent in question should be referred to the local authority's adult learning disability team (or its equivalent) for help and advice. If that team thinks that further investigations are required, it can undertake them: it should, moreover, have the necessary contacts and resources to commission a report so that as soon as the pre-proceedings letter is written, and proceedings are issued, the legal advisers for the parent can be in a position, with public funding, to address the question of a litigation friend. It is, I think, important that judgments on capacity are not made by the social workers from the child protection team.'

3.93 It is important to note that a parent who lacks capacity is extremely unlikely to be able to give consent under the Children Act 1989, s 20 for their child to become looked after. Even where a party does have capacity, any consent must be fully informed.[19]

---

14 https://www.basw.co.uk/resource/?id=5816.

15 See *A County Council v A Mother* (above) paras 132–135.

16 This is the recommendation of Toolkit 6 of the Advocate's Gateway (theadvocatesgateway.org) and implicitly covers any person with the relevant communication deficit.

17 For a thorough review of the need to follow proper ABE procedures see, eg: *AS v TH, BC, NC, SH (by their Children's Guardian)* [2016] EWHC 532 (Fam).

18 [2008] EWCA Civ 462.

19 *Coventry City Council v C, B CA and CH* [2012] EWHC 2190 (Fam); *Newcastle City Council v WM & Others* [2015] EWFC 42.

Chapter 4

VULNERABLE PEOPLE IN THE INITIAL STAGES OF PROCEEDINGS

CRIMINAL PROCEEDINGS

Introduction

4.1 Once criminal proceedings have been instigated there will be the first hearing in the magistrates' court (for adult defendants) or in the youth court (for youth defendants – see **Chapter 7**). This hearing is very important and the need for special measures both for defendants and potential witnesses at that hearing and during the rest of the proceedings should be considered. Further, there will need to be the consideration of any possible defences that may specifically arise from the defendant's mental health – and what if any expert evidence may need to be obtained to address this see **Chapter 6**.

4.2 With respect to vulnerable witnesses at initial hearings in criminal proceedings (ie before trial) there will be no requirement for the witness to attend these initial hearings; that does not mean that they *cannot* attend, although usually a witness is not present at court for initial hearings. Once a decision has been made to bring a case to court, the care of a prosecution witness is handled by the witness support unit who act as a key point of contact for all prosecution witnesses. The witness support unit is run by the police and CPS – see **Chapter 9**. For defence witnesses there is no specific support unit, the provision of information and consideration of special measures falls to the defence solicitors though support will also be available from the voluntary organisation who create the at court witness support service which also assists the Crown witnesses when at court – see **Chapter 9**.

At the initial hearings, although the witness is most likely not present at court, the witness's needs – in particular re potential special measures and the impact of the proceedings upon them – will be considered by the court. Further, if there is a guilty plea then it is standard for a victim impact statement to have been prepared which will be provided to the court.

4.3 With respect to vulnerable defendants, it is helpful to have in mind Article 6 of ECHR, as enacted in the Human Rights Act 1998, s 1(3), Sch 1.

The basic principle of right to a fair trial is well known and often stated, however the full wording of Article 6 is helpful for practitioners to be aware of and to be able to cite:

> 'Article 6
>
> (1) In the determination of his civil rights and obligations or of any criminal charge against him, everyone is entitled to a fair and public hearing within a reasonable time by an independent and impartial tribunal established by law. Judgment shall be pronounced publicly but the press and public may be excluded from all or part of the trial in the interests of morals, public order or national security in a democratic society, where the interests of juveniles or the protection of the private life of the parties so require, or to the extent strictly necessary in the opinion of the court in special circumstances where publicity would prejudice the interests of justice.
>
> (2) Everyone charged with a criminal offence shall be presumed innocent until proved guilty according to law.
>
> (3) Everyone charged with a criminal offence has the following minimum rights:
>
> (a) to be informed promptly, in a language which he understands and in detail, of the nature and cause of the accusation against him;
>
> (b) to have adequate time and facilities for the preparation of his defence;
>
> (c) to defend himself in person or through legal assistance of his own choosing or, if he has not sufficient means to pay for legal assistance, to be given it free when the interests of justice so require;
>
> (d) to examine or have examined witnesses against him and to obtain the attendance and examination of witnesses on his behalf under the same conditions as witnesses against him;
>
> (e) to have the free assistance of an interpreter if he cannot understand or speak the language used in court.'

This principle of a right to a fair trial underpin the right of a vulnerable defendant and it should be noted the Article 6(3) rights are the *minimum* rights.

THE VULNERABLE DEFENDANT AT THE FIRST HEARING IN THE MAGISTRATES' COURT

4.4 At the first hearing (and beforehand) those representing vulnerable defendants need to be alive to the specific needs of any defendant and what special measures/assistance they may require in order for the first hearing to be effective; this is in line with the overriding objective that cases are 'dealt with justly' (CPR 2015, r 1.1(1)). If a defendant has been identified as requiring special measures at an interview/investigation stage then this will assist in identifying whether such measures will be necessary during the court proceedings.

4.5 The way this first hearing proceeds will depend on a number of factors; in particular whether the case is to be sent for trial to the Crown Court and whether the matter is to be contested at trial or if there is to be a guilty plea.

4.6 In the matters where the offence alleged is indictable only and therefore the case must be sent to the Crown Court, the absence of specific assistance for defendants (for example no intermediary or no interpreter) is unlikely to prevent the case being sent to the Crown Court. However, there is a need for a defendant to be able to follow the proceedings brought against them, so there should be careful consideration as to how much can be fairly achieved if the special measures or assistance are not available. The court will be mindful of the need for proceedings to be progressed and will balance this against any needs or assistance required by a defendant.

4.7 If there is an absence of key special measures for the defendant, and this is having a significant impact on the defendant's ability to understand or participate in the proceedings, it may be that an adjournment will need to be considered in order to allow for the hearing to be fully effective. If the requirement is clear before the hearing then the party should try and seek an adjournment in advance to avoid a wasted hearing. Furthermore, those acting for a defendant have a duty to ensure that a defendant is aware of the credit for an early guilty plea; this still applies to vulnerable defendants. For example, if it is the view of counsel for a vulnerable defendant that it is not possible to take instructions without the assistance of an intermediary and one is not available at the first hearing it may be advisable to ask the court to order that the credit for a guilty plea has not therefore been lost in these circumstances or at the very least will be considered at the next hearing. It should be noted that not being able to have an in intermediary during a trial, even though it had been recommended, has in some cases not resulted in a finding that the defendant was unable to have a fair trial (see para **13.10**) and therefore it seems that it is unlikely that the higher courts would find that the absence of an intermediary at an initial hearing is likely to have caused such unfairness that the defendant had subsequently had a unfair trial.

4.8 If, on the first hearing in the magistrates' court, no adjournment is required and the case is to remain in the magistrates' court then the matters set out at **4.27** should be considered. The case management form for magistrates' courts proceedings assists in identifying the matters to be considered at this stage to assist vulnerable defendants and witnesses.

DISCLOSURE AT OR BEFORE THE FIRST HEARING IN THE MAGISTRATES' COURT

4.9 At the magistrates' court the CPS provide the defence with initial disclosure, which is known by a number of acronyms including the IPDC. The CPR

2015, r 8.2 provides that the disclosure should be provided no later than the start of the day of the first hearing:

> '8.2.—(1) The prosecutor must serve initial details of the prosecution case on the court officer— (a) as soon as practicable; and (b) in any event, no later than the beginning of the day of the first hearing.
>
> (2) Where a defendant requests those details, the prosecutor must serve them on the defendant— (a) as soon as practicable; and (b) in any event, no later than the beginning of the day of the first hearing.
>
> (3) Where a defendant does not request those details, the prosecutor must make them available to the defendant at, or before, the beginning of the day of the first hearing.'

4.10 It is of note that this applies in the magistrates' court and does not specifically refer to the youth court. However, the case of *R(P) v Barking Youth Court*[1] clearly sets out that a youth court is a magistrates' court.

4.11 The CPR 2015, r 8.3 provides that the initial details of the prosecution case must include:

> '(a) where, immediately before the first hearing in the magistrates' court, the defendant was in police custody for the offence charged—
>
> (i) a summary of the circumstances of the offence, and
>
> (ii) the defendant's criminal record, if any;
>
> (b) where paragraph (a) does not apply—
>
> (i) a summary of the circumstances of the offence,
>
> (ii) any account given by the defendant in interview, whether contained in that summary or in another document,
>
> (iii) any written witness statement or exhibit that the prosecutor then has available and considers material to plea, or to the allocation of the case for trial, or to sentence,
>
> (iv) the defendant's criminal record, if any, and
>
> (v) any available statement of the effect of the offence on a victim, a victim's family or others.'

4.12 Further, there is the common law duty of disclosure. The Crown must disclose material which may assist the defence at bail hearings or in the early preparation of their case or in mitigation: *R v DPP, ex parte Lee.*[2] The common law principle is that the Crown should act fairly, disclosing as soon as possible material that may assist the defence.

---

1 [2002] EWHC 134 (Admin).

2 [1999] 1 WLR 1950.

A key factor with a vulnerable defendant is the need to have sufficient time to go through the material with the defendant and to consider all relevant matters.

THE FURTHER STAGES OF STANDARD DISCLOSURE IN CRIMINAL PROCEEDINGS FOLLOWING THE FIRST HEARING IN THE MAGISTRATES' COURT

Disclosure stages in criminal proceedings

4.13 It is not the purpose of this book to set out in any detail the stages of disclosure in criminal cases. However, it is likely to be of assistance for family practitioners to have knowledge of the standard stages of disclosure in a criminal case (they are referred to as stages) – these are set out below.

In addition, it is also important to remember that the Crown have a common law duty of disclosure as evaluated in *R v DPP, ex parte Lee.*[3]

Stage 1

4.14 For the service of the prosecution case and unused material under the Criminal Procedure and Investigations Act 1996. This date will ordinarily be 50 days (custody cases) or 70 days (bail cases) after the sending of the case to the Crown Court. This is in line with the timetable for the service of the prosecution case provided in the Crime and Disorder Act 1998 (Service of Prosecution Evidence) Regulations 2005.[4] The court does not have power to abridge this time (without consent) but does have power to extend it.

Stage 2

4.15 For the service of the defence response, ie service of the defence case statement. This date will ordinarily be 28 days after Stage 1.

Stage 3

4.16 For the prosecution response to the defence statement and other defence items. This date will ordinarily be 14 or 28 days after Stage 2 depending on the anticipated date of trial.

Stage 4

4.17 For the defence to provide final materials or make applications[5] that will commonly arise out of prosecution disclosure.

3 [1999] 1 WLR 1950.
4 SI 2005/902.
5 Usually under CPIA 1996, s 8.

4.18 When considering the joint hearings and cross-disclosure into family proceedings at the date of the PTPH it will not be the case that all the Crown's papers will have been disclosed/be available.

4.19 Almost the whole case in the Crown Court is now served via DCS and this applies to both the prosecution and the defence. As from 5 January 2016 all cases were sent for a PTPH (rather than a preliminary hearing or PCMH) and since March 2016 in the Crown Court all cases sent are DCS cases. The following link provides general guidance and some explanation for the changes: http://www.justice.gov.uk/courts/procedure-rules/criminal/docs/october-2015/cm007-eng.pdf.

OVERVIEW OF INITIAL CASE MANAGEMENT AND DIRECTIONS FOR VULNERABLE WITNESSES AND DEFENDANTS

4.20 In line with the overriding objective that cases are 'dealt with justly' (CPR 2015, r 1.1(1)) it is imperative that vulnerable witnesses and vulnerable defendants are identified early on within criminal proceedings. The CPR 2015, Pt 3 sets out the courts' and the parties' duties with respect to case management. The duty of the court is that it must 'further the overriding objective by actively managing the case' (CPR 2015, r 3.2(1)) Actively managing the case includes 'the early identification of the needs of witnesses' (CPR 2015, r 3.2(2)(b)).

4.21 The CRR 2015, r 3.9 requires as follows:

- CPR 2015, r 3.9(3):

  'In order to prepare for the trial, the court must take every reasonable step—

  (a) to encourage; and to facilitate the attendance of witnesses when they are needed; and

  (b) to facilitate the participation of any person, including the defendant.'

- CPR 2015, r 3.9(6):

  'Facilitating the participation of any person includes giving directions for the appropriate treatment and questioning of a witness or the defendant, especially where the court directs that such questioning is to be conducted through an intermediary.'

- CPR 2015, r 3.9(7):

  'Where directions for appropriate treatment and questioning are required, the court must—

  (a) invite representations by the parties and by any intermediary; and

(b) set ground rules for the conduct of the questioning, which rules may include—

(i) a direction relieving a party of any duty to put that party's case to a witness or a defendant in its entirety,

(ii) directions about the manner of questioning,

(iii) directions about the duration of questioning,

(iv) if necessary, directions about the questions that may or may not be asked,

(v) where there is more than one defendant, the allocation among them of the topics about which a witness may be asked, and

(vi) directions about the use of models, plans, body maps or similar aids to help communicate a question or an answer.'

4.22 With respect to case management lawyers should have regard to the Advocate's Tool Kit in particular 1a entitled Case management when a witness or defendant is vulnerable and also the Essential questions checklist.

4.23 Given the structure of criminal cases under the better case managements system, for magistrates' court and youth court cases the is likely only to be the first hearing and then the trial date (where there is a not guilty plea) and for Crown Court cases only the hearing in the magistrates' court sending the matter to the Crown Court, the PTPH and then the trial date (again where there is a not guilty plea).

4.24 Therefore, it is imperative that at the PTPH the representatives for the parties should be able to identify the potential vulnerable witnesses/defendants to ensure that appropriate directions can be made. It should be noted that this may only be such that the preliminary directions can be made to ensure that the vulnerable person or defendant is going to be properly assisted/the appropriate course is going to be taken – for example for the instruction of a report with respect to an intermediary.

4.25 Further, where necessary, a further hearing can be sought by the parties and given that a ground rules hearing is likely to be required it maybe that a combined pre-trial hearing and ground rule hearing can also be listed.

4.26 The PTPH form (see **Appendix A**) helps the representatives to identify the matters that need to be considered at this stage with respect to vulnerable witnesses and defendants including.

4.27 Matters that should be considered at the PTPH include:

(a) Special measures and intermediaries (see **Chapters 8** and **12**).

(b) Fitness to plead/stand trial (see **Chapter 6**).

(c) Defences that require the need for expert evidence including those that relate to the mental health of the defendant, for example insanity or diminished responsibility (see **Chapter 6**).

(d) *Witness summons*: Unfortunately, it is not unusual for witnesses who are vulnerable to also be reluctant to attend court and there is often the need to consider at the PTPH the need for such a measure to be in place to ensure the attendance of the witness and the effectiveness of the trial.

(e) *Reporting restrictions*: Protection of parties' and other connected persons' identities. It may be necessary for there to be reporting restrictions to protect vulnerable persons connected with proceedings – in particular children.

(f) *Bail conditions*: Consideration will need to be given to the appropriate conditions to protect vulnerable witnesses.

(g) *Anonymous witnesses*: An application for a witness anonymity order may be made by either the prosecution or defence. For procedure see CPR 2015, r 18. The Attorney General has issued guidelines: https://www.gov.uk/applications-for-witness-anonymity-orders-the-prosecutors-role as well as the DPP: http://www.cps.gov.uk/publications/directors_guidance/witness_anonymity.html. Three conditions as set out in the Act must be shown to be satisfied. A witness anonymity order prevents the identity of the witness from being disclosed in the proceedings, although the witness cannot be screened from the judge or jury. It is to be regarded as a 'special measure of last practicable resort'; save in the exceptional circumstances set out in the Act, 'the ancient principle that the defendant is entitled to know the identity of witnesses who incriminate him is maintained.' There is no common law or statutory power permitting the statement of an anonymous witness to be read.

4.28 Case management will require specific consideration of witnesses in sexual offences cases in particular the need for directions in relation to cross-examination of previous sexual behaviour of the complainant.

CRIMINAL PRECEDENTS AND STANDARD FORMS

4.29 There are a number of standard forms and standard precedents for those practising in both family law and criminal law A number of these relate either specifically to vulnerable people or give pointers as to considerations that practitioners should consider with respect to vulnerable people within the court system.

For both criminal and family law the Ministry of Justice website contains helpful standard forms and there are specific sections for both crime and family.

The following standard forms can be found in **Appendix A**:

- Magistrates' court case management form
- PTPH form
- Bail application form
- Witness summons form

- Application for special measures
- Application to give evidence by live link

The following precedents can be found in **Appendix B**:

- A draft skeleton for obtaining LAA funding for a psychologist report in order to then obtain approval for an intermediary.
- A draft application to adduce the complainant's previous sexual behaviour.

FAMILY PROCEEDINGS (AND IN PARTICULAR CARE PROCEEDINGS)

4.30 A substantial consideration of the regulations governing application forms and time limits for case management hearings as part of the PLO (see **Chapter 2**) are beyond the scope of this handbook and practitioners are referred to the *Family Court Practice* for details of procedural guidelines. As set out in **Chapter 2**, in November 2017 the Family Proceedings Rules 2010 were amended to include Part 3A Vulnerable persons participation in proceedings and giving evidence and Practice Direction (PD) 3AA Vulnerable persons: participation in proceedings and giving evidence. These rules and practice direction do provide a structure as to how to approach a vulnerable witness and importantly it is a mandatory requirement to consider whether a party's participation in the proceedings (other than by way of giving evidence) is likely to be diminished by reason of vulnerability.

This part of the handbook deals with parties who are so vulnerable that the initial stages of proceedings are affected by their inability to conduct proceedings on their own behalf.

Parties' ability to conduct proceedings[6]

4.31 Parties who do not have capacity to conduct proceedings are referred to as 'protected parties'. A party will be a protected party if they lack capacity under the Mental Capacity Act 2005, s 2(1). The participation of a protected party in proceedings is governed by FPR 2010, Part 15 and Practice Directions 15A and 15B.

4.32 In care proceedings, where there is often substantial pre-proceedings involvement, the Local Authority is expected to be on alert for parents who may lack capacity during these pre-proceedings stages. Pre-proceedings issues are addressed above in **Chapter 2**.

6 Key guidance documents in this area include:
Parents Who Lack Capacity to Conduct Public Law Proceedings – Family Justice Council, April 2010.
President's Guidance – Family Proceedings: Parents with a learning disability – April 2018.

4.33 Once proceedings are issued, the issue of capacity should be considered by the party's legal representative and, if there are concerns, an urgent application should be made to the court for an expert assessment by a psychologist/psychiatrist. There are some situations in which a letter from a treating clinician will suffice (see FPR 2010 PD15B). Once concerns about a party's capacity have been raised, no further steps involving that party should be taken in proceedings until the matter is resolved.

4.34 There is a presumption of capacity. Simply because a party has a learning difficulty (for example) this should not automatically prompt an investigation into their capacity to conduct proceedings.

4.35 The issue of capacity must be kept under review throughout proceedings. In *Re W (Children) (Care Proceedings: Litigation Capacity)*[7] the father's litigation capacity fluctuated throughout proceedings. The court had to assess on the balance of probabilities whether he could take part in proceedings on the whole and whether he could make the necessary decisions. The court was mindful in making this assessment of the full package of support which was available to the father.

4.36 The protected party's own legal representative will usually take the lead in the instruction of an expert. A draft letter of instruction can be found annexed to 'Parents who Lack Capacity to Conduct Public Law Proceedings', Family Justice Council, April 2010. This can be adapted to private law proceedings. It is important, if the person to be assessed is a litigant in person, that the letter of instruction states that the disadvantage faced by a litigant in person facing legal representatives does not of itself mean that they lack capacity. The assessment must include a consideration of whether the party would have capacity with the benefit of other assistance (eg a lay advocate).

4.37 If there is a dispute between experts as to a party's capacity, the issue must be determined by the court. In the case of *Re D (Children)*[8] this did not happen, with the litigation friend being dismissed on the basis of one expert's evidence (despite it conflicting with the evidence of previous expert). The Court of Appeal described this as a serious procedural irregularity, albeit they then validated the proceedings retrospectively as they felt that notwithstanding the discharge of the litigation friend, the parent's difficulties had been accounted for in other ways (eg through the use of a lay advocate). Per Lady Justice King:

> '[56] … This case does however perhaps provide a cautionary tale and a reminder that issues of capacity are of fundamental importance. The rules providing for the identification of a person, who lacks capacity, reflect society's proper understanding of the impact on both parent and child of the making of an order which will separate them permanently. It is therefore essential that the evidence which informs the issue of capacity complies with the test found in the

7 [2008] EWHC 1188 (Fam).
8 [2015] EWCA Civ 749.

MCA 2005 and that any conflict of evidence is brought to the attention of the court and resolved prior to the case progressing further. It is in order to avoid this course causing delay that the PLO anticipates issues of capacity being raised and dealt with in the early stages of the proceedings.'

4.38 Once a party is deemed to lack capacity to conduct proceedings, their participation in proceedings must be by way of a litigation friend. The 'Protected Parties in Family Proceedings: Checklist For the Appointment of a Litigation Friend (including the Official Solicitor)' provides useful guidance at this stage and should be completed by those representing the protected party.

4.39 The court can appoint anybody to be a litigation friend providing that their interests do not conflict with those of the protected party, and they are able to make decisions about the case in a fair and competent way. The proposed litigation friend must file a Certificate of Suitability (Form FP9).

4.40 If there is nobody suitable to act as a litigation friend, or if the court refuses a certificate of suitability, the Official Solicitor will be appointed to act as the litigation friend. This must be a last resort. The role of the Official Solicitor is considered in more detail at **Chapter 7**.

4.41 Unless it would be harmful (not merely distressing) the protected party should be informed of the appointment of the litigation friend and their role in proceedings (see 'Parents who Lack Capacity'). The order appointing the litigation friend should provide for them to receive a detailed letter of background information and a paginated bundle.

4.42 The litigation friend has a duty to conduct proceedings fairly and competently on behalf of the protected party and in their best interests having regard to the evidence. All decisions taken must be taken in the interests of the protected party.

4.43 In public law proceedings, where a child is to remain looked after at the conclusion of proceedings, the fact that a parent was deemed to lack capacity should be recorded clearly on the fact of any final order or care plan as a specific issue for consideration by the Independent Reviewing Officer.

4.44 The fact that a party lacks capacity does not mean that they are unable to give evidence. It may be advisable to ask any expert to consider as part of their assessment of capacity what safeguards or support would be necessary to enable the protected party to give evidence.

When looking at persons who have capacity but are vulnerable enough to require assistance in order to participate and give instructions or evidence, see **Chapter X**.

Chapter 5

JOINT HEARINGS – FAMILY AND CRIME

INTRODUCTION

5.1 Joint family and criminal hearings can have an invaluable role to play in cases involving vulnerable defendants and vulnerable witnesses and are unfortunately not yet used to their fullest extent, possibly because of the lack of knowledge about the possibility of such hearings or possibly because not enough is done soon enough in order for the necessary matters to be in place for a joint hearing to take place. This chapter provides a summary of the background to these hearings and a general overview to the rules and procedures governing them.

BACKGROUND

5.2

PROTOCOL AND GOOD PRACTICE MODEL ('2013 PROTOCOL') DISCLOSURE OF INFORMATION IN CASES OF ALLEGED CHILD ABUSE AND LINKED CRIMINAL AND CARE DIRECTIONS HEARINGS

Key documents:

1 The 2013 Protocol

2 The standard order template: 2013 Protocol and good practice model disclosure of information in cases of alleged child abuse and linked criminal and care directions hearings

Link: https://www.judiciary.gov.uk/publications/protocol-good-practice-model-2013/

5.3 *Joint Hearings – Family and Crime*

On 17 October 2013, the then Senior Presiding Judge for England and Wales, Lord Justice Goss, the then President of the Family Division, The Rt Hon Sir James Munby and the then Director of Public Prosecutions, Keir Starmer QC signed 'Disclosure of information in cases of alleged child abuse and linked criminal and care directions hearing' ('The Protocol and Good Practice Model'). Joint hearings in family and crime is not a new concept and the Public Law Proceedings Guide to Case Management – Practice Direction 12A at para 39 states:

> 'Where there are parallel care proceedings and criminal proceedings against a person connected with the child for a serious offence against the child, linked directions hearings should where practicable take place as the case progresses. The timing of the proceedings in a linked care and criminal case should appear in the Timetable for the Child.'

5.3 Since that Protocol, joint hearings in connected family and criminal proceedings have become more common, although they are still somewhat rare and arguably underused. These hearings can be mutually beneficial to both sets of proceedings and are something that those in the initial stages of proceedings should be alive to – a joint hearing is particular beneficial in a case involving vulnerable witnesses as it ensures that advocates in both sets of proceedings are made aware of the needs of the vulnerable witnesses (or vulnerable defendants or other parties to the proceedings) and there can be a joint approach. The Protocol applies where a person connected with the child who is subject of the care proceedings or the child themselves is to be tried at the Crown Court for any violent or sexual offence or for an offence of child cruelty against the child or any person connected with the child, and either:

- the local authority, CPS or any party to the care proceedings (including the children's guardian) considers that the care and criminal proceedings do, or may, impinge on one another; or
- in any public law proceedings in the High Court or county court or in any proceedings in the Crown Court, a judge is satisfied that the protocol does, or may, apply.

5.4 The timetable of the criminal proceedings in a linked care and criminal case should appear on the Case Management Order in the family proceedings as part of the relevant timetable for the child. As always, the 26-week time limit will apply in the care proceedings unless a longer timetable has been set by the court. In these proceedings, early disclosure and listing of hearings is necessary.

PRACTICALITIES/PROCEDURAL MATTERS

5.5 As to the practicalities/procedure at these joint hearings, the following are some general matters:

Where – Crown Court or Family Court?

5.6 The joint hearing will be heard before a judge (or judges) at the Crown Court. Para 16.5 of the *Protocol and Good Practice Model:* states:

> 'The criminal case shall be listed before the judge at the Crown Court in public with the linked directions appointment in the care proceedings listed for a hearing in private immediately thereafter.'

In private or open court?

5.7 As stated above although the hearings are listed together they are still conducted to some extent separately as the criminal proceedings are in open court (unless an order is in place to the contrary) and the family proceedings will as usual be in private. This makes considerable procedural sense. It will therefore be important for the practitioners to keep in check what matters should be dealt with in open court and what matters should be dealt with in private. Further, given the family proceedings are in private the Protocol and Good Practice Model addresses the right of the criminal lawyers to remain and states:

> 'Subject to any specific objections raised, by the parties, the advocates appearing in the criminal case may be invited to remain during the directions appointment in the care proceedings.'

The wording that it is an *invitation* makes it clear that this is not a foregone conclusion and it may still be that there will be matters that will not be dealt with when those solely connected with the criminal proceedings are present.

5.8 What will need to be carefully managed is where there are multiple defendants in the criminal proceedings who are not all concerned with the interconnecting family proceedings and what is discussed before those parties both inside and outside court.

Advocates robed or not?

5.9 There is no reason for the lawyers acting in the family proceedings to be robed although they may be invited to make representations during the criminal proceedings, in which the criminal advocates will be robed. If you acting for a party in both sets of proceedings then you will need to be robed.

One or more judges?

5.10 This will be a matter for the judges in the proceedings. From experience it is sometimes both a criminal and a family judge or simply one judge which is most likely to be the Crown Court judge, given the case is to be heard in the Crown Court. However, the Family Court judge could also sit alone, providing he/she is authorised to sit in the relevant category of crime. Joint hearings are clearly most advantageous for combined court buildings. However, there is clearly the possibility of contacting the allocated judge for the care proceedings during the combined hearing and it may be that the two judges will have discussed the best method to be contacted should the need arise during the hearing.

Procedure

5.11 Not less than five days prior to the hearing the local authority must serve on the CPS and the Crown Court a case summary and not less than two days prior to the hearing the local authority must circulate a schedule of issues for the hearing that it has agreed with the CPS. Paragraphs 16.6 and 16.7 of the Protocol sets out the matters to be considered at the linked directions hearing and Annex I contains a template directions order.

5.12 Where a Crown Court judge will be sitting on his/her own at the joint hearing it may be advisable for those acting in the care proceedings to agree between the parties any proposed directions that solely relate to the care proceedings (or where the permission of the Family Court is required in advance of the hearing) and where possible have those agreed in principle by the allocated judge for the care proceedings.

Which hearings will be joint hearings?

5.13 The relevant hearings are the Joint Plea and Trial Preparation Hearing (PTPH) and the Case Management Hearing (CMC). Given the implementation of Better Case Management in criminal proceedings and the intention that there should only be one hearing prior to the trial, that being the PTPH, it is most likely to be the PTPH and CMH that are combined into a joint hearing. However, a directions hearing can be directed and if the parties and the court agree that a joint hearing would be beneficial after the PTPH then this could still take place.

Chapter 6

FITNESS TO PLEAD AND SPECIFIC DEFENCES ARISING FROM BEING A VULNERABLE DEFENDANT

FITNESS TO PLEAD IN THE CROWN COURT

Introduction

6.1 In cases involving vulnerable defendants, the first step within court proceedings is often to take a preliminary view of whether the a defendant is fit to plead; at the initial stage those acting for a defendant will often, without a formal report, have to make a judgement call when first engaging with their client, which may be at the first hearing, whether fitness to plead is a matter that needs to be considered. One clear difficulty is that by its very nature fitness to plead is not something that specific instructions can be taken for or on, as the very decision being considered is often based on the view that the client's ability to give instructions is impaired.

The legal concept of 'fitness to plead' is not used in the magistrates' court although there is a similar procedure which is set out in the Mental Health Act 1983, s 37(3) (when read in conjunction with the Powers of Criminal Courts (Sentencing) Act 2000, s 11(1)). The procedure in the youth court is the same as in the magistrates' court see **Chapter 7**.

6.2 Fitness to plead is a matter that needs to be raised as soon as possible; if apparent it should be raised at the outset of proceedings (in summary proceedings this will be at the first hearing) and in Crown Court proceedings although helpful to be identified at the sending hearing it should be identified at the PTPH. The trial preparation forms identify fitness to plead as matter for consideration. It should be remembered that fitness to plead is something that needs to be considered irrelevant of whether it is likely the person committed the offence, so even if the defendant confessed all in the police station and the evidence is such that it is apparent that the person committed the offence (eg CCTV evidence) this does not negate the possibility of the defendant not being fit to plead/stand trial.

6.3 Further, it must be remembered that fitness to plead can be a transient matter and representatives should be alive to the fact that the stresses and strains of criminal proceedings can result in a defendant who was fit to plead initially not being fit to plead by the time of trial or at the very least now requiring special measures, for example the assistance of an intermediary which had not been previously required. There is a wealth of case law with respect to fitness to plead some of which is set out below. The case of *R v Patrick Orr*[1] highlights that fitness to plead is something that may alter even during the trial process. In this case the defendant became unwell after giving his evidence in chief. Two psychiatrists attended court and assessed him as unfit to be cross-examined. The judge allowed the trial to proceed and likened the defendant to a vulnerable witness who had difficulty in dealing with part of the trial process and who should not be disadvantaged by not being cross-examined. The Court of Appeal found that this was not the correct approach and that the issue of fitness to plead could be raised at any time prior to verdict and could not be determined by reference to only part of the trial process. So although the defendant had been fit up to the point of cross-examination, the fitness to plead process could still be commenced see paras 29 and 30:

> '29. Once the issue of fitness to plead has been raised it must be determined. In this case, the judge explicitly found that the appellant had been fit to participate in his trial up to the point of cross examination and thereby implicitly determined that the appellant was no longer able to fully participate in his trial within the 'Pritchard' refined criteria. In these circumstances, the procedure to be adopted was clearly set out by section Criminal Procedure (Insanity) Act 1964, 4A.
>
> 30. We agree with the submission that this is a statutory mandatory requirement which cannot be avoided by the court's general discretion to order proceedings otherwise, however beneficial to the defendant they may appear. It follows that, in this case, the jury should not have been allowed to return a verdict, other than a verdict of acquittal if they were not satisfied on the evidence already given in the trial that the appellant did the act charged against him.'

Procedure

6.4 For those interested in the history of criminal law and the significant changes that have occurred, fitness to plead is an area that has changed significantly over time. For example past procedures include the 16th century punishment for those found mute by malice; they were subjected to the *peine forte et dure* which was a process which amounted to being confined in a narrow cell, starved and gradually crushed under an increasing weight until such time as the defendant either reconsidered their decision not to enter a plea or died. Unfitness to plead was first introduced into statute in the Criminal Lunatics Act 1800, s 2.

Today the key legal provisions governing fitness to plead are the Criminal Procedure (Insanity) Act 1964, ss 4, 4A and 5 and CPR 2015, 25.10

1 [2016] EWCA Crim 889.

6.5

> **Finding of unfitness to plead (Criminal Procedure (Insanity) Act 1964, s 4)**
>
> (1) This section applies where on the trial of a person the question arises (at the instance of the defence or otherwise) whether the accused is under a disability, that is to say, under any disability such that apart from this Act it would constitute a bar to his being tried.
>
> (2) If, having regard to the nature of the supposed disability, the court are of opinion that it is expedient to do so and in the interests of the accused, they may postpone consideration of the question of fitness to be tried until any time up to the opening of the case for the defence.
>
> (3) If, before the question of fitness to be tried falls to be determined, the jury return a verdict of acquittal on the count or each of the counts on which the accused is being tried, that question shall not be determined.
>
> (4) Subject to subsections (2) and (3) above, the question of fitness to be tried shall be determined as soon as it arises.
>
> (5) The question of fitness to be tried shall be determined by the court without a jury.
>
> (6) The court shall not make a determination under subsection (5) above except on the written or oral evidence of two or more registered medical practitioners at least one of whom is duly approved.

The test in determining fitness to plead is for the the judge and is not one of insanity or mental illness but the test as set out in *Pritchard*[2] and clarified in *John M*:[3]

> 'The court considers the defendant's ability at the time of the trial:
>
> (i) to understand the charges;
>
> (ii) to understand the plea;
>
> (iii) to challenge jurors;
>
> (iv) to instruct legal representatives;
>
> (v) to understand the course of the trial; and
>
> (vi) to give evidence if he chooses.'

6.6 As set out in the Criminal Procedure (Insanity) Act 1964, s 4 above, whether, a person is fit to plead is for the judge to determine and not a matter for the jury. If the judge concludes on the basis of expert medical evidence of two registered medical practitioners, one of which must be approved under the Mental Health Act 1983, s 12, that the defendant lacks any of the above capabilities the

2 (1836) 7 C & P 303.
3 [2003] EWCA Crim 3452.

judge will determine that he is unfit to plead (Criminal Procedure (Insanity) Act 1964 s 4 (2)).

6.7 Conversely a judge is entitled to conclude, on the evidence before them at the time, that the defendant is fit without evidence from two registered medical practitioners and that the trial proceeds on the assumption that a defendant is fit to plead until otherwise established: *R v Ghulam*.[4] However, there is no statutory presumption of fitness to plead in criminal law although there is such a presumption in civil law under the Mental Capacity Act 2005, s 1, where a person is assumed to have capacity unless the contrary is established. Further, should a judge at the PTPH take the view that there is not sufficient evidence supporting a defendant's unfitness to plead and in effect forces a plea, those acting on behalf of the defendant are not prevented legally from still seeking to ascertain whether the defendant is fit to plead.

6.8 However, it is clearly sensible that a defendant who may not be fit to plead should not be asked to enter a plea until the matter of his fitness to plead has been properly considered.

6.9

Finding that the accused did the act or made the omission charged against him (Criminal Procedure (Insanity) Act 1964, s 4A

'(1) This section applies where in accordance with section 4(5) above it is determined by a court that the accused is under a disability.

(2) The trial shall not proceed or further proceed but it shall be determined by a jury—

(a) on the evidence (if any) already given in the trial; and

(b) on such evidence as may be adduced or further adduced by the prosecution, or adduced by a person appointed by the court under this section to put the case for the defence,

whether they are satisfied, as respects the count or each of the counts on which the accused was to be or was being tried, that he did the act or made the omission charged against him as the offence.

(3) If as respects that count or any of those counts the jury are satisfied as mentioned in subsection (2) above, they shall make a finding that the accused did the act or made the omission charged against him.

(4) If as respects that count or any of those counts the jury are not so satisfied, they shall return a verdict of acquittal as if on the count in question the trial had proceeded to a conclusion.

(5) Where the question of disability was determined after arraignment of the accused, the determination under subsection (2) is to be made by the jury by whom he was being tried.'

4 [2009] EWCA Crim 2285.

The burden of proof is on the party alleging unfitness: *R v Robertson*.[5]

The procedure once a defendant has been found not fit to plead is set out in the Criminal Procedure (Insanity) Act 1964, s 4(A). Pausing before the case moves to the stage of considering if the defendant performed the alleged acts there is then the possibility for the Crown to seek to end the proceedings against the defendant. For example, in a case where the defendant is not fit to plead and the likely outcome (should they be found to have performed the alleged acts) is an absolute discharge, it may be that the Crown will take a view that it is not in the public interest to proceed against that defendant. Before the indictment has been preferred the Crown can discontinue the proceedings. However, once the indictment has been preferred then the proceedings cannot be discontinued (Prosecution of Offences Act 1985, s 23A). The procedure once the indictment is preferred is that Crown can either offer no evidence or ask that the matter lie on the file. From the perspective of a defendant it is preferable that the Crown offers no evidence so that the case has been finalised.

6.10 If, however, the Crown proceeds against the defendant when they have been found not fit to plead then there is a hearing to determine whether the defendant did the act or made the omission charged against them as set out in the Criminal Procedure (Insanity) Act 1964, s 4A. Using the word 'trial' would be a misnomer as there can be no finding of guilt. At that hearing any confession or incriminating statement made by a defendant should not ordinarily be relied upon by the Crown unless the defendant's unfitness arose after the making of the statement *R v Swinbourne*.[6]

6.11 The hearing is before a jury and it is for the Crown to prove beyond reasonable doubt that the defendant did the act alleged, ie to the normal criminal standard of proof. If the act is not proved then the jury return a verdict of not guilty: *R v Antoine (Pierre Harrison)*;[7] *R v Chal*.[8]

It should be noted that those acting for a defendant at this trial are appointed by the court. In practice it is usually the team that were already acting on behalf of the defendant.

6.12

Powers to deal with persons not guilty by reason of insanity or unfit to plead etc (Criminal Procedure (Insanity) Act 1964, s 5)

'(1) This section applies where—

(a) a special verdict is returned that the accused is not guilty by reason of insanity; or

(b) findings have been made that the accused is under a disability and that he did the act or made the omission charged against him.

5 [1968] 1 WLR 1767.
6 [2013] EWCA Crim 2329.
7 [2001] 1 AC 340.
8 [2007] EWCA Crim 2647.

(2) The court shall make in respect of the accused—

(a) a hospital order (with or without a restriction order);

(b) a supervision order; or

(c) an order for his absolute discharge.

(3) Where—

(a) the offence to which the special verdict or the findings relate is an offence the sentence for which is fixed by law, and

(b) the court have power to make a hospital order,

the court shall make a hospital order with a restriction order (whether or not they would have power to make a restriction order apart from this subsection).

(4) In this section—

"hospital order" has the meaning given in section 37 of the Mental Health Act 1983;

"restriction order" has the meaning given to it by section 41 of that Act;

"supervision order" has the meaning given in Part 1 of Schedule 1A to this Act.'

If the jury find that defendant did the act then the court has three options as to how the proceed with the defendant: (i) a hospital order (with or without a restriction order); (ii) a supervision order; or (iii) an absolute discharge.

6.13 See **Chapter 14** with respect to jury directions and defendants being unfit to plead.

The case of *R v Walls*[9] sets out, at para 37, a helpful summary re fitness to plead:

'It is important to underline three matters:

i) A finding that a defendant is unfit to plead has the consequence that the court must determine whether he did the act in accordance with the procedure set out in s.4A of the Criminal Procedure (Insanity) Act 1964. The court appoints a representative to put the case for the defence, but the defendant himself will not give evidence and ex hypothesi, his ability to give instructions or the ability to obtain an account from the defendant is limited. Depriving the defendant of these very significant rights is a very serious step.

ii) There are available to those with learning disabilities in this age, facilities that can assist. Consideration can now be given to the use of

9 [2011] EWCA 443.

an intermediary under the court's inherent powers as described in the Sevenoaks case, pending the bringing into force of s.33BA (3) and (4) of the Youth and Criminal Evidence Act 1999 (added by the Coroners and Justice Act 2009). Plainly consideration should be given to the use of these powers or other ways in which the characteristics of a defendant evident from a psychological or psychiatric report can be accommodated with the trial process so that his limitations can be understood by the jury, before a court takes the very significant step of embarking on a trial of fitness to plead.

iii) A finding that a defendant did the act in question, has the consequence that the court's powers of disposal are limited to a hospital order (where the issues are too well known to need stating), a supervision order for a specified period of no more than two years or an absolute discharge – see s.5 of the Criminal Procedure (Insanity) 1964. The court's ability either to protect the public or to assist the defendant is severely limited.'

Check list/key considerations

- *Pre-arraignment*: Are there concerns about the defendant's fitness to plead/stand trial? Consider all factors including: behaviour at the police station; during the alleged incident; known medical information; and presentation to legal professionals.
- *Arraignment*: If it is before the first hearing then it may be inappropriate for the defendant to be arraigned. Consider if the court and the Crown should be put on notice prior to the first hearing that this is a live issue as it may be that the first hearing can be adjourned by agreement until preliminary medical evidence has been obtained.
- *Post-arraignment*: If the defendant has already been arraigned and the issue of fitness to plead or to stand trial has arisen during the process, consider what steps need to be taken to inform the court and the Crown. Does the case need to be listed to put the court and the Crown on notice and set a timetable?
- *Expert evidence*:
  - If it is a concern does the defendant already have a treating team that can provide an initial preliminary view?
  - Which experts need to be instructed to provide reports on the defendant? Does a psychologist need to be instructed re cognitive function? Does an intermediary report need to be prepared (can the defendant's difficulties be reduced by assistance to the extent that the defendant can participate in the trial)? If fitness to plead is to be found by the court the court requires evidence from two registered medical practitioners, one of whom must be approved under the Mental Health Act 1983, s 12.
  - What funding needs to be applied for in order to obtain the reports? Does counsel need to provide advice to support the extension of LAA funding for the expert's reports?

Templates and forms

- The Plea and Trial preparation form has a section to record issues with respect to fitness to plead.
- See the **Appendices** at pp 155 et seq for an example of advice to obtain LAA funding for an expert.

Insanity and automatism (internal and external causation)

6.14 Insanity and automatism are two defences that can often become confused. In simplistic terms insanity is when there is an internal cause and automatism is when there is an external cause of the behaviour.

6.15 In the case of vulnerable defendants, it is most likely that the defence that will be being considered is one of insanity.

6.16 A successful defence of insanity results in a verdict of not guilty by reason of insanity; such a verdict is an acquittal in that the defendant is found not to be to blame for his actions, however such an acquittal does not necessarily result in there being no consequences for the defendant. Therefore those representing such defendants will still need to be alive to whether, even if such a defence is made out, in fact the defendant has a full defence resulting in a full finding of not guilty rather than a special verdict.

Insanity

6.17

> **Special verdict where accused found guilty, but insane at date of act or omission charged, and orders thereupon (Trial of Lunatics Act 1883, s 2)**
>
> (1) Where in any indictment or information any act or omission is charged against any person as an offence, and it is given in evidence on the trial of such person for that offence that he was insane, so as not to be responsible, according to law, for his actions at the time when the act was done or omission made, then, if it appears to the jury before whom such person is tried that he did the act or made the omission charged, but was insane as aforesaid at the time when he did or made the same, the jury shall return a special verdict that the accused is not guilty by reason of insanity.

6.18 The key case is that of *M'Naughten*;[10] in order for there to be a verdict of not guilty by reason of insanity it must be found that:

(1) at the time of the commission of the actus reus the defendant was suffering from a disease of the mind

10 (1843) 8 ER 718.

(2) That disease of the mind gave rise to a defect of reason such that either:

(a) they did not know the nature and quality of the act they were doing or

(b) that what they were doing was legally wrong.

6.19 The Trial of Lunatics Act 1883, s 2 sets out the procedure for the jury to return the special verdict. If the defence rely on the defence of not guilty by reason of insanity the burden of proof is on the defence and the standard of proof is the balance of probabilities. However, it is the case that the Crown must still prove the actus reus to the normal criminal standard of proof (beyond a reasonable doubt).

6.20 There must be evidence from two registered practitioners and at least one must be approved under the Mental Health Act 1983, s 12.

Powers to deal with persons guilty by reason of insanity or unfit to plead etc (Criminal Procedure (Insanity) Act 1964, s 5)

'(1) This section applies where—

(a) a special verdict is returned that the accused is not guilty by reason of insanity; or

(b) findings have been made that the accused is under a disability and that he did the act or made the omission charged against him.

(2) The court shall make in respect of the accused—

(a) a hospital order (with or without a restriction order);

(b) a supervision order; or

(c) an order for his absolute discharge.

(3) Where—

(a) the offence to which the special verdict or the findings relate is an offence the sentence for which is fixed by law, and

(b) the court have power to make a hospital order,

the court shall make a hospital order with a restriction order (whether or not they would have power to make a restriction order apart from this subsection).

(4) In this section—

"hospital order" has the meaning given in section 37 of the Mental Health Act 1983;

"restriction order" has the meaning given to it by section 41 of that Act;

"supervision order" has the meaning given in Part 1 of Schedule 1A to this Act.'

6.21 In order for the cause to amount to a disease of the mind it must be an internal factor.[11] Examples of internal causes from previous case law have included epilepsy, brain tumours, hyperglycaemic episodes.

6.22 It is for the jury to return a special verdict of not guilty by reason of insanity as set out in the Trial of Lunatics Act 1883, s 2 and is not as result of the defendant's plea. Further, even if it is the case that both the defence and the Crown agree that the defence is made out and there should be no trial, it is still for the jury to decide although they can be told that the defence and Crown agree. However, if the jury return a verdict which is perverse on the evidence then the Court of Appeal can substitute a special verdict under the Criminal Appeal Act 1968, s 6.

6.23 As stated above where a special verdict is returned it is not the case that the court has no powers to impose any further orders. As can be seen from the Criminal Procedure (Insanity) Act 1964, s 5 (set out at **6.21**) the court has a number of orders available to it. However, in cases where the sentence is fixed by law and there would be the power to make a hospital order (eg in a case of murder) a hospital order with a restriction order must be made.

Sane automatism (internal factor)

6.24 This defence applies when an external cause is such that at the time of the offence an external factor has caused the defendant's actions to be wholly involuntary.

6.25 In the case of defendants and often vulnerable defendants, the impact of any medication they were taking at the time of the offences may be something that has caused sane automatism.

OTHER DEFENCES

6.26 As well as insanity there are a number of defences that may arises in cases with vulnerable people.

Diminished responsibility

6.27

Persons suffering from diminished responsibility (Homicide Act 1957, s 2)

'(1) A person ("D") who kills or is a party to the killing of another is not to be convicted of murder if D was suffering from an abnormality of mental functioning which—

11 *R v Coley & Ors* [2013] EWCA Crim 223.

(a) arose from a recognised medical condition,

(b) substantially impaired D's ability to do one or more of the things mentioned in subsection (1A), and

(c) provides an explanation for D's acts and omissions in doing or being a party to the killing.

(1A) Those things are—

(a) to understand the nature of D's conduct;

(b) to form a rational judgment;

(c) to exercise self-control.

(1B) For the purposes of subsection (1)(c), an abnormality of mental functioning provides an explanation for D's conduct if it causes, or is a significant contributory factor in causing, D to carry out that conduct.

(2) On a charge of murder, it shall be for the defence to prove that the person charged is by virtue of this section not liable to be convicted of murder.

(3) A person who but for this section would be liable, whether as principal or as accessory, to be convicted of murder shall be liable instead to be convicted of manslaughter.

(4) The fact that one party to a killing is by virtue of this section not liable to be convicted of murder shall not affect the question whether the killing amounted to murder in the case of any other party to it.'

Duress

6.28 Duress affords a defence which if raised and not disproved, exonerates the defendant altogether. Lord Wilberforce in *DPP for Northern Ireland v Lynch*[12] described duress as follows:

> 'the victim completes the act and knows that he is doing so; but the addition of the element of duress prevents the law from treating what he has done as a crime.'

6.29 A two-stage test was set out in *R v Graham*[13] (which was approved by *R v Howe*).[14] The two stages are:

> '(a) Was the defendant, or may he have been, impelled to act as he did because, as a result of what he reasonably believed [the threatener] had said or done, he had good cause to fear that if he did not so act the [threatener] would kill him or ... cause him serious injury?

12 [1975] AC 653.
13 [1982] 1 All ER 801.
14 [1987] AC 417.

(b) If so have the prosecution made the jury sure that a sober person of reasonable firmness, sharing the characteristics of the defendant, would not have responded to whatever he reasonably believed [the threatener] said or did by taking part [in the offence].'

6.30 There are circumstances and offences where it has been held that the defence of duress should not be available; for example when a person has voluntarily associated with the people/person that have been the source of the duress, knowing that they could act in that way: *R v Fitzpatrick*.[15]

In the case of *R v Howe*[16] duress was found not to be a defence to murder however, arguably this law has been somewhat left unclear after duress was held to be an available defence to conspiracy to murder in *R v Ness and Awan*[17] and the Law Commission recommended that the defence of duress should be available in its Report Murder, Manslaughter and Infanticide (Law Com No 304, 2006).

Provocation/loss of control:

6.31 The statutory defence of loss of control is under the Coroners and Justice Act 2009, ss 54 and 55 and s 56 of that Act abolished the common law defence of provocation in relation to killings. These provisions came into force on 4 October 2010.

6.32 This defence arises where there is a vulnerable person who has been subjected to abuse or mistreatment.

Partial defence to murder: loss of control (Coroners and Justice Act 2009, s 54)

'(1) Where a person ("D") kills or is a party to the killing of another ("V"), D is not to be convicted of murder if—

(a) D's acts and omissions in doing or being a party to the killing resulted from D's loss of self-control,

(b) the loss of self-control had a qualifying trigger, and

(c) a person of D's sex and age, with a normal degree of tolerance and self-restraint and in the circumstances of D, might have reacted in the same or in a similar way to D.

(2) For the purposes of subsection (1)(a), it does not matter whether or not the loss of control was sudden.

15 [1977] NI 20.
16 [1987] AC 417.
17 2011 Crim LR 645.

(3) In subsection (1)(c) the reference to "the circumstances of D" is a reference to all of D's circumstances other than those whose only relevance to D's conduct is that they bear on D's general capacity for tolerance or self-restraint.

(4) Subsection (1) does not apply if, in doing or being a party to the killing, D acted in a considered desire for revenge.

(5) On a charge of murder, if sufficient evidence is adduced to raise an issue with respect to the defence under subsection (1), the jury must assume that the defence is satisfied unless the prosecution proves beyond reasonable doubt that it is not.

(6) For the purposes of subsection (5), sufficient evidence is adduced to raise an issue with respect to the defence if evidence is adduced on which, in the opinion of the trial judge, a jury, properly directed, could reasonably conclude that the defence might apply.

(7) A person who, but for this section, would be liable to be convicted of murder is liable instead to be convicted of manslaughter.

(8) The fact that one party to a killing is by virtue of this section not liable to be convicted of murder does not affect the question whether the killing amounted to murder in the case of any other party to it.'

6.33 The burden and standard of proof is such that, once evidence has been raised by the defence to support the defence of loss of control, the Crown must disprove it to the criminal standard of proof.

6.34 The Coroners and Justice Act 2009, s 55 and the definition of the qualifying trigger highlights that this provision is likely to relate to that person being a victim in some way or to someone else being a victim.

Meaning of "qualifying trigger" (Coroners and Justice Act 2009, s 55)

'(1) This section applies for the purposes of section 54.

(2) A loss of self-control had a qualifying trigger if subsection (3), (4) or (5) applies.

(3) This subsection applies if D's loss of self-control was attributable to D's fear of serious violence from V against D or another identified person.

(4) This subsection applies if D's loss of self-control was attributable to a thing or things done or said (or both) which—

(a) constituted circumstances of an extremely grave character, and

(b) caused D to have a justifiable sense of being seriously wronged.

(5) This subsection applies if D's loss of self-control was attributable to a combination of the matters mentioned in subsections (3) and (4).

(6) In determining whether a loss of self-control had a qualifying trigger—

(a) D's fear of serious violence is to be disregarded to the extent that it was caused by a thing which D incited to be done or said for the purpose of providing an excuse to use violence;

(b) a sense of being seriously wronged by a thing done or said is not justifiable if D incited the thing to be done or said for the purpose of providing an excuse to use violence;

(c) the fact that a thing done or said constituted sexual infidelity is to be disregarded.

(7) In this section references to "D" and "V" are to be construed in accordance with section 54.'

Chapter 7

YOUNG DEFENDANTS AND THE YOUTH COURT

INTRODUCTION

7.1 The principles governing how young defendants – children – are to be treated within the criminal justice system is to some extent different from the principles for adult defendants. A key difference for youth defendants is that the principal aim of youth justice is as set out in the Crime And Disorder Act 1998, s 37, which requires the principal aim of agencies involved in the youth justice system to be the prevention of offending by young persons. This is a positive approach to child offenders and makes it clear that rehabilitation is a key consideration.

REQUIREMENT TO BE REGISTERED AS COMPETENT TO ACT IN YOUTH PROCEEDINGS

7.2 Barristers undertaking youth court work must be aware of the Bar Standards Board guidance entitled 'Youth Proceedings Competences' which was issued in February 2017 see the link at https://www.barstandardsboard.org.uk/media/1821763/bsb_youth_competencies_2017_for_website.pdf.

This is an invaluable document for those undertaking youth court work. It should be noted that this document applies not only to proceedings in the youth court but all cases involving young defendants. The document makes it clear that the competences are relevant at all stages of a case 'including any engagement a barrister has with young people outside the courtroom.'

7.3 The document is divided into five sections:

1 Law and procedure;

2 Dealing with vulnerability;

3 Awareness of background and needs;

4 Communication and engagement; and

5 Awareness of key organisations

Further, the Bar Standards Board introduced a regulatory requirement that barristers who intend to undertake Youth Court work must register that intention with the Bar Standards Board. This is usually done when renewing their practising certificates. Barristers can register and unregister through the MyBar portal.

DEFINITION OF A CHILD

7.4 There has been an inconsistent use of terminology when referring to child defendants and the definition of who is to be considered as a child defendant. The UN Convention on the Rights of the Child defines 'children' as being under 18, therefore, unless stated otherwise, the use of the word 'child' means a person under 18.

The Youth Court Bench Book which provides guidance to those presiding over youth court proceedings and is again an invaluable resource for practitioners acting in youth proceedings.

The Youth Court Bench Book states that those children under the age of 14 are referred to as 'children' and those aged 14–17 as 'young people' so care is need with terminology.

AGE OF CRIMINAL LIABILITY

7.5 It should be noted that a child under the age of ten has not reached the age of criminal liability. Since 30 September 1998 all children aged ten and over are treated as having the same capacity as adults to commit criminal offences. The presumption that a child between the ages of 10 and 13 years inclusive is incapable of forming criminal intention (known as *doli incapax*) was abolished by the Crime and Disorder Act 1998, s 34 and therefore that presumption only remains of relevance for offences committed before its abolition, ie before 30 September 1998. In cases under the old law the presumption is a rebuttable presumption where the Crown must establish that the defendant knew what they were doing was seriously wrong.

DECISION TO PROSECUTE AND OUT OF COURT DISPOSALS

7.6 Even before a prosecution has commenced the fact that an alleged offender is a child is a key consideration: this includes how they are dealt with if arrested, if they are interviewed and how they may be detained. See **Chapter 3** re arrest, police interviews and detention of youth defendants.

When deciding whether to bring a case against a child, the Code for Crown Prosecutors states that Crown Prosecutors must consider the interests of a youth, amongst other public interest factors, when deciding whether a prosecution is needed.

Practitioners both for the defence and the prosecution, when dealing with/ considering cases involving child suspects, need to be aware that the fact that a suspect is a child is a key factor. As stated above it is one that should be considered by a prosecutor when making the decision to prosecute and the defence should ensure this factor has been properly considered before any decision to prosecute has been made. It may be a successful ground for a judicial review of a decision to prosecute a child if it can be demonstrated that the decision was made regardless of, or without any or sufficient inquiry into, the circumstances and general character of the accused. *R v Chief Constable of Kent and Another ex parte L, R v DPP ex parte B*[1] highlights the importance in appropriate cases of the Crown obtaining sufficient information about the child's home circumstances and background from sources such as the police, youth offending service and children's services before making the decision whether to prosecute. This is something that those acting for children in care cases should also be alive to, as it may be that they will have useful information which will assist the prosecution in determining the public interest to prosecute.

7.7 The CPS website provides practitioners with assistance as to the steps that should be considered by the CPS which deciding if it is appropriate to prosecute a child; see https://www.cps.gov.uk/legal-guidance/youth-offenders.

7.8 When applying the public interest factors in the Full Code Test in a case involving a youth, paragraph 4.17(b) will always be a particularly important one. This paragraph provides that:

> 'A prosecution is less likely to be required if … the seriousness and the consequences of the offending can be appropriately dealt with by an out-of-court disposal which the suspect accepts and with which he or she complies.'

7.9 Another alternative to a court prosecution of a child is a youth caution or youth conditional caution. A youth caution can be offered provided that the statutory criteria are satisfied these being:

- the police are satisfied that there is sufficient evidence to charge the youth with an offence;
- the youth admits the offence to the police;
- the police do not consider that the youth should be prosecuted or given a youth conditional caution for the offence; and
- the police cannot issue a youth caution for an offence that is indictable only in the case of an adult without the authority of the CPS.

1 [1991] 93 Cr App R 416.

Practitioners should have in mind that there is no statutory restriction on the number of youth cautions that a youth can receive, and a youth may receive a youth caution even if he or she has previous convictions, reprimands, warnings, youth cautions and youth conditional cautions.

Youth conditional cautions

7.10 The Crime and Disorder Act 1998, ss 65 and 66A–66H (as amended) provide that a youth conditional caution (YCC) can be given to a youth provided that the following conditions are satisfied:

- The authorised person has evidence that the youth has committed an offence.
- The prosecutor is satisfied that there is sufficient evidence to charge the youth with the offence and that a YCC should be given in respect of the offence.
- The youth admits the offence to an authorised person.
- The authorised person has explained the effect of the YCC to the youth and has warned him or her that failure to comply with any of the conditions may result in a prosecution. If the youth is 16 or under this must be done in the presence of an appropriate adult.
- The youth signs a document that contains details of the offence, an admission that he committed the offence, consent to the YCC and the conditions attached to the caution.

7.11 Youth conditional cautions are available for any offence, except an offence of hate crime or domestic violence that has a gravity core of 4 on the Youth Gravity Factor Matrix but a YCC can only be given for an indictable only offence on the authority of the CPS. The police may issue a YCC for any either way or summary offence, except an offence of hate crime or domestic violence with a gravity score of 4, without reference to the CPS. The YCC is no longer restricted to youths with no previous convictions and there is no statutory restriction on the number of YCCs that a youth can receive.

THE OBJECTIVES OF THE YOUTH JUSTICE SYSTEM

7.12 Once a prosecution has started, the Children and Young Persons Act (CYPA) 1933, s 44 requires the courts to have regard to the welfare of a young person during the proceedings.

The Youth Justice Board have identified six key objectives of the youth justice system:

- Swift administration of justice.
- Confronting young offenders with their offending behaviour.

- Intervention that tackles particular factors that lead youths to offend.
- Punishment proportionate to the offending.
- Encouraging reparation.
- Reinforcing the responsibility of parents/guardians.

GENERAL MATTERS RELATING TO THE YOUTH COURT

The power to constitute a youth court

7.13 The power to constitute a youth court is set out in the CYPA 1933, s 45 which is set out below:

> 'Constitution of Youth courts.
>
> (1) Magistrates' courts—
>
> (a) constituted in accordance with this section or section 66 of the Courts Act 2003 (judges having powers of District Judges (Magistrates' Courts)), and
>
> (b) sitting for the purpose of—
>
> (i) hearing any charge against a child or young person, or
>
> (ii) exercising any other jurisdiction conferred on youth courts by or under this or any other Act,
>
> are to be known as youth courts.
>
> (2) A justice of the peace is not qualified to sit as a member of a youth court for the purpose of dealing with any proceedings unless he has an authorisation extending to the proceedings.
>
> (3) He has an authorisation extending to the proceedings only if he has been authorised by the Lord Chief Justice, with the concurrence of the Lord Chancellor, to sit as a member of a youth court to deal with—
>
> (a) proceedings of that description, or
>
> (b) all proceedings dealt with by youth courts.'

7.14 As is clear from these provisions a magistrate must be authorised in order to sit in the youth court. Further, under the Justices of the Peace Rules 2016, SI 2016/709, r 30 a magistrate can only be authorised when they have completed the relevant training.

Composition and those present in youth court hearings

7.15 The composition of the youth court is as in the adult magistrates' court.

Not in open court

7.16 The youth court sits largely in private. Those permitted to be in attendance in a youth court hearing are set out under the CYPA 1933, s 47(2) which states:

> 'No person shall be present at any sitting of a youth court except—
>
> (a) members and officers of the court;
>
> (b) parties to the case before the court, their legal representatives, and witnesses and other persons directly concerned in that case;
>
> (c) bona fide representatives of newspapers or news agencies;
>
> (d) such other persons as the court may specially authorise to be present.'

7.17 The key group of those permitted to attend that may cause concern for those considering the welfare of a child defendant is the representatives of newspapers or news agencies.

Reporting restrictions

7.18 However, the CYPA 1933, s 49 does impose reporting restrictions on identifying children. It should be noted these restrictions, unless other orders are made, are only in place while the person is a child. The court also has the power to lift the reporting restrictions (CYPA 1933, s 49(8)).

For a child being tried in the adult magistrates' court or Crown Court the court can make reporting restrictions under the Youth Justice and Criminal Evidence Act (YJCEA) 1999, s 45.

How trials/hearings are conducted

7.19 The procedure is as in the adult magistrates' court save it is more informal. The Youth Court Bench Book states: 'Magistrates are encouraged to sit on the same level as the other people present, and the parent/guardian should sit next to their child and remain seated throughout the proceedings.'

The requirement for the attendance at youth court hearing of a parent or guardian

7.20 Under the CYPA 1933, s 34, where a child is before a court, the court may, and shall in the case of a child or a young person who is under the age of

16 years, require a person who is a parent or guardian, or a relevant person of the local authority who has care of the child, to attend at the court during all the stages of the proceedings, unless and to the extent that the court is satisfied that it would be unreasonable to require such attendance, having regard to the circumstances of the case.

Differing Terminology

7.21 When a child is tried in the youth court or adult magistrates' court the correct terminology is a 'Finding of guilt' rather than a conviction and 'Order made on a finding of guilt' rather than sentence.

DETERMINING THE CORRECT VENUE FOR CHILD DEFENDANTS

7.22 There is a presumption under the MCA 1980, s 24(1) that a person under the age of 18 shall be tried summarily, with some exceptions, as follows:

> '24 Summary trial of information against child or young person for indictable offence.
>
> (1) Where a person under the age of 18 years appears or is brought before a magistrates' court on an information charging him with an indictable offence he shall, subject to sections 51 and 51A of the Crime and Disorder Act 1998 and to sections 24A and 24B below, be tried summarily.'

7.23 Leveson J stated in *R on the application of H,A and O v Southampton Youth Court;*[2]

> 'The general policy of the legislature is that those who are under 18 years of age and in particular children of under 15 years of age should, wherever possible, be tried in the youth court. It is the court which is best designed to meet their specific needs. A trial in the Crown Court with the inevitably greater formality and greatly increased number of people involved (including a jury and the public) should be reserved for the most serious cases.'

It is correct that most children charged with offences have their cases heard in the youth court rather than in the adult magistrates' court or Crown Court. However, there are cases with a child defendant that are not heard in the youth court (CYPA 1933, s 46, Children and Young Persons Act 1963, s 18 and Magistrates'

2 [2004] EWHC 2912 Admin.

Court Act 1980, ss 24 and 29). The Youth Bench Book summarises the position as follows:

7.24 When the circumstances below arise a child or young person shall be sent forthwith to the Crown Court for trial:

> 'a. When charged with homicide.
>
> b. When charged with a relevant firearms offence, which if convicted would be subject to a minimum statutory sentence.
>
> c. When notice is given to the court that there is evidence of a fraud of such seriousness or complexity that the management of the case should, without delay, be taken over by the Crown Court.
>
> d. When notice is given by the DPP that a child will be called as a witness and for the purpose of avoiding any prejudice to the welfare of the child, the case should be taken over and proceeded with, without delay, by the Crown Court.
>
> e. When charged with a specified offence and it appears to the court that an extended sentence (minimum four years detention), under the dangerous offender provisions, is likely to be needed.'

7.25 Homicide is not defined in statute but would ordinarily include murder and manslaughter. From the guidance provided in the Youth Court Jurisdiction in the Modern Approach (July 2015) it appears that deaths from road traffic incidents are not offences of homicide. However, these offences carry a maximum of 14 years' imprisonment and so are capable of being grave crimes.

7.26 In certain other cases, the court must follow the plea before venue procedure, ie the court may determine that the young defendant's case should not remain in the Crown Court, namely where:

> 'a. The youth is charged jointly with an indictable offence (and appears on the same or subsequent occasion) with an adult who is sent to the Crown Court for trial for that offence …
>
> b. The youth is charged with an indictable or summary offence (punishable with imprisonment or disqualification from driving) where they have been sent for trial for a related offence on the same or previous occasion.
>
> c. When charged with an offence capable of being a grave crime.'

7.27 Where a child reaches the age of 18 during the proceedings, the Youth Court may, if it thinks fit, proceed with the hearing and conclude the case or it may transfer the case to the adult court. It cannot deal with a further charge once it is known that a child or young person has reached the age of 18.

7.28 Even where a child is tried in the Youth Court or magistrates' court, they can still be committed to the Crown Court for sentence where they have been convicted of a 'specified offence' (Criminal Justice Act (CJA) 2003, s 224) and the magistrates decide that the criteria for the imposition of a sentence of detention for life (CJA 2003, s 226) or an extended sentence (CJA 2003, s 226B) now appear to be met (Powers of Criminal Courts (Sentencing) Act (PCC(S)A) 2000, s 3C).

7.29 A grave crime is defined in the PCC(S)A 2000, s 91(1) as:

'(a) an offence punishable in the case of a person aged 21 or over with imprisonment of 14 years or more, not being an offence for which the sentence is fixed by law;

(b) an offence of sexual assault contrary to the Sexual Offences Act 2003, s 3; or

(c) an offence of child sexual offences committed by children or young persons under 18 contrary to the Sexual Offences Act 2003, s 13; or

(d) an offence of sexual activity with a child family member contrary to the Sexual Offences Act 2003, s 25; or

(e) an offence of inciting a child family member to engage in sexual activity contrary to the Sexual Offences Act 2003, s 26.'

7.30 If a child is sent for trial for a grave crime, the court may also send that child for trial for any indictable offence that is related to the grave crime and for any summary offence that is punishable with imprisonment or carries mandatory or discretionary disqualification from driving that is related to the grave crime or to the indictable offence that is related to the grave crime (Crime and Disorder Act 1998, s 51A(4)). Where the youth appears on a subsequent occasion, he may be sent for trial for any indictable or summary offence (punishable with imprisonment or mandatory or discretionary disqualification from driving) that is related to the grave crime. There is no power to send for trial summary offences that are not related to the grave crime (Crime and Disorder Act 1998, s 51A(5)).

7.31 When considering the appropriate venue and the relevant test practitioners should have regard to The Sentencing Guidelines Council Definitive Guideline: Overarching Principles Sentencing Youths paragraph 12.11 which sets out the following guidance:

'i) a young person aged 10 or 11 (or aged 12–14 but not a persistent offender) should be committed to the Crown Court under this provision (grave crimes) only where charged with an offence of such gravity that, despite the normal prohibition on a custodial sentence for a person of that age, a sentence exceeding two years is a realistic possibility;

ii) a young person aged 12–17 (for which a detention and training order could be imposed) should be committed to the Crown Court under this provision only where charged with an offence of such gravity that a sentence substantially beyond the 2 year maximum for a detention and training order is a realistic possibility.'

7.32 The CPS guidance states that prosecutors should assist the court to determine venue in grave crimes by:

- Drawing to the court's attention relevant sentencing authorities, eg the Sentencing Guidelines Council Definitive Guideline on Robbery and recent and relevant appellate sentencing cases.
- Informing the court of the aggravating and mitigating features of the offence.
- Providing the court with an accurate and agreed list of the youth's previous convictions, youth conditional cautions, youth cautions, warnings and reprimands. This will assist the court to determine both the nature and length of sentence: *R (on the application of T) v Medway Youth Court.*[3]

7.33 A child who has been sent for trial with an adult may be remitted back to the Youth Court for trial if the indictment no longer includes the 'main offence', and the youth has not been arraigned. The definition of the 'main offence' includes the offence for which the youth and the adult were sent where the conditions for that sending are no longer satisfied. This includes cases in which the adult will not be tried for that offence because he has pleaded guilty or the case against him will not proceed. The Crown Court will need to determine venue and the child should be tried in the Crown Court only if there is a real prospect of a custodial sentence of two years. If there is no real prospect of such a sentence the youth should be remitted for trial in the Youth Court.

YOUTH OFFENDING TEAM (YOT)

7.34 A key part of the Youth Justice System both in and out of court is the Youth Offending Team.

YOTs are part of the local council and are independent from the police and the courts, although they do work with both. They work with the police, probation officers, health, housing and children services, schools and education authorities, charities and the local community (see the Government website at: https://www.gov.uk/youth-offending-team).

A YOT officer would be present at hearings in the Youth Court and would have made contact with/tried to make contact with the youth and their appropriate adult prior to the hearing. The Youth Justice Board have provided guidance as to the role of YOT including a guidance entitled 'Work in court: section 2 case management guidance'.

SENTENCING CHILDREN AND YOUNG PEOPLE

7.35 Those practising in the area of Youth Justice must be aware of the very different approach to sentence for Young Offenders. The Sentencing Council have

3 [2003] EWHC 2279 Admin.

issued sentencing Guidelines entitled: Sentencing Children and Young People – Overarching Principles and Offence Specific Guidelines for Sexual Offences and Robbery – Definitive Guideline.

Again the court must have regard to the principal aim of the youth justice system as set out above to prevent offending by children and young people (Crime and Disorder Act 1998, s 37(1)) and also the welfare of the child or young person (Children and Young Persons Act 1993, s 44(1)). These principals do not apply when imposing a mandatory life sentence, when imposing a statutory minimum custodial sentence, when imposing detention for life under the dangerous offender provisions or when making certain orders under the Mental Health Act 1983.

The guidelines provide helpful consideration of the principals of sentencing youths: that the approach to sentencing should 'be individualistic and focused on the child or young person, as opposed to offence focused.' 'It is important to avoid 'criminalising' children and young people unnecessarily.

It notes that the principals 'do not undermine the fact that the sentence should reflect the seriousness of the offence'.

The guidelines set out a table of available sentences for youth offenders by age:

	Age of child and young person			
Sentence	**10–11**	**12–14**	**15–17**	**Rehabilitation period**
Absolute or conditional discharge or reparation order	√	√	√	Absolute discharge and reparation: spent on day of sentence Conditional discharge: spent on last day of the period of discharge
Financial order	√	√	√	Spent 6 months after the finding of guilt
Referral order	√	√	√	Spent on day of completion
Youth rehabilitation order (YRO)	√	√	√	Spent 6 months after the last day the order is to have effect
YRO with intensive supervision and surveillance or fostering	×	√ For persistent offenders **only**	√	Spent 6 months after the last day the order is to have effect

	Age of child and young person			
Sentence	**10–11**	**12–14**	**15–17**	**Rehabilitation period**
Detention and training order	×	√ For persistent offenders **only**	√	6 months or under: spent 18 months after the sentence is completed (including supervision period) More than 6 months: spent 24 months after the sentence is completed (including supervision period)
PCC(S)A 2000, s 91 detention (grave crime)	√	√	√	More than 6 months – 30 months: spent 24 months after sentence completed (including licence period) More than 30 months – 48 months: spent 42 months after sentence completed (including licence period) More than 48 months: never spent
Extended sentence of detention*	√	√	√	Never spent

* If found guilty of a specified violent or sexual offence and the court is of the opinion that there is a significant risk to the public of serious harm caused by the child or young person committing further specified offences.

Chapter 8

INTERMEDIARIES AND GROUND RULES HEARINGS

8.1 Where a case involves either vulnerable parties or witnesses both criminal and family law have regulations which deal with the identification of, and the making of directions to assist, vulnerable and protected parties.

CRIMINAL LAW

Intermediaries

8.2 **Chapter 11** provides a detailed analysis of the special measures available in criminal cases, including an in-depth analysis of the use of intermediaries for both witnesses and defendants in criminal cases.

Funding for intermediaries in criminal cases

Prosecution use of intermediaries

8.3 The CPS website provides helpful guidance setting out the division of funding for the use of intermediaries for prosecution witnesses, in summary the police are responsible for the cost pre-proceedings and the CPS once the proceedings have commenced:

> '**Annex D: Cost Split between the Police and CPS**
>
> The police are responsible for the costs of the investigation. Where an intermediary is to be used, the following costs will be met by the police:
>
> a. the use of the intermediary to assist the witness in interviews/making statements and in subsequent enquiries, regardless of what stage proceedings might have reached;

b. the preparation of any reports that support the witness interview/ statement taking process;

c. where a new witness comes to light post-charge and an intermediary assessment is needed before the witness is interviewed, the cost of the report and the use of the intermediary to assist the witness in interviews/ making statements;

d. the preparation of a report by an intermediary to justify termination of an investigation.

The CPS is responsible for the presentation of evidence in court. Where an intermediary is to be used, the following costs will be met by the CPS:

a. intermediary attendance at a pre-trial witness interview (in accordance with the Guidance about Pre-trial Witness Interviews);

b. intermediary attendance at a pre-court familiarisation visit with a vulnerable witness, because this is part of the preparation for the presentation of evidence in court;

c. intermediary reports that set out the witness's communication abilities and weaknesses for use in court;

d. intermediary attendance at all court hearings and preparation by the intermediary for the presentation of evidence at court;

e. intermediary attendance at a Direct Communication with Victim meeting.

Responsibility for any other potential intermediary costs should be agreed locally by the police and CPS on a case by case basis before the intermediary is commissioned to do the work. A record should be kept and the intermediary informed so that the appropriate organisation can pay the invoice.'

The funding for the use of an intermediary for a defendant

8.4 The funding for intermediaries for defendants is dependent upon when the intermediary will be providing the assistance. At court hearings the intermediary is paid for by the court. However, for assistance outside of court hearings, for example if the intermediary's assistance is sought in helping the defendant prepare for trial, this funding is not as a general rule covered by the inherent jurisdiction of the court. Therefore, for legally aided defendants, an application for funding through their legal aid certificate will be required.

Ground rules hearings

8.5 The key statutory provisions/protocols/case law etc:

- Criminal Procedure Rules (CPR) 2015, SI 2015/1490, r 3.9(7):

  '(7) Where directions for appropriate treatment and questioning are required, the court must—

(a) invite representations by the parties and by any intermediary; and

(b) set ground rules for the conduct of the questioning, which rules may include—

  (i) a direction relieving a party of any duty to put that party's case to a witness or a defendant in its entirety,

  (ii) directions about the manner of questioning,

  (iii) directions about the duration of questioning,

  (iv) if necessary, directions about the questions that may or may not be asked,

  (v) where there is more than one defendant, the allocation among them of the topics about which a witness may be asked, and

  (vi) directions about the use of models, plans, body maps or similar aids to help communicate a question or an answer.'

- Criminal Practice Directions para 3E: Ground rules hearing to plan the questioning of a vulnerable defendant.
- Advocate's Gateway Toolkit: 1. Ground rules hearings and the fair treatment of vulnerable people in court.
- Youth Justice and Criminal Evidence Act (YJCEA) 1999, s 28 – re pre-recorded cross-examination.
- *R v Lubemba.*[1]

8.6 In summary, the above provide:

- The ground rules hearing should take place prior to trial commencing: *R v Lubemba.*[2]
- The purpose of a ground rules hearings is for the court to make directions for the fair treatment and effective participation of vulnerable defendants and vulnerable witnesses. Courts must take reasonable steps to ensure the effective participation of vulnerable defendants and witnesses.
- Where directions for the appropriate treatment and questioning are required, the court must set ground rules (CPR 2015, r 3.9(7)(b)).
- 'The ground rules hearing should cover, amongst other matters, the general care of the witness, if, when and where the witness is to be shown their video interview, when, where and how the parties (and the judge if identified) intend to introduce themselves to the witness, the length of questioning and frequency of breaks and the nature of the questions to be asked.' (*R v Lubemba; R v JP*)[3] Requirement of ground rules hearing in intermediary cases and intermediaries must be included in those discussions: 'Discussion of ground rules is required

1 [2014] EWCA Crim 2064.
2 Ibid at para 42.
3 [2014] EWCA Crim 2064, at para 43.

in all intermediary trials where they must be discussed between the judge or magistrates, advocates and intermediary before the witness gives evidence' (CPD 3E.2) and when there is an intermediary they 'must' be invited to make representations (CPR 2015, r 3.9(7)(a));

- In the YJCEA 1999, s 28 cases (pre-recorded cross-examination), advocates are required to complete the s 28 Defence GRH Form from the HM Courts and Tribunal Service (HMCTS) which includes space at section 8 to set out for the judge 'all proposed questions which should be drafted taking into account the relevant Toolkit'.
- Advocates and judges should consider special measures and other reasonable adjustments throughout proceedings. Thus, it may be necessary to revisit the ground rules set at the start of the proceedings by way of a further GRH.
- Guidance for family courts, including on GRHs, is available in Toolkit 13 – Vulnerable witnesses and parties in the family courts.

FAMILY LAW

Introduction

8.7 Until very recently there was no formal rule-based procedure for the assessment of vulnerable witnesses or the employment of intermediaries in family proceedings. Unlike criminal cases in which there has been for some time a statutory foundation for the use of intermediaries[4] the use of intermediaries in family proceedings began largely in the early 2010s as a result of representatives seeking such assistance under the inherent jurisdiction of the court to permit of the best evidence from vulnerable parties. It was not until November 2017 that the Family Procedure Rules (FPR) 2010, SI 2010/2955, Part 3A and Practice Direction 3AA set out a formal requirement to assess and assist vulnerable witnesses.[5]

8.8 There is still no scheme similar to that in criminal cases whereby an application is made to the National Crime Agency for the identification of a 'registered intermediary' from their database. In family cases there is usually resort to one or two commercial agencies which employ registered intermediaries for both criminal and family cases.[6] The use of intermediaries and their assistance in evidence is therefore largely undertaken as a result and under the powers of the court's general and wide jurisdiction to regulate evidence in family proceedings as set out in the FPR 2010 both in the overriding objective and in its case management powers[7] as supplemented by the FPR 2010, Part 3A.

4 Eg, YJCEA 1999, ss 16(1) and 29(2).

5 It is notable that the Advocate's Toolkit in the COIC Advocate's Gateway in relation to family proceedings was published in 2014 and has no reference to the updated approach (Toolkit 13).

6 It is notable however that the NCA database has more registered intermediaries than are often employed by those agencies and family practitioners who sometimes struggle to find intermediaries might benefit from being able to access the NCA database.

7 See **Chapter 1**.

Intermediaries – definition

8.9 Intermediaries are professionals, usually qualified in psychology, speech and language therapy or related disciplines, whose function is to:

'(a) communicate questions put to a witness or party;

(b) communicate to any person asking such questions the answers given by the witness or party in reply to them; and

(c) explain such questions or answers so far as is necessary to enable them to be understood by the witness or party or by the person asking such questions;[8] '

Use and employment of intermediaries in family proceedings

8.10 The power to order the use of intermediaries now exists in FPR 2010, Part 3A, PD 3AA. There is earlier authority as to the use of intermediaries and their instruction and it is likely that courts will be assisted by reference to those reported cases in which the use of intermediaries and other persons trained to assist in communication and the giving of evidence was considered and in which the timing and funding of that participation was considered.

8.11 In *Re A (Care Proceedings: Learning Disabled Parent)*[9] the court set out the approach:[10]

(1) Practitioners should identify the need for intermediaries as soon as possible and preferably at time of instruction and should come to a view as to capacity to give instructions and competence to give evidence. If there is a perceived need for support that should be addressed at the earliest opportunity; if, as is often the case, the local authority is already aware of a serious issue or makes the party's representative aware of it then the court should be made aware also and should appoint a litigation friend the day following issue.

(2) If not at the time of instruction then at least by the time of the first case management hearing the questions of capacity and competence should have been addressed and if necessary directions as to assistance from a litigation friend and/or an intermediary applied for; if there is doubt or concern as to capacity and competence then an appropriate expert should have been identified and an application made to the court for a report on the same.

8.12 Similar considerations apply in the cases of disabilities which are other than intellectual, so that the outline approach approved by the High Court in the case of *Re A* above was further approved by the Court of Appeal in relation

8 FPR 2010, Pt 3A, r 3A.1.
9 [2013] EWHC 3502 Fam, [2014] 2 FLR 591.
10 Ibid at paras 76–79.

to deaf parents and will surely apply to other aspects of disability which affect communication and understanding.[11]

Deaf parents

8.13 In *Re C (Care Proceedings: Deaf Parent)*[12] the Court of Appeal gave guidance about the approach to profoundly deaf parents. In particular:

(1) It must be understood that communication with a deaf person is not simply a question of interpretation or translation; there is need for expert insight at an early stage.

(2) The parents and the local authority (or legal representatives) should make the court aware of the issues at the earliest stage.

(3) An expert should be appointed to address the impact of the disability on the individual concerned. A 'relay interpreter' – a form of intermediary – should be considered.

(4) The issue of funding should be considered at if not before the case management hearing.

The modern law – FPR 2010, Part 3A

8.14 The previous case law on the use of intermediaries remains relevant but the power of the court in relation to intermediaries is now contained in FPR 2010, Part 3A. The nature and role of intermediaries is defined.[13] The court has the power to order the employment of an intermediary to assist 'participation' in the proceedings (that is participation other than by giving evidence, which presumably includes the receipt of advice and the giving of instructions, help with understanding expert reports and assistance in understanding the procedure and any other evidence given in the course of the proceedings).[14] The court also has power to order the employment of an intermediary to assist in the giving of evidence in court.[15]

8.15 FPR 2010, Part 3A is supplemented by Practice Direction 3AA. The practice direction, insofar as it is applicable to intermediaries, places the duty on the court and all the parties to identify any party or witness who is a vulnerable person at the earliest possible stage of any family proceedings.[16] All parties are required to work together with the court to ensure that the person can participate in proceedings without the quality of their evidence being diminished and without being put in fear or distress as a result of their vulnerability.[17]

---

11 *Re C (Care Proceedings: Deaf Parent)* [2014] EWCA Civ 128, [2014] 1 WLR 2495.
12 [2014] EWCA Civ 128, [2014] 1 WLR 2495.
13 FPR 2010, r 3A.1.
14 FPR 2010, r 3A.8(1)(d).
15 FPR 2010, r 3A.8(1)(e).
16 FPR 2010, PD3AA para 1.3.
17 FPR 2010, PD3AA para 1.4.

8.16 The requirement to address questions of vulnerability (and therefore the potential need for an intermediary) at an early stage is enhanced by the provisions of FPR 2010, r 3A.10 which allow that the application for an assessment of vulnerability and/or participation directions may be included within the application initiating the proceedings. If not in that application then an application within the proceedings may follow when matters of vulnerability and the need for assistance become evident. The application for an intermediary should set out: (1) why the party or witness would benefit from assistance; (2) why an intermediary would be likely to improve the person's ability to participate in the proceedings; and/or (3) why an intermediary would be likely to improve the quality of the person's evidence.[18]

PARTICIPATION DIRECTIONS AND GROUND RULES HEARINGS

Assessment of vulnerability – purpose

8.17 Participation directions and the potential need for ground rules hearings require an initial assessment of vulnerability (or child or protected party status) and then consideration of applications for specific measures to improve the quality of evidence given. The guidance for the conduct and purpose of ground rules hearings is in FPR 2010, PD3AA, para 5 and is addressed below.

8.18 A precursor to making participation directions and the ground rules hearing is the assessment of vulnerability or the designation of a party or witness as a child or protected party. The arrangement of the rules suggests that the involvement of children as witnesses and of protected persons both as witnesses and parties shall always require the court to consider participation directions in those cases. In every other case an adult with capacity who is nevertheless thought to be vulnerable will be subject to the assessment process set out below.

8.19 A child is a person under the age of 18.[19] A protected party is a person who lacks capacity to litigate under the Mental Capacity Act 2005[20] and therefore acts by a litigation friend (often the Official Solicitor in family proceedings). The Mental Capacity Act 2005, s 2(1) is dealt with elsewhere in this handbook but in summary it provides that a person lacks capacity in relation to a matter if, at the material time, he is unable to make a decision for himself in relation to the matter because of an impairment of or disturbance in the functioning of the mind or brain, whether the impairment or disturbance is permanent or temporary.

8.20 The purpose of assessment of vulnerability has two aspects: (1) to decide whether *participation* in proceedings is likely to be diminished without participation directions; and (2) to decide whether the quality of the *evidence* given by a party or a witness is likely to be diminished without participation directions.

---

18 FPR 2010, PD3aa para 6.1.

19 FPR 2010, r 3A.1.

20 FPR 2010, r 2.3 contains the definition.

Children

8.21 In relation to children the duty of the court is to consider directions to prevent the quality of their *evidence*[21] being diminished but not the requirement to consider how their *participation* in proceedings may be diminished.[22] This is presumably since most children who are parties will have a litigation friend or a Children's Guardian. There may be a lacuna here in relation to 'Gillick' competent children who instruct their own legal representatives; however it is likely that any court would revert to its plenary powers in relation to the conduct of proceedings[23] to make directions to assist where necessary. The question of whether a child should give evidence at all is dealt with below.

Protected parties

8.22 The court must consider both the likely ability to participate in proceedings and the likely quality of evidence in relation to protected parties.[24]

Adults with capacity

8.23 The court must consider whether an adult party or witness who does not lack capacity is likely to suffer in relation to both participation[25] and evidence.[26]

Vulnerability – considerations

8.24 Because of the automatic requirement to consider participation directions in the cases of children and protected persons, vulnerability assessments occur only in cases where an adult with capacity is the subject of concern. In deciding upon whether a person's participation or evidence is likely to be diminished in quality the court is mandated to have regard in particular to the 'checklist' of matters in FPR 2010, r 3A.7. The use of the phrase 'in particular' suggests that the checklist is not exclusive and that any relevant circumstance will be open to consideration.

8.25 The checklist is divided into a number of subject areas:

(1) Those matters which are extrinsic to the person concerned such as whether they would suffer from real or perceived intimidation from another person, a party, a witness or a member of the family of such person.[27]

---

21 FPR 2010, r 3A.5.
22 FPR 2010, r 3A.4 dealing with participation in proceedings is disapplied in relation to children.
23 See **Chapter 1**.
24 FPR 2010, r 3A.6.
25 FPR 2010, r 3A.4.
26 FPR 2010, r 3A.5.
27 FPR 2010, r 3A.7(a).

(2) Those matters intrinsic so the person concerned such as mental disability or limitation, ill-health or physical disability.[28]

(3) Matters concerning the nature of the proceedings such as whether a matter is contentious or concerns allegations of abuse, and the nature and extent of the information before the court.[29] Thus the court, in deciding on whether and how a person is to give evidence or participate, may find that there is sufficient other evidence in relation to an issue that evidence on the point may be limited or dispensed with, or that representatives may make submissions on certain matters without having to engage in cross-examination on them.

(4) Matters concerning the social and personal characteristics of the relevant person such as their age, maturity and understanding, social and cultural background, religious beliefs and domestic circumstances, and any other characteristic which is relevant to the exercise.[30]

(5) Any questions that the court may put or cause to be put to a witness under the Matrimonial and Family Proceedings Act 1984, s 31G(6).[31]

(6) Practical issues such as the availability and cost of the measures which may assist a party.[32]

(7) Any other matter set out in FPR 2010, PD3AA.[33]

8.26 With regard to allegations of abuse the nature of the potential abuse is the subject of further guidance in FPR 2010, PD3AA, para 2.1 and encompasses a wide range of categories from the definitions of domestic abuse already dealt with in the FPR 2010[34] to sexual and physical abuse, 'honour-based' violence, female genital mutilation and abuse as a result of sexual and gender discrimination.[35]

8.27 When looking at the question of vulnerability overall the court should have regard to all the matters set out above and should require the assistance of all relevant parties at the earliest possible stage in the proceedings.[36] This echoes the requirement in previous authority.

8.28 In looking at vulnerability overall the court must also have regard to FPR 2010, PD3AA, para 3.1 which adds a further layer of considerations as to the potential *effect* of the various potential reasons for vulnerability set out above. The court should require the assistance of the relevant parties when

---

28 FPR 2010, r 3A.7(b).

29 FPR 2010, r 3A.7(c)–(e).

30 FPR 2010, r 3A.7(f)–(h) and (j).

31 FPR 2010, r 3A.7(i); this little-known provision *requires* a court: (a) to ascertain from any unrepresented litigant the matters as to which any witness may depose or on which he may be cross-examined; and (b) to put or cause to be put questions which in the interests of that party appear to be proper.

32 FPR 2010, r 3A.7(k) and (l).

33 FPR 2010, r 3A.7(m).

34 FPR 2010, PD12J.

35 FPR 2010, PD3AA, para 2.1 (a)–(h).

36 FPR 2010, PD3AA, paras 1.3–1.4.

considering whether any of the factors set out above may mean that participation may be diminished and should consider the ability of the person concerned to: (a) understand the proceedings and their role in the proceedings when in court; (b) put their views to the court; (c) give instructions before, during and after the hearing; and (d) attend the hearing without significant distress.

Participation directions

8.29 Once the court has decided that a party is either a child, a protected party or a vulnerable person, the court must consider participation directions. Insofar as the vulnerability affects the giving of instructions or requires early assessment those directions may be made at the stage when that vulnerability becomes evident and the powers of the court both under its general case management powers and the particular powers given by the FPR 2010, Part 3A are sufficiently wide to allow directions to be made at any time, including if necessary orders for more specialist assessment under the FPR 2010, Part 25.

8.30 With regard to participation other than by way of giving evidence the court's powers are contained in FPR 2010, r 3A.8 as supplemented by PD3AA, para 4.

8.31 Participation directions permitted by the FPR 2010, r 3.8 are those which:

(a) prevent a party or witness from seeing another party or witness;
(b) allow a party or witness to participate in hearings and give evidence by live link;
(c) provide for a party or witness to use a device to help communicate;
(d) provide for a party or witness to participate in proceedings with the assistance of an intermediary;
(e) provide for a party or witness to be questioned in court with the assistance of an intermediary; or
(f) do anything else which is set out in the FPR 2010, PD 3AA.

8.32 The FPR 2010, PD3AA gives guidance that the court should also have regard to its general case management powers and its general power to control the evidence and gives particular examples of directions that may be made, such as the structure and timing of the hearing, the formality of language to be used and whether a witness may use a different court entrance.[37]

If a measure is not available at a particular court centre the court may direct that it will sit at the nearest or most convenient location at which that level of court sits

37 FPR 2010, PD3AA, paras 4.1 and 4.2.

and where the relevant measure is available.[38] The court may not direct that public funding be made available for any measure.[39]

8.33 Participation directions under the general power in the FPR 2010, PD3AA are now commonly used to make significant inroads into the usual discretion given to advocates to cross-examine and the use of the advocates' toolkits which apply to criminal cases is widespread in assisting advocates to deal with the various problems that arise in individual cases. The court may take the following measures: require sight of written questions before the witness gives evidence; require the parties to agree a limited number of questioning advocates; require questions to be reviewed and altered by any intermediary; and restrict 'follow up' questions so as to prevent oppressive and distorting cross-examination.

8.34 In cases where a party suffers distress upon attendance at court provision can be made for separate rooms for cross-examination so that only the judge and the questioning advocate is present (others being linked by audio or video). In one case a video link was arranged to the court room from the relevant party's bedsit a few miles away.[40] The ability of the court to use media such as 'Skype' has also been approved in other cases.[41]

Children giving evidence

8.35 The FPR 2010, PD3AA, para 5.1 makes clear that the question of whether children are to give evidence is a matter governed by 'relevant case law and the guidance of the Family Justice Council in relation to children giving evidence in family proceedings'.

8.36 The relevant case law is found in *Re W (Children)(Abuse: Oral Evidence)*[42] and *Re E (A Child) (Evidence)*.[43] It is very important that all practitioners are familiar with the essential passages of those cases and they are therefore quoted extensively below. There is a balance to be struck in deciding whether to call a child to give evidence which is addressed by Lady Hale in *Re W*. In *Re E* McFarlane LJ is critical of the failure of practitioners to apply properly and rigorously the guidance in that case and that contained in the later guidelines from the Family Justice Council.

8.37 *In Re W (Children) (Abuse: Oral Evidence)* (above), Lady Hale said:

> '[22] … The existing law erects a presumption against a child giving evidence which requires to be rebutted by anyone seeking to put questions

38 FPR2010, r 3A.8(2) and (3).

39 There is already authority that the use of intermediaries at court is one to be met by HMCTS: see *Re D (A child) (No 2)* [2015] EWFC 2 and *Re K & H (Children)* [2015] EWCA Civ 543.

40 See *Medway v Others* [2016] EWFC B104 http://www.bailii.org/ew/cases/EWFC/OJ/2016/B104.html.

41 See *Re ML (Use of Skype Technology)* [2013] EWHC 2091 (Fam).

42 [2010] UKSC 12, [2010] 1 FLR 1485.

43 [2016] EWCA Civ 473, [2017] 1 FLR 1675.

to the child. That cannot be reconciled with the approach of the European Court of Human Rights, which always aims to strike a fair balance between competing European Convention rights. Article 6 requires that the proceedings overall be fair and this normally entails an opportunity to challenge the evidence presented by the other side. But even in criminal proceedings account must be taken of the Art 8 rights of the perceived victim: see SN v Sweden (Application No 34209/96) (2002) 39 EHRR 304. Striking that balance in care proceedings may well mean that the child should not be called to give evidence in the great majority of cases, but that is a result and not a presumption or even a starting point.

[23] The object of the proceedings is to achieve a fair trial in the determination of the rights of all the people involved. Children are harmed if they are taken away from their families for no good reason. Children are harmed if they are left in abusive families. This means that the court must admit all the evidence which bears upon the relevant questions: whether the threshold criteria justifying State intervention have been proved; if they have, what action if any will be in the best interests of the child? The court cannot ignore relevant evidence just because other evidence might have been better. It will have to do the best it can on what it has.

[24] When the court is considering whether a particular child should be called as a witness, the court will have to weigh two considerations: the advantages that that will bring to the determination of the truth and the damage it may do to the welfare of this or any other child. A fair trial is a trial which is fair in the light of the issues which have to be decided. Mr Geekie accepts that the welfare of the child is also a relevant consideration, albeit not the paramount consideration in this respect. He is right to do so, because the object of the proceedings is to promote the welfare of this and other children. The hearing cannot be fair to them unless their interests are given great weight.

[25] In weighing the advantages that calling the child to give evidence may bring to the fair and accurate determination of the case, the court will have to look at several factors. One will be the issues it has to decide in order properly to determine the case. Sometimes it may be possible to decide the case without making findings on particular allegations. Another will be the quality of the evidence it already has. Sometimes there may be enough evidence to make the findings needed whether or not the child is cross-examined. Sometimes there will be nothing useful to be gained from the child's oral evidence. The case is built upon a web of behaviour, drawings, stray remarks, injuries and the like, and not upon concrete allegations voiced by the child. The quality of any ABE interview will also be an important factor, as will be the nature of any challenge which the party may wish to make. The court is unlikely to be helped by generalised accusations of lying, or by a fishing expedition in which the childis taken slowly through the story yet again in the hope that something will turn up, or by a cross-examination which is designed to intimidate the child and pave the way for accusations of inconsistency in a future criminal trial. On the other hand, focused questions

which put forward a different explanation for certain events may help the court to do justice between the parties. Also relevant will be the age and maturity of the child and the length of time since the events in question, for these will have a bearing on whether an account now can be as reliable as a near-contemporaneous account, especially if given in a well-conducted ABE interview.

[26] The age and maturity of the child, along with the length of time since the events in question, will also be relevant to the second part of the inquiry, which is the risk of harm to the child. Further specific factors may be the support which the child has from family or other sources, or the lack of it, the child's own wishes and feelings about giving evidence, and the views of the child's guardian and, where appropriate, those with parental responsibility. We endorse the view that an unwilling child should rarely, if ever, be obliged to give evidence. The risk of further delay to the proceedings is also a factor: there is a general principle that delay in determining any question about a child's upbringing is likely to prejudice his welfare: see the Children Act 1989, s 1(2). There may also be specific risks of harm to this particular child. Where there are parallel criminal proceedings, the likelihood of the child having to give evidence twice may increase the risk of harm. The parent may be seeking to put his child through this ordeal in order to strengthen his hand in the criminal proceedings rather than to enable the family court to get at the truth. On the other hand, as the family court has to give less weight to the evidence of a child because she has not been called, then that may be damaging too. However, the court is entitled to have regard to the general evidence of the harm which giving evidence may do to children, as well as to any features which are particular to this child and this case. That risk of harm is an ever present feature to which, on the present evidence, the court must give great weight. The risk, and, therefore, the weight, may vary from case to case, but the court must always take it into account and does not need expert evidence in order to do so.

[27] But on both sides of the equation, the court must factor in what steps can betaken to improve the quality of the child's evidence and at the same time to decrease the risk of harm to the child. These two aims are not in opposition to one another. The whole premise of Achieving Best Evidence and the special measures in criminal cases is that this will improve rather than diminish the quality of the evidence to the court. It does not assume that the most reliable account of any incident is one made from recollection months or years later in the stressful conditions of a courtroom. Nor does it assume that an 'Old Bailey style' cross-examination is the best way of testing that evidence. It may be the best way of casting doubt upon it in the eyes of a jury but that is another matter. A family court would have to be astute both to protect the child from the harmful and destructive effects of questioning and also to evaluate the answers in the light of the child's stage of development.

[28] The family court will have to be realistic in evaluating how effective it can be in maximising the advantage while minimising the harm. There are

things that the court can do but they are not things that it is used to doing at present. It is not limited by the usual courtroom procedures or to applying the special measures by analogy. The important thing is that the questions which challenge the child's account are fairly put to the child so that she can answer them, not that counsel should be able to question her directly. One possibility is an early videoed cross-examination as proposed by Pigot. Another is cross-examination via video-link. But another is putting the required questions to her through an intermediary. This could be the court itself, as would be common in continental Europe and used to be much more common than it is now in the courts of this country.

[29] In principle, the approach in private family proceedings between parents should be the same as the approach in care proceedings. However, there are specific risks to which the court must be alive. Allegations of abuse are not being made by a neutral and expert local authority which has nothing to gain by making them, but by a parent who is seeking to gain an advantage in the battle against the other parent. This does not mean that they are false but it does increase the risk of misinterpretation, exaggeration or downright fabrication. On the other hand, the child will not routinely have the protection and support of a Cafcass guardian. There are also many more litigants in person in private proceedings. So if the court does reach the conclusion that justice cannot be done unless the child gives evidence, it will have to take very careful precautions to ensure that the child is not harmed by this.

[30] It will be seen that these considerations are simply an amplification of those outlined by Smith LJ in the Medway case, at para [45], but without the starting point, at para [44]. The essential test is whether justice can be done to all the parties without further questioning of the child. Our prediction is that, if the court is called upon to do it, the consequence of the balancing exercise will usually be that the additional benefits to the court's task in calling the child do not outweigh the additional harm that it will do to the child. A wise parent with his child's interests truly at heart will understand that too. But rarity should be a consequence of the exercise rather than a threshold test (as in Huang v Secretary of State for the Home Department; Kashmiri v Secretary of State for the Home Department [2007] UKHL 11, [2007] 2 AC 167, [2007] 2 WLR 581, [2007] 1 FLR 2021, para [20]).'

8.38 In *Re E* McFarlane LJ said:

'[56] It is of note that, despite the passage of some 6 years since the Supreme Court decision in Re W, this court has been told that the previous culture and practice of the family courts remains largely unchanged with the previous presumption against children giving evidence remaining intact. That state of affairs is plainly contrary to the binding decision of the Supreme Court which was that such a presumption is contrary to Art 6 of the European Convention for the Protection of Human Rights and Fundamental Freedoms 1950 (the European Convention).

[57] In any case where the issue of children giving oral evidence is raised it is necessary for the court to engage with the factors identified by Baroness Hale in Re W, together with any other factors that are relevant to the particular child or the individual case, before coming to a reasoned and considered conclusion on the issue.

[58] It is crucial that any issue as to a child giving evidence is raised and determined at the earliest stage, and in any event well before the planned trial date. The court will not, however, be in a position to come to a conclusion on that issue unless it has undertaken an evaluation of the evidence which is otherwise available. Where there has been an ABE interview, and the quality and/or content of that interview are to be challenged, it is likely that the judge will have to view the DVD before being in a position to decide the Re W issue.

[59] The court should also have regard to the Working Party of the Family Justice Council Guidelines on the issue of Children Giving Evidence in Family Proceedings.

[60] Whilst not all of the elements described by Baroness Hale in Re W or in para 9 of the Guidelines will be relevant in every case, it is plain that the court undertaking a Re W determination will need to engage in a relatively full and sophisticated evaluation of the relevant factors; simply paying lip-service to Re W is not acceptable. By 'full' I do not wish to suggest that a lengthy judgment is required, but simply that the judge must consider each of the relevant points with that process recorded in short form in a judgment. Such a detailed process is in my view justified given the importance of the decision for the welfare of the child and for the fairness of hearing.'

8.39 The Family Justice Council Guidelines in relation to children giving evidence in family proceedings are published and available online.[44] The guidelines give a full set of considerations not only as to the criteria for consideration when deciding whether a child should give evidence but also, if that decision is that the child should do so, guidance as to ground rules and practical measures at final hearing.

8.40 With regard to the question of whether the child is to give evidence the guidelines give a long list of considerations. All should be addressed, even if only to discount them because of the circumstances of a particular case. All relevant considerations should, however, be fully addressed in a report to the court (often by the children's guardian but if necessary by a local authority or independent social worker).

44 https://www.judiciary.uk/wp-content/uploads/2014/10/fjc_guidelines_-in_relation_children_-giving_evidence_-in_-family_-proceedings_dec2011.pdf.

8.41 The criteria as set out in the Family Justice Council Guidelines, are:

'a. the child's wishes and feelings; in particular their willingness to give evidence; as an unwilling child should rarely if ever be obliged to give evidence;

b. the child's particular needs and abilities;

c. the issues that need to be determined;

d. the nature and gravity of the allegations;

e. the source of the allegations;

f. whether the case depends on the child's allegations alone;

g. corroborative evidence;

h. the quality and reliability of the existing evidence;

i. the quality and reliability of any ABE interview;

j. whether the child has retracted allegations;

k. the nature of any challenge a party wishes to make;

l. the age of the child; generally the older the child the better;

m. the maturity, vulnerability and understanding, capacity and competence of the child; this may be apparent from the ABE or from professionals discussions with the child;

n. the length of time since the events in question;

o. the support or lack of support the child has;

p. the quality and importance of the child's evidence;

q. the right to challenge evidence;

r. whether justice can be done without further questioning;

s. the risk of further delay;

t. the views of the guardian who is expected to have discussed the issue with the child concerned if appropriate and those with parental responsibility;

u. specific risks arising from the possibility of the child giving evidence twice in criminal or other and family proceedings taking into account that normally the family proceedings will be heard before the criminal; and

v. the serious consequences of the allegations i.e. whether the findings impact upon care and contact decisions.'

GROUND RULES HEARINGS

Basic rules

8.42 Where a decision has been made that a child, or a protected or vulnerable person is to give evidence the court must hold a ground rules hearing. This must be prior to any hearing at which evidence is heard and is the hearing at which the necessary participation directions are given in relation to questioning and support.[45]

8.43 The court should consider the form of the evidence (oral or by other means including sign language) and must consider whether the evidence may be heard at some point before the main hearing and either recorded or transcribed.[46] The court must consider the range of possible participation directions and must also consider directions in relation to whether:

'(a) any questions that can be asked by one advocate should not be repeated by another without the permission of the court;

(b) questions or topics to be put in cross-examination should be agreed prior to the hearing;

(c) questions to be put in cross-examination should be put by one legal representative or advocate alone, or, if appropriate, by the judge; and

(d) the taking of evidence should be managed in any other way.'[47]

8.44 The court must also consider whether the witness has given evidence or an interview in other proceedings and whether that evidence has been recorded and whether such recordings are available for use in the family proceedings.[48]

8.45 All advocates are expected to be familiar with the resources in the Advocate's Gateway and any Guidance on the MOJ websites.[49]

Best practice at ground rules hearings

8.46 It is at the ground rules hearings that the shape of the case involving vulnerable witnesses of whatever category is decided. The requirement that

45 FPR 2010, PD3AA, para 5.2.
46 FPR 2010, PD3AA, paras 5.3; 5.4.
47 FPR 2010, PD3AA, para 5.5.
48 FPR 2010, PD3AA, para 5.6.
49 FPR 2010, PD3AA, para 5.7.

advocates be familiar with the toolkits in the Advocate's Gateway, and that such a requirement is not limited to Toolkit 13 (Family Cases) suggests that the scope of participation directions will be very wide. Family practitioners should first look to Toolkit 1 on ground rules hearings which although aimed firmly at criminal practice notes in its introduction that 'the ground rules approach is also being applied in other parts of the justice system' and cites a number of cases in the Family Court and the Court of Protection. Present practice suggests that the Family Court will look to Toolkit 1 as a guide to potential ground rules ideas and potential participation directions, particularly in the light of the fact that Toolkit 13 which applies to family law has not been updated since 2014 and does not address the matter of ground rules and participation directions except in the broadest way.

8.47 Those representing the vulnerable witness should be the first to propose the means by which the diminution of the quality of their evidence or their participation in proceedings can be mitigated. Although the court retains a residual jurisdiction to make participation directions of its own motion (FPR 2010, r 3A.11) the usual practice will be that the party seeking assistance will make an application within the proceedings in accordance with the FPR 2010, PD3AA, para 6. The application must address the following:[50]

> '(a) why the party or witness would benefit from assistance;
>
> (b) the measure or measures that would be likely to maximise as far as practicable the quality of that evidence;
>
> (c) why the measure or measures sought would be likely to improve the person's ability to participate in the proceedings; and
>
> (d) why the measure or measures sought would be likely to improve the quality of the person's evidence.'

8.48 As well as the usual form of direction by audio and video link therefore it can be seen that the scope for participation directions is largely unlimited except by resources. Participation directions have included:

(a) Provision for the cross-examination of a child by a single advocate in the ABE suite used for her initial interview prior to commencement of the final hearing;

(b) Use of a 'round table' format for cross-examining witnesses;

(c) The use of written and agreed questions in questionnaire form;

(d) The review and alteration of written questions by the intermediary for the witness;

(e) Use of a 'structured interview' conducted by an independent social worker using agreed questions;

---

50 FPR 2010, PD3AA, para 6.1.

(f) A video link to a separate flat near the court for an agoraphobic and highly anxious party.[51]

8.49 The ground rules hearing should also address practical issues such as where and when an ABE interview should be viewed by parties and witness, the likely need for breaks (and therefore the likely length of the hearing); the length and time of day of questioning; the need for a separate 'break out room' for the witness and whether the witness should enter and leave the court and court building by a separate entrance from others in the case.

8.50 In criminal cases there is available to the court a specific direction relieving a party of the duty to 'put his case'.[52] It is in theory just as important in civil and family cases that a party should put to a witness any serious challenge to them or the evidence that they give.[53] It is likely that the court in family cases has a discretion to relieve an advocate of this duty where appropriate under the very wide powers to control the evidence that exists in non-criminal cases. Good practice would suggest that the advocate should raise the issue and have the matter resolved in advance of cross-examination of the witness. It would seem sensible that a recital or declaration of the court to that effect should be clear on the face of the order.

8.51 If there are intermediaries involved in the case they will be significantly involved in deciding what ground rules there should be and what would be the most effective participation directions. Similarly, in cases where there have been psychiatric or psychological reports the opinion of those experts should be sought by way of addendum if not in their initial report as to any suggestions for enhancing the quality of evidence given.

8.52 Family practitioners are urged to become familiar with Toolkit 1 of the Advocate's Gateway which contains a number of imaginative examples of the way in which the powers of the court can be used to assist vulnerable witnesses.

---

51 *Medway v Others* [2016] EWFC B104; a case which also names the agency used to facilitate the link and a clear review of the scope of the court's power.

52 CPR, r 3.9(7).

53 See **Chapter 1**.

Chapter 9

ADDITIONAL PRE-GIVING EVIDENCE CONSIDERATIONS FOR VULNERABLE WITNESSES

WITNESS SUPPORT

9.1 In criminal cases there are witnesses for the prosecution and witnesses for the defence (and occasionally witnesses called by the court); the responsibility for ensuring that the needs of a vulnerable witness are meet is primarily the responsibility of the party calling that witness.

Prosecution witnesses: A vulnerable witness is entitled to be offered a full needs assessment by the Witness Care Unit to make sure that they are supported to give their best evidence, including an explanation of the special measures available. It is possible, and often beneficial, for the WCU to arrange for the witness to visit the court before the trial date to familiarise themselves with the court building and court room and practise using the Special Measures equipment if appropriate. The Witness Care Unit should inform child witnesses about what will happen at court and provide a Young Witness Pack to help them understand what will happen when they give evidence. The witness should have the opportunity to see their video or written statement shortly before the trial. This should be organised by the police.

Defence witnesses: For defence witnesses the primary responsibility to ensure that the appropriate support is available falls on those acting for the defendant (if that defendant is represented). Those acting for a defendant need to be alive to possible special measures that any defence witnesses may need at trial, including the use of interpreters, screens or intermediaries. Those acting for a defendant need to ensure that matters are brought to the court's attention as soon as is practicable and where necessary the appropriate application made in advance of trial. In some cases it may be that relevant information will be available from the unused material if a witnesses has given a statement for the prosecution.

The Witness Service: The Witness Service is a voluntary and invaluable organisation that offers support to witnesses, both defence and prosecution in the criminal courts throughout the country. They often have their own area within the court building where they can support witnesses prior to giving evidence. The volunteers are often willing to show witnesses (both defence and prosecution) around the court room prior to giving evidence and will come into court with a witness to provide them with support. This is the link to The Witness Service advice page: https://www.citizensadvice.org.uk/about-us/citizens-advice-witness-service/about-the-citizens-advice-witness-service/.

9.2 There is no formal witness support system within the Family Courts. Victim support deals solely with victims and witnesses of crime. There is therefore considerable variation across the country and funding arrangements for alternative support is unclear. Consideration should be given on case-by-case basis as to how this support can be provided to vulnerable witnesses, either with assistance from the child's guardian and his/her solicitor in the case of a child, the advocate for the vulnerable party or from the local authority or police where relevant.

There are, however, charitable organisations that are available to assist people within the courts system, in particular the Personal Support Unit (PSU) whose website states that they have 'Over 700 trained volunteers, providing a free service across the country'. They 'provide comfort, support and guidance before, during and after court. We ensure people facing court alone feel prepared and supported to access justice.' This may be useful when practitioners are faced with a litigant in person who they would wish to ensure is able to access some support within court proceedings.

ATTENDING COURT FOR A PRE-TRIAL VISIT

9.3 The Advocacy Training Council Working Group, in 'Raising the Bar: The Handling of Vulnerable Witnesses, victims and defendants in court', emphasises that pre-trial familiarisation visits have been shown to be enormously beneficial. They should be conducted in a manner that will reassure the witness and so advocates should be sensitive to possible sources of anxiety such as a vulnerable witness in a sex abuse case meeting a male advocate in a small, enclosed room. A 'rapport' session in which the advocate can build a better understanding of the witness's capacity and communication needs appears to be essential in some cases. It is sensible to research the names of the witness's siblings and friends, where they attend school or where have been on holiday to put the witness at ease; knowing the layout of the witness's house may also be useful if the complaint relates to a domestic setting.

9.4 Preparing vulnerable witnesses for court by providing them with sufficient time for them to absorb information and having access to material in good time will be important in ensuring that a witness doesn't become unsettled or confused on the day of the hearing.

OTHER SOURCES OF ASSISTANCE

Interpreters

9.5 The court has a responsibility to fund interpreters for deaf and hearing-impaired litigants (presumably this also includes witnesses) and for foreign language speakers. Always use registered and qualified interpreters with legal training and experience. It is not appropriate to use family members or friends as there is no way of ensuring the accuracy of the interpretation. The interpreter should not be giving advice or opinions. Interpreters need to be provided with documentation with some background information and contextual understanding about what they will be asked to translate. Remember that additional time will need to be allowed whilst interpretation takes place and to allow written documents to be translated.

Meeting the judge in family cases

9.6 *Guidelines for Judges Meeting Children who are Subject to Family Proceedings* were published by the Family Justice Council in April 2010. This document sets out what should happen in circumstances when a child expresses a wish to see the judge, after this is discussed with them by a CAFCASS officer or guardian. The primary purpose of such a meeting is for the child to feel more involved and connected with the proceedings. If the judge feels that meeting the child would be inappropriate, he/she should consider providing a brief written explanation for the child.

9.7 The judge has significant discretion about where and how such a meeting should be conducted, having considered representations for the parties. A judge should usually never see a child alone and a minute of the meeting should be taken (or a transcript obtained if recorded). The purpose of the meeting is not to gather evidence – that remains the responsibility of the CAFCASS officer. It is to help the child understand the court process and be reassured that the judge has understood him/her. The judge should explain that they cannot hold secrets and what is said will be communicated to the child's parents other than in exceptional circumstances. The judge should ensure that the child understands that the decisions in the case are solely the responsibility of the judge and that the outcome is never the responsibility of the child. The meeting also provides an opportunity for the judge to discuss how the child wants decisions to be communicated. The parties or their representatives shall have the opportunity to respond to the content of the meeting, whether by way of oral evidence or submissions once the minutes/transcript are made available.

9.8 The Hague Convention case of *Re: KP (A Child)*,[1] provided the Court of Appeal with an opportunity to emphasise some of the points made in the guidelines:

> 'i) During that part of any meeting between a young person and a judge in which the judge is listening to the child's point of view and hearing what they have to say, the judge's role should be largely that of a passive recipient of whatever communication the young person wishes to transmit.
>
> ii) The purpose of the meeting is not to obtain evidence and the judge should not, therefore probe or seek to test whatever it is that the child wishes to say …
>
> iii) A meeting, such as in the present case, taking place prior to the judge deciding upon the central issues should be for the dual purposes of allowing the judge to hear what the young person may wish to volunteer and for the young person to hear the judge explain the nature of the court process …. It is difficult to envisage circumstances in which such a meeting would last for more than 20 minutes or so
>
> iv) If the child volunteers evidence that would be or might be relevant to the outcome of the proceedings, the judge should report back to the parties and determine whether, and if so how, the evidence should be best adduced …'

9.9 The Court of Appeal disapproved of the approach taken by Parker J at first instance where she had sought to 'probe' the child's wishes and feelings over the course of more than an hour. The judge had been in error in regarding the meeting as being an opportunity for the child to make representations or submissions to them.

---

1 [2014] EWCA Civ 554.

Chapter 10

THE OFFICIAL SOLICITOR

INTRODUCTION

10.1 The Official Solicitor to the Senior Courts ('OS') is an independent statutory office holder who acts in three primary capacities:

- as a last resort litigation friend and, in rare cases, solicitor, for children (though only exceptionally for those who are the subject of family proceedings) and for adults who lack mental capacity;
- on behalf of the Lord Chancellor in cases of international child abduction, through the International Child Abduction and Contact Unit ('ICACU'); and,
- on behalf of the Lord Chancellor in cases of international maintenance claims through the Reciprocal Enforcement of Maintenance Orders Unit ('REMO').

10.2 The OS also has a rarely used role as advocate to the court, but it is the first role with which this work is concerned. This role, in various forms, has existed since the 18th century and the continued existence of the OS is now provided for by the Senior Courts Act 1981, s 90.

10.3 The OS acts within the courts of England and Wales only and in civil, family and Court of Protection proceedings. The OS plays no role in criminal and tribunal proceedings.

10.4 The office of the OS is now combined with that of the Public Trustee, though the roles of the two remain legally separate and distinct.

THE OFFICIAL SOLICITOR AS A LITIGATION FRIEND – GENERAL

10.5 The primary function of the OS has historically been to help those who are vulnerable due to lack of capacity in litigation. The OS continues this role and will accept an appointment as a litigation friend where:

- A party requires a litigation friend;

- There is confirmation of security for the protected party's legal costs; and,
- There is no other person who is suitable and willing to act.

10.6 There are two broad groups who may require the OS to act as a litigation friend. These are adults who lack capacity and children.

ADULTS WHO LACK CAPACITY

10.7 If an adult party or intended party to family proceedings lacks capacity (within the meaning of the Mental Capacity Act 2005) to conduct the proceedings, they are a 'protected party': FPR 2010, r 2.3.

10.8 As a protected party, they require a litigation friend to conduct the proceedings on their behalf: FPR 2010, r 15.2. Without one, unless the court orders otherwise, a protected party is limited in the steps he or she may take in the litigation to applying for a litigation friend or filing an application form: FPR 2010, r 15.3.

10.9 The court can appoint the OS as a litigation friend to a protected party: FPR 2010, r 15.6.

10.10 There must be undisputed satisfactory evidence or a finding by the court that the party lacks capacity to conduct the proceedings and is therefore a protected party. The party or intended party is entitled to dispute an opinion that they lack capacity and there may be cases where their capacity is the subject of dispute between competent experts. In either case, a formal finding by the court under FPR 2010, r.2.3 will be appropriate.

10.11 Capacity is issue specific and must be kept under review. If there is evidence that the protected party has regained capacity, the OS will apply to the court to be discharged.

CHILDREN

10.12 The OS acts as a litigation friend to children who are party to proceedings though, with the advent of CAFCASS, only exceptionally for those who are the subject of family proceedings.

10.13 Generally, where a child is a party to proceedings but not the subject of those proceedings, the child must have a litigation friend to conduct proceedings on the child's behalf: FPR 2010, r 16.5.

10.14 The most common examples where the OS will act as a litigation friend for a child are where:

- a child is also the parent of a child and is a respondent to a Children Act 1989 or Adoption and Children Act 2002 application;
- a child wishes to make an application for an order under the Children Act 1989 naming another child (typically a Child Arrangements Order for contact with a sibling). The OS will need to be satisfied that the proposed proceedings would benefit the child applicant;
- a child has been joined as an intervener in a public law children case to response to allegations;
- a child is witness to some disputed factual issue in a children case and may require intervener status;
- a child is an intervenor in divorce or financial remedy proceedings;
- a child is an applicant or respondent in an application for an order under Part IV of the Family Law Act 1996;
- a child is party to applications for declarations of status under the Family Law Act 1986, Part III other than s 55A applications; and
- a child is an applicant or respondent in an application for an order under the Family Law Act 1996, Part IV (Family Homes and Domestic Violence) or Part 4A (Forced Marriage).

10.15 Since 1 April 2001, the OS has largely ceased to represent children who are the subject of family proceedings and these children are now represented by CAFCASS. The OS will only represent such children in exceptional circumstances and only then after having liaised with CAFCASS in order to avoid duplication and ensure the most suitable arrangements are made.

SECURITY OF LEGAL COSTS

10.16 The OS will only act where there is confirmation of security for the protected party's legal costs: FPR 2010, PD15A. The OS is specifically excluded from having to undertake to pay any costs which the protected party may be ordered to pay in relation to the proceedings (as other litigation friends are required to do).

10.17 Sources of security include:

- the Legal Aid Agency where the protected party or child is eligible for legal aid;
- the protected party's or child's own funds. If they have financial capacity, then this may be with their consent. If they do not, then where the Court

of Protection has given the OS the authority to recover the costs from the protected party's or child's funds; or

- an undertaking from another party to pay the OS's costs.

THE OFFICIAL SOLICITOR AS A LAST RESORT

10.18 The OS will only act as a litigation friend in the absence of another willing and suitable person. Pursuant to FPR 2010 r.15.4(3), a person may act as a litigation friend if that person:

- consents to act;
- can fairly and competently conduct proceedings on behalf of the protected party/child;
- has no interest adverse to that of the protected party/child; and
- undertakes to pay any costs which the protected party may be ordered to pay in relation to the proceedings, subject to any right the litigation friend may have to be repaid from the assets of the protected party.

WHERE THE OFFICIAL SOLICITOR HAS ACCEPTED AN APPOINTMENT AS LITIGATION FRIEND

10.19 The OS only becomes formally involved when appointed by the court. At this point, the OS will need time to prepare the case and, if there are ongoing proceedings, may wish to make submissions about any substantive hearing date.

10.20 The OS's duty is to act in the protected party's best interests by supplementing their want of capacity and judgement. The OS can only make decisions on behalf of the protected party within the litigation. In determining the protected party's best interests, the OS will consider all of the circumstances and facts of each case, but will take into account:

- the protected party's past and present wishes and feelings, the beliefs and values that would be likely to influence their conduct of the proceedings if they had capacity, and the other factors they would be likely to consider if able to do so;
- the need, so far as reasonably practical, to permit and encourage the protected party to participate, or to improve their ability to participate, as fully as possible in decisions relating to the conduct of the proceedings
- the need to respect the emotional bond between parent and child;
- the fact that the court will view the child's welfare as the paramount consideration and apply the welfare checklist;

- the matters to which the court is to have regard; and
- the overriding objective: FPR 2010, r 1.1

10.21 In order to properly consider the circumstances of each case, the OS is under a further duty to gather and assess all relevant evidence to enable the OS to make a balanced judgement of the merits of the case and the likely outcome: *Re B (children) (evidence: expert evidence)*.[1]

10.22 Not only can the OS act as a litigation friend but he can also act as solicitor. Far more usually, however, the OS will instruct a private firm of solicitors to represent the protected party (where the protected party has not already done so). In all cases, the OS requires from the solicitors who have been instructed:

- a reading list identifying the material documents;
- identification of the issues including those which require consideration on behalf of the protected party or child;
- a summary of the background to, and major steps in, the proceedings;
- advice as to the steps the OS, as litigation friend, should now take in the proceedings on behalf of the protected party or child;
- copies of all notes of attendance on the protected party or child (so that the OS is properly informed as to the views and wishes expressed by the protected party or child to date); and,
- confirmation of the protected party's or child's ascertainable present views and wishes in relation to the proceedings.

10.23 The protected party is still the solicitor's client, but the solicitor will take his or her instructions from the OS and the protected party does not have the power to terminate the relationship with their solicitor. Typically, the solicitor has contact with the protected party and will relay the wishes and feelings of the protected party to the OS.

10.24 When acting for a protected party, it is important to ensure that any information given to them is given in a form which can be understood and in a way that is commensurate with their circumstances. This can include using simple language, visual aids and/or any other means. As Mr Justice Gillen highlighted, with subsequent approval from Sir James Munby in *Re D (A Child) (No 3)*,[2] in *Re G and A (Care Order: Freeing Order: Parents with a Learning Disability)*:[3]

> '[5(d)] … The court must also take steps to ensure there are no barriers to justice within the process itself. Judges and magistrates must recognise that parents with learning disabilities need extra time with solicitors so that

1 [2010] EWCA Civ 363, [2010] All ER (D) 212 (Feb).
2 [2016] EWFC 1.
3 [2006] NI Fam 8.

everything can be carefully explained to them. Advocates can play a vital role in supporting parents with learning difficulties particularly when they are involved in child protection or judicial processes … This approach should be echoed throughout the whole system including LAC reviews. All parts of the Family justice system should take care as to the language and vocabulary that is utilised … the courts must be careful to ensure that the supposed inability of parents to change might itself be an artefact of professionals ineffectiveness in engaging with the parents in appropriate terms …'.

Chapter 11

COMPETENCE OF WITNESSES IN A CRIMINAL TRIAL

11.1 The issue of competence and whether a witness should be sworn before giving evidence are both matters that any practitioner considering a case involving vulnerable witnesses will need to be aware of, together with the provisions that govern these matters.

COMPETENCE OF WITNESSES

A presumption that all persons are competent

11.2 A person is competent if they can be legally called to give evidence in proceedings; this should not be confused with compellability. There is a statutory presumption that a witness is competent and age or disability is not a presumptive barrier to being competent, as set out in YJCEA 1999, s 53(1):

> '53 Competence of witnesses to give evidence.
>
> (1) At every stage in criminal proceedings all persons are (whatever their age) competent to give evidence.'

The two statutory exceptions to being competent

11.3 YJCEA 1999, s 53(3)–(5) set out the test for competence:

> '(3) A person is not competent to give evidence in criminal proceedings if it appears to the court that he is not a person who is able to—
>
> (a) understand questions put to him as a witness, and
>
> (b) give answers to them which can be understood.

> (4) A person charged in criminal proceedings is not competent to give evidence in the proceedings for the prosecution (whether he is the only person, or is one of two or more persons, charged in the proceedings).
>
> (5) In subsection (4) the reference to a person charged in criminal proceedings does not include a person who is not, or is no longer, liable to be convicted of any offence in the proceedings (whether as a result of pleading guilty or for any other reason).'

11.4 There are therefore two exceptions to a witness being competent to give evidence at a criminal trial. The first set out in YJCEA 1999, s 53(3) applies to all witnesses, both for the defence and the prosecution and does not expressly exclude the defendant. However, the exception set out in s 53(4) and (5) is purely as to competence to give evidence for the prosecution.

11.5 As regards vulnerable witnesses YJCEA 1999, s 53(3) is the key provision that will need to be considered. In order to be competent a witness must have an ability to understand questions and answer them and clearly special measures can assist in ensuring competence.

The test for determining competence

11.6 The test for determining competence is set out in YJCEA 1999, s 54. In summary the procedure is as follows:

- *Who can raise the issue of competence*: The issue of competence can be raised by the court by its own motion or by either party.
- *A matter for the court*: Once the issue of competence is raised it a matter that is to be determined by the court irrespective of how the matter has been raised (YJCEA 1999, s 54(1)).
- *In the absence of the jury*: Any proceedings held for the determination of the question of competence shall take place in the absence of the jury (if there is one) (YJCEA 1999, s 54(4)).
- *Balance of probabilities*: Once the issue of competence is raised it is for the party calling the witness to satisfy the court that, on a balance of probabilities, the witness is competent to give evidence in the proceedings (YJCEA 1999, s 54(2)). It is important to note that when determining the question of competence:

  > 'the court shall treat the witness as having the benefit of any directions under section 19 YJCEA' which means that the court will consider the witness's competence with the use of special measures where it has been determined that these are appropriate.' (YJCEA 1999, s 54(3).)

- *Expert evidence*: Expert evidence may be received on the question of competence (YJCEA 1999, s 54(5)) but there is no requirement that expert evidence is given on the issue.

- *Questioning of the potential witness*: It is also of note that if the court considers that it is necessary for there to be any questioning of the witness this shall be conducted by the court in the presence of the parties (YJCEA 1999, s 54(6)).

CASE LAW

11.7 *R v B*:[1] In this case the court considered whether a conviction can be regarded as safe when it is heavily dependent upon the evidence of a child witness. In this case the witness giving evidence was four and a half and giving evidence about events that had taken place when she was three. In particular it was submitted that the competency requirement was not satisfied.

Practitioners' attention is particularly drawn to paras 38–43 of this judgment where the principles in YJCEA 1999, ss 53 and 54 are considered by the court. The case highlighted the fact that the question is not whether a witness is a child or infirm, etc but whether they are competent and that there are no presumptions or preconceptions (at para 38):

> 'These statutory provisions are not limited to the evidence of children. They apply to individuals of unsound mind. They apply to the infirm. The question in each case is whether the individual witness, or, as in this case, the individual child, is competent to give evidence in the particular trial. The question is entirely witness or child specific. There are no presumptions or preconceptions. The witness need not understand the special importance that the truth should be told in court, and the witness need not understand every single question or give a readily understood answer to every question. Many competent adult witnesses would fail such a competency test. Dealing with it broadly and fairly, provided the witness can understand the questions put to him and can also provide understandable answers, he or she is competent. If the witness cannot understand the questions or his answers to questions which he understands cannot themselves be understood he is not. The questions come, of course, from both sides. If the child is called as a witness by the prosecution he or she must have the ability to understand the questions put to him by the defence as well as the prosecution and to provide answers to them which are understandable. The provisions of the statute are clear and unequivocal, and do not require reinterpretation. (*R v MacPherson* [2006] 1 CAR 30: *R v Powell* [2006] 1 CAR 31:
>
> *R v M* [2008] EWCA Crim 2751 and *R v Malicki* [2009] EWCA Crim 365.)'

Para 41 reminds practitioners that the question is not one of whether a witness is telling the truth or not:

> 'The judge determines the competency question, by distinguishing carefully between the issues of competence and credibility. At the stage when the

1 [2010] EWCA Crim 4.

> competency question is determined the judge is not deciding whether a witness is or will be telling the truth and giving accurate evidence. Provided the witness is competent, the weight to be attached to the evidence is for the jury.'

Para 43 confirms that 'the competency test may be re-analysed at the end of the child's evidence'. In practice if the evidence has already gone before the jury then the jury may have to be told to disregard that evidence. However, if the child's evidence is the main evidence in a trial and the judge then excludes this evidence it may also follow that the court will find no case to answer.

In this case the Lord Justice noted that the summing up was 'meticulous, comprehensive and fair' and therefore the comments may provide helpful assistance for those acting in cases involving issues of competency of a child witnesses (for further details on summing up in such cases see **Chapter 14**). At para 29:

> 'In the course of the summing up the jury was given detailed and fair directions about the way in which they should approach X's evidence. The judge began by reminding the jury that the procedure adopted in her case was not "intended to pre-judge the evidence" that she would give, and went on to remind the jury that the question whether she was "reliable, credible and truthful" had to be decided in exactly the same way as it would with any other witness. The jury was to judge "her accuracy, reliability and credibility, both in the interview and at court" and he advised them to take 5 specific matters which were said to undermine confidence in X's credibility into account. In very brief summary (the judge dealt with them in much more detail) they were: the child's age at the time of the alleged offence, the date of the interview, and her age when she gave evidence; the various gaps in time which might effect (sic) her memory; the sequence of events which culminated in her evidence at trial; the need for the jury to make their assessment of whether she was able to understand and be intelligible both in her video interview and her evidence; the way she gave evidence, and in particular whether her evidence about what the appellant had done was spontaneous or simply responding to questions which suggested the answers, and whether she agreed with everything suggested to her, or whether she was prepared to "stick to her guns and disagree" when she thought the question was wrong. Finally, he asked the jury to consider the way in which X had given evidence, making appropriate allowances for her age.'

11.8 Other key cases include:

- *R v Sed (Ali Dahir)*:[2] considers whether the hearsay provisions engage the principals of competency.

2 [2004] EWCA Crim 1294.

- *R v Watts (James Michael)*:[3] approves the use of intermediaries for witnesses to ensure a witness is able to meet the test for competency.
- *R v F*:[4] the approach in *R v B* was considered and confirmed and paragraphs 25 to 28 highlight the need for care when addressing competency and also the requirement by the courts that practitioners in cases involving vulnerable witnesses are themselves able to effectively assist such witnesses:

  '25 As this court indicated at paragraph 42 in *R v B* [2010] EWCA Crim 4, the trial process must cater for the needs of witnesses. The competency test is not failed because the forensic techniques of the advocate or the processes of the court have to be adapted to enable the witness to give the best evidence of which he or she is capable. It is our clear conclusion that the hearing did not effectively explore H's ability to communicate.

  '26 We do not underestimate the difficulties of questioning vulnerable witnesses. It requires not only training, flexibility and sensitivity, but also time and patience. It seems to us that when difficulties were encountered, it became apparent that the intermediary had not had sufficient time to carry out a full assessment of H's skills which might enable communication to take place. Questions of time and more abstract concepts ran into difficulty when the judge, in an effort to obtain an answer to the witness' understanding of the seasons, posed questions about what a daffodil looked like. When the intermediary said that she did not think that the witness knew a daffodil as such, the judge said that she did not wish to ask any further questions.

  '27 We have come to the conclusion that in the circumstances the exercise carried out was not a fair test of the witness' competency. The shortcomings of this process seem to us to owe much to a lack of preparation and a lack of ability to respond flexibly to the difficulties which arose. There are now substantial materials available to those who have to deal with the questions of competency and the use of intermediaries. We draw attention to the publication "Raising the Bar: the Handling of Vulnerable Witnesses, Victims and Defendants in Court" — a Report of the Working Group of the Advocacy Training Council of the Bar published in 2011. In the same vein the Crown Court Bench Book has a section dealing with intermediaries. Relevant issues are also discussed by this Court in *R v B* (already referred to), particularly at paragraphs 33 to 43.'

DETERMINING WHETHER A WITNESS SHOULD BE SWORN

11.9 Following on from consideration of competence is whether a witness should be sworn to give evidence or not. The provisions governing whether a

3 [2010] EWCA Crim 1824.
4 [2013] EWCA Crim 424.

witness should be sworn to give evidence are set out in YJCEA 1999, s 55. As with competence it can be raised by the court on its own motion or by a party to the proceedings (YJCEA 1999, s 55(1)). The general test is set out in YJCEA 1999, s 55(2) and says that unless the witness meets that test they may not be sworn:

> 'The witness may not be sworn for that purpose unless—
>
> (a) he has attained the age of 14, and
>
> (b) he has a sufficient appreciation of the solemnity of the occasion and of the particular responsibility to tell the truth which is involved in taking an oath.'

YJCEA 1999, s 53(3) sets out a presumption that a 'witness shall, if he is able to give intelligible testimony, be presumed to have a sufficient appreciation of those matters if no evidence tending to show the contrary is adduced (by any party).' The test of intelligible testimony set out in YJCEA 1999, s 54(8) is as per the test for competency in s 53.

If an issue is raised as to whether the witness should be sworn it is for the party seeking to have the witness sworn to satisfy the court that, on a balance of probabilities, the witness has attained the age of 14 and has a sufficient appreciation of the matters mentioned in YJCEA 1999, s 55(4)(2)(b).

The provisions as to how the questions should be determined mirror those for competency:

- When the court is determining competency any proceedings such determination shall take place in the absence of the jury (if there is one) (YJCEA 1999, s 54(5)).
- Expert evidence may be received on the question but is not required (YJCEA 1999, s 55(6)).
- Any questioning of the witness (where the court considers that necessary) shall be conducted by the court in the presence of the parties (YJCEA 1999, s 55(7)).

YJCEA 1999, s 56 addresses the position if the court receives unsworn evidence and s 56(3) states:

> 'A deposition of unsworn evidence given by a person to whom this subsection applies may be taken for the purposes of criminal proceedings as if that evidence had been given on oath.'

And importantly YJCEA 1999, s 56(5) states:

> 'Where a person ("the witness") who is competent to give evidence in criminal proceedings gives evidence in such proceedings unsworn, no conviction, verdict or finding in those proceedings shall be taken to be unsafe for the purposes of any of sections 2(1), 13(1) and 16(1) of the Criminal Appeal Act 1968 (grounds for allowing appeals) by reason only that it appears to the Court of Appeal that the witness was a person falling within section 55(2) (and should accordingly have given his evidence on oath).'

Chapter 12

VULNERABLE WITNESSES DURING A CRIMINAL TRIAL

INTRODUCTION

12.1 The purpose of this chapter is to address the special measures available for vulnerable witnesses, both those for the defence and the crown, during the trial process. There are different provisions governing special measures for vulnerable defendants and these are considered in **Chapter 13**.

Previous chapters have addressed the measures and steps that may or should have been taken with respect to vulnerable witnesses prior to the trial date including during the investigation and in the pre-proceedings. These include the procedure for 'Achieving Best Evidence' (ABE) interviews for vulnerable witnesses, the use of appropriate adults for vulnerable suspects at the police station and the use of intermediaries to assist both vulnerable witnesses and vulnerable defendants throughout each stage of proceedings. However, it should be remembered that a failure to apply special measures or give proper consideration to vulnerable witnesses can be relevant at the trial stage not only with respect to the witness themselves but also the validity of their evidence or how it can be used at trial. For example if it can be argued that a defendant should have had a appropriate adult in interview it may be possible to have the interview excluded under PACE 1984, s 78.

As set out in previous chapters, vulnerability comes in many forms and careful consideration should be given as to how best to assist the vulnerable person. There are a number of special measures that are available within the criminal justice system, as considered below, and they can be combined where such an approach is better able to address the witness's specific needs.

12.2 Courts and practitioners are now very conscious of the need to consider vulnerable witnesses and defendants at an early stage of proceedings so that where possible the special measures that are available to vulnerable people during the trial process are identified well in advance of a trial and will have already been ordered in advance of trial. This early identification can provide vulnerable people with reassurance that they will be able to provide their best evidence during the trial process and also helps the trial process to run smoothly and avoids wasting court time. Further, if they are not ordered in advance it may be that some special measures will not be able to be facilitated by the court – for example if the case has not been listed in a court room with live link facilities.

However, even though the court process seeks to identify relevant vulnerable people early on and consider the relevant special measures or necessary directions that may assist them during the trial, the court and the lawyers must be alive to the fact of possible changes in circumstances and the need to reconsider the relevant special measures that a vulnerable person may need or what further directions may be required. This can even be once they have begun giving evidence.

This chapter focuses on the measures available inside the court room, but assistance is also available while the witness waits to give evidence see **Chapter 9**. Witness Support are usually available at court to assist witnesses and measures can be taken to ensure the witness is waiting somewhere they feel comfortable and where they will not come into contact with another person who may cause them distress prior to giving evidence. In some cases, there may also be a family liaison officer who will be present at court to assist a vulnerable witness.

The witness should know who will contact them or who they can contact for further information after they have given evidence. This will provide them with further reassurance.

12.3 With respect to special measures directed by the court, there is often a balancing act between protecting a vulnerable witness and ensuring a defendant has a fair trial as considered by Lady Hallett in her judgment in the recent case of *R v YGM*:[1]

> 'In recent years the criminal justice system has made huge strides in its efforts to ensure that vulnerable witnesses are treated fairly and appropriately during the trial process. This court has strived to ensure that a proper balance is maintained between the interests of a witness and the rights of a defendant.'

Considering the term 'special measures' and in particular the word 'special', the reality is that these measures to assist witnesses have become commonplace during criminal trials and it is not unusual for a trial to incorporate the use of measures to assist witnesses to give their best evidence.[2] From the author's experience it is not unusual for a trial judge to remind a jury that 'special measures' are now very much commonplace. It is interesting from an academic perspective to note that in the Family Procedure Rules (FPR) 2010, r 3A the measures are simply known as that and the word 'special' is not included, possibly showing that there is now an understanding that these measures are not 'special' but are in many ways standard measures to assist vulnerable witnesses in giving their evidence.

1 [2018] EWCA Crim 2458.

2 This was noted by the former Lord Chief Justice, Baron Judge of Draycotte in 'Half a Century of Change: The Evidence of Child Victims – Toulmin Lecture in Law and Psychiatry'.

12.4 The consideration of vulnerable witnesses in the preparation for trial was considered in **Chapter 4** and is encapsulated in the CPR 2015, r 3.9(3):

> 'In order to prepare for the trial, the court must take every reasonable step—
>
> (a) to encourage and to facilitate the attendance of witnesses when they are needed; and
>
> (b) to facilitate the participation of any person, including the defendant.'

'Every reasonable step' – these are key words for every practitioner to have in mind when addressing the court as to what steps should be taken with respect to vulnerable people during a criminal trial.

12.5 The CPR 2015 go further, stating that facilitating the participation of any person includes giving directions for the appropriate treatment and questioning of a witness or the defendant, especially where the court directs that such questioning is to be conducted through an intermediary (CPR 2015, r 3.9(6)).

One of the key ways in which a vulnerable person's participation is reasonable facilitated is through special measures.

KEY LEGAL PROVISIONS FOR SPECIAL MEASURES AT TRIAL

12.6 The use of special measures in criminal proceedings is predominately governed by:

(i) Youth Justice and Criminal Evidence Act 1999 (YCJCEA 1999);

(ii) Criminal Practice Direction I, paras 3D–3G, October 2015; and

(iii) CPR 2015, Part 18.

12.7 Further guidance is provided by:

(iv) Children and Young Persons Act 1933, s 44;

(v) The Advocate's Gateway (Inns of Court College of Advocacy), and in particular the Toolkits to assist advocates;

(vi) Raising the Bar: The Handling of Vulnerable Witnesses, Victims and Defendants in Court' (2011) (Advocacy Training Council);

(vii) Special Measures Guidance issued by the Professional Practice Committee of the General Council of the Bar; and

(viii) 'Achieving Best Evidence in Criminal Proceedings' (Ministry of Justice 2011).

12.8 Vulnerable and intimidated witnesses (as defined by the YJCEA 1999) are eligible for special measures. The Act introduced 'Special Measures Directions in Case of Vulnerable and Intimidated Witnesses' to the criminal trial process. The YJCEA 1999, ss 16 and 17 set out the circumstances in which witnesses are eligible for a special measures direction (see below). It should be noted that both prosecution and defence witnesses are potentially eligible for a special measures direction under these provisions, but that the defendant is specifically excluded from a direction by the words 'other than the accused' in the YJCEA 1999, ss 16(1), 17(1) and 19(1)(a) notwithstanding that that a defendant may have identical needs to those of a prosecution or defence witness in order to give evidence, see **Chapter 13** for the provisions available for defendants.

WHO IS ELIGIBLE FOR SPECIAL MEASURES?

12.9 There is a wide set of categories of witness who are eligible for special measures. These are set out in YJCEA 1999, ss 16 and 17, see below:

Under YJCEA 1999, s 16:

- Child witnesses (YJCEA 1999, s 16(1)(a)).
- Witnesses suffering from a mental disorder (YJCEA 1999, s 16(2)).
- Witnesses suffering from a physical disability (YJCEA 1999, s 16(2)).

Under YJCEA 1999, s 17:

- Witnesses whose evidence would be diminished by fear or distress (YJCEA 1999, s 17(1)).
- Complainants in sexual offence cases (YJCEA 1999, s 17(4)).
- Complainants in other relevant offences (YJCEA 1999, s 17(5)).

The provisions with respect to witnesses about whom the court is satisfied that the quality of their evidence is likely to be diminished by reason of fear or distress very much open special measures up and have allowed them to become very much standard measures for witnesses who are vulnerable, not necessarily in general terms but as a result of being involved within the proceedings.

CHILD WITNESSES

12.10 Child witnesses are automatically eligible for special measures, under the YJCEA 1999, s 16(1)(a). However, a determination of what, if any, special measures will assist the particular child witness is still required.

The act introduces a 'primary rule' for child witnesses (YJCEA 1999, s 21(3)).

> '(3) The primary rule in the case of a child witness is that the court must give a special measures direction in relation to the witness which complies with the following requirements—
>
> (a) it must provide for any relevant recording to be admitted under section 27 (video recorded evidence in chief); and
>
> (b) it must provide for any evidence given by the witness in the proceedings which is not given by means of a video recording (whether in chief or otherwise) to be given by means of a live link in accordance with section 24.'

Under YJCEA 1999, s 21(4) the primary rule is subject to limitations. These include availability and the witness's wishes. In the latter case the rule does not apply to the extent that the court is satisfied that not complying with the rule would not diminish the quality of the witness's evidence and also to the extent that the court is satisfied that compliance with it would not be likely to maximise the quality of the witness's evidence so far as practicable (whether because the application to that evidence of one or more other special measures available in relation to the witness would have that result or for any other reason). If the witness does not seek to give evidence via live link the presumption is then that the witness shall give evidence with the assistance of screens under YJCEA 1999, s 23. Again, this is unless the witness indicates that is not their wish and the court determines that the witness' evidence would not be diminished without such special measures.

12.11 YJCEA 1999, s 21 (4C) provides as follows:

> 'In making a decision under subsection (4)(ba) or (4B)(a), the court must take into account the following factors (and any others it considers relevant)—
>
> (a) the age and maturity of the witness;
>
> (b) the ability of the witness to understand the consequences of giving evidence otherwise than in accordance with the requirements in subsection (3) or (as the case may be) in accordance with the requirement in subsection (4A);
>
> (c) the relationship (if any) between the witness and the accused;
>
> (d) the witness's social and cultural background and ethnic origins;
>
> (e) the nature and alleged circumstances of the offence to which the proceedings relate.'

YJCEA 1999, s 22 extends the provisions of s 21 to witnesses who are over 18 at the time of the hearing, but who were under 18 at the time that the video recorded interview was made.

12.12 For guidance about the questioning of child witnesses: see *R v W & M*,[3] *R v Wills*[4] and *R v Edwards*.[5]

Fast tracking for cases involving child witnesses

12.13 Cases involving witnesses under the age of ten should be fast tracked. The protocol proposes that there should be no more than eight weeks between the first complaint and charge and no more than eight weeks from plea to trial.[6]

PHYSICAL OR MENTAL IMPAIRMENT

12.14 The YJCEA 1999, s 16(1) and (2) provide that witnesses with physical or mental impairments are eligible for consideration for special measures:

- witnesses under 18 at the time of the hearing (child witnesses, see above) (YJCEA 199, s 16(1)(a)); and
- witnesses the quality of whose evidence the court considers will be diminished by reason of any of the circumstances set out in the YCEA 1999, s 16(2) (YJCEA 199, s 16(1)(b)).

12.15 The prescribed circumstances to be considered are:

- witnesses suffering from a mental disorder within the meaning of the Mental Health Act 1983, or who otherwise have a significant impairment of intelligence and social functioning (YJCEA 1999, s 16(2)(a)(i) and (ii)); and
- witnesses who have a physical disability or who suffer from a physical disorder (YJCEA 1999, s 16(2)(b)).

12.16 The reference to 'at the time of the hearing' in the YJCEA 1999, s 16(1)(a) is defined in s 16(3) as 'the time at which the court gives a special measures direction' in respect of the witness. Therefore, to be eligible under the YJCEA 1999, s 16(1)(b) the witness must have one of the prescribed circumstances and the court must consider that the witnesses' evidence will be diminished as a result of that circumstance – or arguably what could be referred to as a vulnerability.

12.17 In determining whether the witness falls within the YJCEA 1999, s 16(1)(b) the court is required (by the YJCEA 1999, s 16(4)) to consider any views expressed by the witness. It should be noted that this section states 'must consider any views expressed by the witness'. So it is a requirement rather than a suggestion.

---

3 [2010] EWCA 1926.
4 [2011] EWCA Crim 1938.
5 [2011] EWCA Crim 3028.
6 A protocol between the Association of Chief Police Officers, the CPS and HMCTS to Expedite cases Involving Witnesses under 10 Years – 2015.

12.18 The quality of a witness's evidence is defined by the YJCEA 1999, s 16(5) as:

> '... completeness, coherence and accuracy; and for this purpose, 'coherence' refers to a witness's ability in giving evidence to give answers which address the questions put to the witness and can be understood both individually and collectively.'

FEAR OR DISTRESS, SEXUAL OFFENCES AND OTHER RELEVANT OFFENCES

12.19 The YJCEA 1999, s 17 sets out the categories of witness eligible for special measures on grounds of fear or distress about testifying. These are:

(i) witnesses about whom the court is satisfied that the quality of their evidence is likely to be diminished by reason of fear or distress in connection with testifying in the proceedings (YCJEA 1999, s 17(1));

(ii) witnesses who are complainants in respect of a sexual offence or an offence under the Modern Slavery Act 2015, s 1 or 2, who will be eligible unless they inform the court that they do not wish to be eligible (YJCEA 1999, s 17(4));

(iii) witnesses in proceedings relating to a 'relevant offence' as set out in the YJCEA 1999, Sch 1A will be eligible unless they inform the court that they do not wish to be eligible (YJCEA 1999, s 17(5)).

12.20 Eligibility as a result of fear and distress provides a wide eligibility criterion as it would not be unusual for a witness to be in fear or distressed by the mere thought of giving evidence. This could be for a wide range of reasons, for example fear of speaking to a group. In determining whether a witness falls within the YJCEA 1999, s 17(1) requirements, the court is required to take into account the factors set out in s 17(2):

- the nature and alleged circumstances of the offence to which the proceedings relate;
- the witness's age;
- any behaviour towards the witness on the part of the accused, his associates and family or any other person likely to be an accused or witness in the proceedings;
- any views expressed by the witness; and, where relevant,
- the witness's social and cultural background and ethnic origins, domestic and employment circumstances and any religious belief or political opinions.

Under the CPR 2015, r 18.10 the application should set out the grounds and provide supporting evidence.

12.21 In addition the YJCEA 1999, s 22A makes special provision for the use of video recorded evidence-in-chief in the case of witnesses who are complainants in criminal proceedings relating to a sexual offence who are not otherwise eligible on grounds of age. This provision does not apply in the magistrates' court.

WHICH OF THE SPECIAL MEASURES IS THE VULNERABLE WITNESS ELIGIBLE FOR?

12.22 Having determined whether a witness is eligible for special measures the next consideration is which special measures a witness may be eligible for, depending on the basis of eligibility. The YJCEA 1999, s 18 sets out the categories of special measures available to witnesses eligible by virtue of the provisions discussed above.

> '18 Special measures available to eligible witnesses.
>
> (1) For the purposes of this Chapter—
>
> (a) the provision which may be made by a special measures direction by virtue of each of sections 23 to 30 is a special measure available in relation to a witness eligible for assistance by virtue of section 16; and
>
> (b) the provision which may be made by such a direction by virtue of each of sections 23 to 28 is a special measure available in relation to a witness eligible for assistance by virtue of section 17;
>
> but this subsection has effect subject to subsection (2).'

12.23 The special measures available for those witnesses eligible under the YJCEA 1999, ss 16 and 17 are:

- Screens (YJCEA 1999, s 23).
- Giving evidence by live link (YJCEA 1999, s 24).
- Giving evidence in private (YJCEA 1999, s 25).
- Removal of wigs and gowns by the judge and barristers (YJCEA 1999, s 26).
- Video recorded evidence in chief (YJCEA 1999, s 27).
- Video recorded cross-examination or re-examination (YJCEA 1999, s 28).

The additional special measures available for those eligible under YJCEA, s 16 are:

- Examination of witness through intermediary (see **Chapter 8**) (YJCEA 1999, s 29).
- Aids to communication (YJCEA 1999, s 30).

When making an application it is important to remember the distinction in measures available as it is very likely that a witness may be eligible for special measures for more than one reason. If one of those reasons is by virtue of a factor under YJCEA 1999, s 16 then there is good sense in including that matter within any application.

The specific statutory provisions relating to special measures are set out in full in **Appendix C**. As stated above, it should be considered whether a vulnerable person needs a combination of special measures. A common combination of special measures is video recorded evidence-in-chief and a live link for cross-examination.

WHO CAN MAKE THE APPLICATION?

12.24 The YJCEA 1999, s 19(1) provides that a party to the proceedings may make an application for a direction in respect of a witness (other than the accused), or that the court may raise the issue of its own motion. The standard templates for making special measures applications are found in **Appendix A**.

12.25 The CPR 2015, r 18.3 sets out the following timetable for applying for special measures:

> Making an application for a direction or order
>
> 18.3. A party who wants the court to exercise its power to give or make a direction or order must—
>
> (a) apply in writing as soon as reasonably practicable, and in any event not more than—
>
>   (i) 28 days after the defendant pleads not guilty, in a magistrates' court, or
>
>   (ii) 14 days after the defendant pleads not guilty, in the Crown Court; and
>
> (b) serve the application on—
>
>   (i) the court officer, and
>
>   (ii) each other party.

The court can vary this standard timetable under CPR, r 18.5.

12.26 In the case of prosecution witnesses the identification of the appropriate special measures to be applied for the trial process is carried out in conjunction with the police and the police should provide the CPS with the following details:[7]

- the ability of the witness to give evidence;

7 https://www.cps.gov.uk/legal-guidance/special-measures.

- whether the witness may have other support needs for which referrals may need to be made;
- the basis upon which the witness is eligible for one or more of the special measures (consideration will need to be given as to whether any expert evidence will be required in order to establish eligibility);
- which of the special measures will be required to assist the particular witness and how the court is to be satisfied of the matters that it must consider under YJCEA 1999, s 19(2) and (3);
- the views of the witness as to which of the special measures should be applied for;
- the appropriate individuals, such as an intermediary, to attend any subsequent meetings between the prosecutor and the witness; and
- whether the witness is receiving therapy.

These somewhat obvious headings may also be of assistance to defence solicitors when assessing defendants or defence witnesses and what steps and application they too should be making.

The test for granting special measures

12.27 Where the court determines that a witness is eligible by virtue of YJCEA 1999, s 16 or 17, s 19(2) provides that it must determine whether any of the special measures available, or a combination of them, would be likely to improve the quality of the evidence given by the witness (YJCEA 1999, s 19(2)(a)), and if so, which special measures would maximise so far as practicable the quality of the evidence (YJCEA 1999, s 19(2)(b)(i)), and give a direction (YJCEA 1999, s 19(2)(b)(ii)). Therefore, simply because a witness is eligible, it does not automatically result in special measures being granted. The court also needs to consider the likely impact of the granting of the special measures.

12.28 The YJCEA 1999, s 19(3) provides that, in determining whether any special measure or measures would or would not be likely to improve or to maximise so far as practicable the quality of the evidence given by the witness, the court must consider all the circumstances of the case, and in particular, any views expressed by the witness, and whether the measure might tend to inhibit such evidence being effectively tested by a party to the proceedings. The YJCEA 1999, s 19 preserves the court's powers, in the exercise of its inherent powers or otherwise, to make orders in relation to witnesses who are not eligible witnesses, or in relation to eligible witnesses for reasons other than the witness's eligibility.

12.29 The YJCEA 1999, s 20 makes provision for the duration, variation and discharge of special measures directions. The YJCEA 1999, s 20(5) requires a court to give reasons in open court for giving, refusing, varying or discharging directions, and in the case of a magistrates' court, to record the reasons in the register.

ADDITIONAL PROTECTIONS FOR VULNERABLE WITNESSES

12.30 In addition to the specific special measures set out above the YJCEA 1999 also provides further protections for vulnerable or intimidated witness to seek to enable them to be able to give their best evidence:

Limits of cross-examination by defendants of witnesses or by the defence in general

12.31 As set out in **Chapter 2** a defendant in criminal proceedings is entitled to – and in fact in normal circumstances must – put their case to the person whose account is challenged. This is the case even where a person is not represented. However, the YJCEA 1999 does provide protections for complainants in specific circumstances to not be cross-examined by defendants:

12.32 The YJCEA 1999, s 34 prohibits the cross-examination in person by defendants of complainants in sexual cases, eg *R v Stephen Hamilton*[8] (at para 62):

> 'it is appropriate to emphasise the vital role that the judge plays in trials of any sexual crime in the pursuit of the interests of justice. He or she must balance, on the one hand, the needs and welfare of the complainant and, on the other, the legitimate interests of the defendant. That is particularly difficult in cases involving children as witnesses, and even more so when considering the evidence of those who are or have been mentally impaired whether as a result of intellectual deficit or by reason of having suffered mental illness.'

12.33 The YJCEA 1999, s 35 prohibits the cross-examination in person by unrepresented defendants of certain 'protected witnesses' (child complainants and other child witnesses).

12.34 The YJCEA 1999, s 36 permits the court to make an order prohibiting the cross-examination in person by a defendant of a witness where the prohibitions in YJCEA 1999, ss 34 and 35 do not apply (such as for certain categories of intimidated witnesses).

Further, the court can limit the questions put by or on behalf of the defence: see *R v Edwards*[9] and *R v Wills*.[10]

8 [2014] EWCA Crim 1555.
9 [2011] EWCA Crim 3028.
10 [2011] EWCA Crim 1938.

The court is also permitted to consider the questions that are to be asked in advance of the cross-examination taking place: see *R v Zafer Dinc*.[11] *R v Lubemba (Cokesix), R v JP*[12] is a key case that all practitioners must be aware of (at para 45):

> 'It is now generally accepted that if justice is to be done to the vulnerable witness and also to the accused, a radical departure from the traditional style of advocacy will be necessary. Advocates must adapt to the witness, not the other way round. They cannot insist upon any supposed right 'to put one's case' or previous inconsistent statements to a vulnerable witness. If there is a right to 'put one's case' (about which we have our doubts) it must be modified for young or vulnerable witnesses. It is perfectly possible to ensure the jury are made aware of the defence case and of significant inconsistencies without intimidation or distressing a witness (see for example paragraph 3E.4 of the Criminal Practice Directions).'

R v Jonas (Sandor)[13] sets out that it may be reasonable for a judge to limit cross-examination, in particular where there has already been cross-examination of the witness by another defence team. Following on from this case CPR 2015, r 3.9(7)(b)(v) now requires the court to set ground rules including, where there is more than one defendant, rules as to the allocation of topics between them when cross-examining the witness. *R v Pipe (Steven)*[14] establishes that the judge can, in some circumstances, stop further cross-examination when a witness has become distressed. It should be noted that in this case the critical element of the defence case had been put to the witness. Specifically it had been made plain to her on a number of occasions that the defendant said that she was lying about what had happened, which the witness repeatedly denied. Further in this case there was no dispute that the witness was not in a fit state to continue her cross-examination.

12.35 There is clear guidance given in the current Compendium updated in June 2018 at section 10-5 of the Judicial College Guidance as to how the jury should be directed with respect to children and vulnerable witnesses who have given evidence.

Lady Hallett in in the recent case of *R v YGM*[15] states the following:

> 'We believe that the following is best practice in a case involving cross examination of a vulnerable witness. First, the identification of any limitations on cross examination should take place at an early stage. We assume that this will occur at the ground rules hearing where the judge will discuss with the advocates the nature and extent of the limitations imposed and whether they are simply as to style or also relate to content. Before the witness is cross examined, it is best practice, (as recommended by the Judicial College) that as well as giving the standard special measures direction, the trial judge

11 [2017] EWCA Crim 1206.
12 [2014] EWCA Crim 2064.
13 [2015] EWCA Crim 562.
14 [2014] EWCA Crim 2570.
15 [2018] EWCA Crim 2458.

> also directs the jury in general terms that limitations have been placed on the defence advocate. If any specific issues of content have been identified that the cross examiner cannot explore, the judge may wish to direct the jury about them after the cross examination is completed. On any view, the judge should direct the jury about them in the summing-up. Finally, we should add that every advocate (and trial judge) is expected to ensure that they are up to date with current best practice in the treatment of vulnerable witnesses.'

However, in this case the judge had not been advised by counsel of the guidance available and the judge did not warn the jury of the limitations placed on cross-examination before it took place, as is recommended as best practice. However, this was not found to be such a fatal error as to render the conviction unsafe. Failures to follow best practice may in some circumstances render the conviction arguably unsafe; however in this case the Court of Appeal found that the judge had given every other direction with care and precision and had also directed the jury in his summing up of the need to limit the cross-examination and he repeated that warning when he reminded the jury of the contents of the cross-examination.

Reporting directions

12.36 In addition to special measures and protections preventing cross-examination the court also has the power to impose reporting restrictions. This may provide further protection and it may make a witness feel more able to give evidence.

The YJCEA 1999, s 46 enables courts to make a reporting direction in relation to adult witnesses which prohibits any matter relating to the witness from being included in any publication during the lifetime of the witness if it is likely to lead members of the public to identify the individual as a witness in criminal proceedings.

Jury directions/consideration for the judge and jury

12.37 **Chapter 14** addresses this in more detail; the directions given to the jury are a fundamental part of the protections available for vulnerable witness (and vulnerable defendants) in particular in ensuring that their evidence is considered fairly: see *R v Uddin and Ali*[16] (at para 54):

> 'The victims of offences of this kind are frequently damaged young people. They are nearly always wholly unused to giving evidence in court. They can be difficult, emotional, contradictory, aggressive and on some occasions

16 [2014] EWCA Crim 2269.

> wholly uncommunicative. Whether in any trial their evidence is so vitiated that it is unsafe to leave the case to the jury will be a matter of careful judicial assessment. However, the courts now have a far greater understanding than hitherto as to the difficulties that exist for vulnerable witnesses and the need for care in assessing whether inconsistent or varying accounts given on different occasions necessarily mean that the underlying allegation is untruthful or unreliable. These are often matters for juries rather than judges to assess because it will be vital for the fact finder to assess the reasons for the changes or the contradictions in the witness's evidence and whether they fatally undermine the prosecution's case as regards the counts on the indictment.'

It is often appropriate in such cases that the trial judge explains these principles to the jury so that a vulnerable witness's evidence is fairly considered.

Chapter 13

VULNERABLE DEFENDANTS DURING THE CRIMINAL TRIAL PROCESS[1]

13.1 The YJCEA 1999 originally excluded the defendant from any of the special measures directions that a court could make in respect of a vulnerable or intimidated witness. The reasoning behind this exclusion appears to derive from the then government's stated aim to redress the balance of the criminal justice system which it perceived as favouring the defendant. However, in the opinion of the authors of this book, this division introduced a potentially unfair disparity when the courts were hearing cases involving vulnerable defendants and in particular child defendants.

In the authors' opinion, in some circumstances it is arguable that a defendant's needs are likely to be greater than those of the other witnesses in a criminal trial, because they will extend throughout the whole trial, not just the part of the trial in which they give evidence. A defendant who gives evidence is a witness in proceedings like any other and not having access to the same assistance that is available for other witnesses could arguably be unfair and contrary to the defendant's ECHR Article 6 right to a fair trial. The defendant will need to follow and understand the evidence given by witnesses, oral and written admissions of fact, legal argument, speeches, the summing up, and to communicate effectively with his lawyers during the trial. Whether it is right or wrong for there to be such a distinction as to the treatment of vulnerable people during a trial, especially in the light of the need for fairness and key principle of innocence until proven guilty is outside the ambit of this handbook – however it is definitely a topic that can sometimes seem to need debate during a trial.

There can be an interconnecting relationship between the provision of special measures and the defendant's fitness to plead and stand trial and this is explored in the section addressing special measures for defendants below.

---

1 See also the discussion in **Chapter 11**.

COMMON LAW

13.2 In the absence of statutory provisions the courts have to some extent redressed the balance by using their inherent jurisdiction to allow special measures for defendants, the inherent jurisdiction being there to ensure the defendant's right to a fair trial as embodied in ECHR Article 6.

13.3 For child defendants in many cases the matter will be dealt with in the Youth Court which (as considered in **Chapter 7**) has its own safeguards and in many respects its own built-in special measures. However, where child defendants are being tried in the Crown Court the case of *V v United Kingdom*[2] provides useful guidance. In this case the ECtHR partly granted the appeal on the basis that Article 6 had been breached by the way that the trial had been conducted:

> 'The Court notes that the applicant's trial took place over three weeks in public in the Crown Court. Special measures were taken in view of the applicant's young age and to promote his understanding of the proceedings. For example, he had the trial procedure explained to him and was taken to see the courtroom in advance, and the hearing times were shortened so as not to tire the defendants excessively. Nonetheless, the formality and ritual of the Crown Court must at times have seemed incomprehensible and intimidating for a child of 11, and there is evidence that certain of the modifications to the courtroom, in particular the raised dock which was designed to enable the defendants to see what was going on, had the effect of increasing the applicant's sense of discomfort during the trial, since he felt exposed to the scrutiny of the press and public. The trial generated extremely high levels of press and public interest, both inside and outside the courtroom, to the extent that the judge in his summing-up referred to the problems caused to witnesses by the blaze of publicity and asked the jury to take this into account when assessing their evidence.
>
> …
>
> 'In conclusion, the applicant was unable to participate effectively in the criminal proceedings against him and was, in consequence, denied a fair hearing in breach of Article 6(1).

13.4 Similarly in *SC v United Kingdom*,[3] which was the trial of an 11-year old boy where it was found that he did not understand the consequences of a conviction. This was held to breach Article 6. The court stated (at para 28):

> 'The right of an accused to effective participation in his or her criminal trial generally includes, inter alia, not only the right to be present, but also to hear and follow the proceedings. In the case of a child, it is essential that

2 (2000) 30 EHRR 121.
3 [2005] 1 FCR 347.

he be dealt with in a manner which takes full account of his age, level of maturity and intellectual and emotional capacities, and that steps are taken to promote his ability to understand and participate in the proceedings, including conducting the hearing in such a way as to reduce as far as possible his feelings of intimidation and inhibition.'

These decisions may provide a useful starting point for those making an application for special measures for child defendants.

With respect to the use of intermediaries, a practice had developed of granting applications for intermediaries to assist the defendant both during their evidence and, where necessary, during the whole trial, using the court's inherent jurisdiction to ensure that the defendant has a fair trial. However, it should be noted that recently this has been somewhat eroded by cases solely granting the use of intermediaries for the defendant's evidence (see **13.7–13.9**). This practice was approved in *R (C) v Sevenoaks Youth Court*,[4] in which it was said that the Youth Court had a duty, under both the CPR 2015 and at common law, to ensure that the defendant had a fair trial, in the context of an application for judicial review of:

(i) the Youth Court's decision to revoke its earlier decision to grant an intermediary to the defendant;

(ii) the LSC's decision to refuse funding for an intermediary; and

(iii) the CPS's decision to continue proceedings against a vulnerable child in the absence of an intermediary.

In that case, the Divisional Court stated that the defendant would require assistance not just during the proceedings, but beforehand, as he and his lawyers prepared for trial, and that he should be given such help as he needed to understand the case against him; to give his own side of the story as his proof of evidence was taken; to speak to his lawyers; to follow the case as it proceeded; to decide whether to question; to decide what line he should take with his co-defendant; to decide if he should give evidence; and help to do so. The Divisional Court said it was in the highest degree unlikely that this level of help could be given by a lawyer, however kind and sympathetic they may be.

As is clear from the case law the use of the court's inherent jurisdiction to ensure a fair trial is not limited to intermediaries; in *Stanford v UK*[5] the matter complained of was that the defendant could not properly hear the proceedings. In this case the defendant's right to a fair trial was not found to have been violated although the ECHR did acknowledge that if a defendant could not hear the proceedings properly that could interfere with his Article 6 rights to participate.

However, some formal statutory provisions and guidance in the criminal procedure rules and practice directions have now been put into place.

4 [2010] 1 All ER 735, DC.

5 [1994] 2 WLUK 324, (1994) Times, 8 March.

Live Link

13.5 The Police and Justice Act 2006, s 47 inserted YJCEA 1999, s 33A, which provides a statutory basis for a defendant to give evidence through a live link in criminal proceedings. The test divides the consideration for adult and child defendants; however, the division does not relate to the time that the special measure is being used but to the time of the application. Therefore, for those acting for defendants who are about to turn 18, there is a need to consider making the application without delay.

33A.— Live link directions

(1) This section applies to any proceedings (whether in a magistrates' court or before the Crown Court) against a person for an offence.

(2) The court may, on the application of the accused, give a live link direction if it is satisfied–

- (a) that the conditions in subsection (4) or, as the case may be, subsection (5) are met in relation to the accused, and
- (b) that it is in the interests of justice for the accused to give evidence through a live link.

(3) A live link direction is a direction that any oral evidence to be given before the court by the accused is to be given through a live link.

(4) Where the accused is aged under 18 when the application is made, the conditions are that–

- (a) his ability to participate effectively in the proceedings as a witness giving oral evidence in court is compromised by his level of intellectual ability or social functioning, and
- (b) use of a live link would enable him to participate more effectively in the proceedings as a witness (whether by improving the quality of his evidence or otherwise).

(5) Where the accused has attained the age of 18 at that time, the conditions are that–

- (a) he suffers from a mental disorder (within the meaning of the Mental Health Act 1983) or otherwise has a significant impairment of intelligence and social function,
- (b) he is for that reason unable to participate effectively in the proceedings as a witness giving oral evidence in court, and
- (c) use of a live link would enable him to participate more effectively in the proceedings as a witness (whether by improving the quality of his evidence or otherwise).

(6) While a live link direction has effect the accused may not give oral evidence before the court in the proceedings otherwise than through a live link.

> (7) The court may discharge a live link direction at any time before or during any hearing to which it applies if it appears to the court to be in the interests of justice to do so (but this does not affect the power to give a further live link direction in relation to the accused).
>
> The court may exercise this power of its own motion or on an application by a party.
>
> (8) The court must state in open court its reasons for–
>
> (a) giving or discharging a live link direction, or
>
> (b) refusing an application for or for the discharge of a live link direction,
>
> and, if it is a magistrates' court, it must cause those reasons to be entered in the register of its proceedings.

Intermediary

13.6 It was anticipated that the YJCEA 1999 will be further amended when the Coroners and Justice Act 2009, s 104 is brought into force: however this is still only prospective. If in force, it would insert new ss 33BA and 33BB into the YJCEA 1999 which would allow a defendant who is under 18 at the time the application is made to give evidence with the assistance of an intermediary (but not to receive assistance during any other stage of the trial) if his ability to participate effectively in the proceedings as a witness giving oral evidence is compromised by his level of intellectual ability or social functioning, and that making the direction is necessary to ensure that the defendant receives a fair trial. A defendant over 18 will be permitted to give evidence with the assistance of an intermediary (but not to receive assistance during any other stage of the trial) only if he suffers from a mental disorder (within the meaning of the Mental Health Act 1983) or otherwise has a significant impairment of intelligence and social function, and for that reason is unable to participate effectively in the proceedings as a witness giving oral evidence, and that making the direction is necessary to ensure that the defendant receives a fair trial. In the opinion of the authors these provisions would be a negative step for the effective active participation of vulnerable defendants.[6]

13.7 The CPR 2015 were amended in April 2016 to include the section in the Direction addressing general matters at CPD 3F.11: Intermediaries for defendants. This section takes a more restrictive approach to the provision of intermediaries to that expressed in *R (C) v Sevenoaks Youth Court*, or to that extended to witnesses by statute.

6 There is helpful and detailed consideration of the provision of special measures for defendants in Criminal Law Review 2017 Rationing defence intermediaries under the April 2016 Criminal Practice Direction.

13.8 At CPD 3F.12 the practice direction states confirms that the court has the power to direct the use of an intermediary under its inherent jurisdiction however what follow is a negative approach:

> 'The court may direct the appointment of an intermediary to assist a defendant in reliance on its inherent powers (*C v Sevenoaks Youth Court* [2009] EWHC 3088 (Admin)). There is however no presumption that a defendant will be so assisted and, even where an intermediary would improve the trial process, appointment is not mandatory (*R v Cox* [2012] EWCA Crim 549).'

It is understood and appreciated that simply 'improving' the trial process may not be sufficient to warrant the direction for an intermediary. However, it is unfortunate that this guidance does not address a test with respect to participation or the giving of evidence which are clearly the key considerations with respect to a vulnerable defendant at trial.

Positively the practice direction does state that:

> 'The court should adapt the trial process to address a defendant's communication needs (*R v Cox* [2012] EWCA Crim 549)" however this is negatively followed by "and will rarely exercise its inherent powers to direct appointment of an intermediary.'(CPD 3F.12)

It is clear that this practice direction does not encourage the regular appointment of intermediaries to assist defendants during the trial process, which is again firmly stated in the following paragraph – again using the word 'rare':

> 'The court may exercise its inherent powers to direct appointment of an intermediary to assist a defendant giving evidence or for the entire trial. Terms of appointment are for the court and there is no illogicality in restricting the appointment to the defendant's evidence (*RvR* [2015] EWCA Crim 1870), when the 'most pressing need' arises (*OP v Secretary of State for Justice* [2014] EWHC 1944 (Admin)). Directions to appoint an intermediary for a defendant's evidence will thus be rare, but for the entire trial extremely rare.' (CPD 3F.13)

In the experience of the authors of the book some well-known intermediary agencies refuse to provide intermediaries solely for defendants giving evidence. Help is found in the Advocate's Toolkits, which the court is also required to have regard to and of which advocates are expected to be aware. Intermediaries are required by Toolkit 16 at para 7.2 which states: 'In the past research has shown that when defendant intermediaries are granted by judges it is usually for the whole trial (Cooper 2014) not just for their testimony, should they decide to give evidence' – this is stated in conjunction with the practice direction. Further, the example in this toolkit of best practice does lend support for those seeking an intermediary for more than just the defendant's evidence.

An application for an intermediary to assist a defendant must be made in accordance with CPR 2015, Part 18. The application form is available on the

Ministry of Justice website and a copy of this is in the template section at **Appendix A**. In addition, where an intermediary report is available, it should be provided with the application (CPD 3F.14). Where the defendant is publicly funded, an application should be made to the Legal Aid Agency for prior authority to fund a pre-trial assessment. It may be that an advice for counsel will be required to assist in obtaining funding, the precedent in **Appendix B** may be of assistance when drafting this advice. If the application is refused, an application may be made to the court to use its inherent powers to direct a pre-trial assessment and funding thereof. Where the court uses its inherent powers to direct assistance by an intermediary at trial (during evidence or for the entire trial), court staff are responsible for arranging payment from central funds (CPD 3F.16).

13.9 Following on in the practice direction there is consideration of the practicalities when a defence intermediary is not available. Where a direction for an intermediary is ineffective due to general unavailability, lack of suitable expertise, or non-availability for the purpose directed (for example, where the direction is for assistance during evidence, but an intermediary will only accept appointment for the entire trial), a trial will not be rendered unfair because a direction to appoint an intermediary for the defendant is ineffective (CPD 3F.20).

This wording may be taking into account the interesting case (from the perspective of defence lawyers) of *R v Akhtar (Siddiqua)*.[7] In this case the court stayed the proceedings when the special measures that the court had directed that the defendant required were unavailable. The Court of Appeal ruled that the judge did have a discretion as to whether to adjourn to another date or to stay the proceedings. Further, the court reiterated the well-known principle that there was no limit on the circumstances in which, in principle, a stay could be ordered. However, the Court of Appeal reiterated that the exercise of the power to order a stay was only to be deployed in special circumstances and that a Crown Court judge could not stay a prosecution simply because he or she considered that to continue the prosecution was a waste of public resources. *R v FB*[8] applied – the basis being that the decision to initiate and continue criminal prosecutions was vested in the Crown Prosecution Service, not the court.

It remains the court's responsibility to adapt the trial process to address the defendant's communication needs, as was the case prior to the existence of intermediaries (*R v Cox*[9]). In such a case, a ground rules hearing should be convened to ensure every reasonable step is taken to facilitate the defendant's participation in accordance with CPR 2015, r 3.9. At the hearing, the court can make new, further and/or alternative directions. This includes setting ground rules to help the defendant follow proceedings and (where applicable) to give evidence (CPD 3F.21). For example, to help the defendant follow proceedings the court may require evidence to be adduced by simple questions, with witnesses being asked to answer in short sentences. Regular breaks may assist the defendant's

7 [2016] EWCA Crim 390.
8 [2010] EWCA Crim 1857, [2011] 1 WLR 844.
9 [2012] EWCA Crim 549.

concentration and enable the defence advocate to summarise the evidence and take further instructions (CPD 3F. 22).

CASE LAW

13.10 The Advocate's Gateway sets out a number of the key cases with respect to vulnerable defendants giving evidence.

Some of the key cases include:

R v Grant-Murray and Henry; R v McGill and Hewitt[10]

The case sets out (at paras 108–110) key considerations for the court and advocates in cases involving child defendants. Para 110 is particularly useful as a list to assist those acting for defendants and to provide support to application for special measures for defendants, should such an application be appropriate:

> '108. As a result the then Lord Chief Justice, Lord Bingham CJ, issued a practice direction in respect of the trial of young persons to ensure compliance with a young person's right to a fair trial. This required significant adaptations and minimum standards of practice to guarantee a child's effective participation.
>
> 109. This practice direction has been modified over the years, in the light of the increased appreciation of the issues judges face when trying children. In 2013, children were recognised as "vulnerable people in court" and a section on intermediaries was introduced. The current *Criminal Practice Directions 2015* [2015] EWCA Crim 1567 consolidated with Amendment no. 2 [2016] EWCA Crim 17, direct a trial judge to consider a number of supporting measures for vulnerable defendants in accordance with the judge's duty to "take every reasonable step to encourage and facilitate the participation of vulnerable defendants (CrimPR 3.9(3)(a) and (b)) so that they may give their best evidence, comprehend the proceedings and engage fully with his or her defence. The pre-trial and trial process should, so far as necessary, be adapted to meet those ends. Regard should be had to the welfare of a young defendant as required by section 44 of the Children and Young Persons Act 1933, and generally to Parts 1 and 3 of the Criminal Procedure Rules (the overriding objective and the court's powers of case management).
>
> 110. The measures include:
>
> i) There should be the provision of an intermediary for the purposes of preparation for the trial and during the trial and a pre-trial visit arranged where appropriate.
>
> ii) Subject to the need for appropriate security arrangements, and if practicable, the trial should be held in a courtroom in which all the

10 [2017] EWCA Crim 1228.

participants are on the same or almost the same level and a vulnerable defendant, especially if young, should normally, if he wishes, be free to sit with members of his family or others in a like relationship, and with some other suitable supporting adult such as a social worker, and in a place which permits easy, informal communication with his legal representatives.

iii) The wearing of robes and wigs should take account of the wishes of a vulnerable defendant.

iv) The conduct of the trial should be according to a timetable which takes full account of a vulnerable defendant's ability to concentrate with frequent and regular breaks, if necessary.

v) The trial judge should ensure, so far as practicable, that the whole trial is conducted in clear language that the defendant can understand and that evidence in chief and cross-examination are conducted using questions that are short and clear. The conclusions of the "ground rules" hearing should be followed, and advocates should use and follow the advocates' "toolkits".'

R v Martin Hamberger[11]

This is an interesting case where the relevant defendant was vulnerable due to physical ill health rather than a mental impairment. The defence had initially made an application to stay the proceedings based upon the provisions of the Criminal Procedure (Insanity) Act 1964, s 4. It was submitted that the medical evidence showed the defendant would suffer serious and irreparable harm to his health and danger to his life if he were to undergo the stress of a trial, and that he was therefore under a disability which constituted a bar to his being tried. The prosecution submitted that on an application of the criteria laid down in *R v Pritchard*,[12] (see **Chapter 6**) and in *R v M*,[13] the medical evidence did not remotely begin to establish that the appellant was unfit for trial. There was nothing to suggest that he did not have sufficient intellect to comprehend the trial proceedings or make a proper defence. The prosecution argued that the defendant's cardiac condition was not a bar to his being tried and the trial process could be adapted by the use of special measures, including, if necessary, his presence by remote link, perhaps even a live link from his home. The judge, having considered the medical evidence which was before the court at that stage, refused the application. Applying the *Pritchard* criteria, the court concluded that he was fit to plead and to stand trial. The court had long experience of trying defendants with various physical conditions and there were many measures which could be taken to enable them to stand trial. In this case the Court of Appeal found that a fair trial could take place even in the circumstances where it may in fact not be possible for a defendant to give oral evidence as part of that trial and considered the possibility of evidence/

11 [2017] EWCA Crim 273.
12 (1836) 7 C & P 303.
13 [2003] EWCA Crim 3452.

an account of the defendant being put before the court by way of a hearsay application (at para 45).

R v Holloway (Adrian)[14]

In this case a vulnerable defendant was found fit to stand trial and then chose to represent himself. The Court of Appeal found (paras 14–15):

> '14 ... This applicant had been certified fit to plead. The judge had no power to force representation on him and there was no basis in fact or law for staying the proceedings. Lord Bingham of Cornhill CJ in *R v Milton Brown* (1988) 2 Cr App R 364, having noted that some jurisdictions require a defendant to be represented, observed:
>
> > "That is not the British tradition, which has permitted individuals to represent themselves in both civil and criminal proceedings. The only notable curtailment is to be found in section 34A of the Criminal Justice Act 1988 which forbids a defendant in a criminal trial to cross-examine a child witness personally. Even in that situation, however, a defendant is not obliged to be professionally represented."
>
> 15. It is clear that a defendant who is fit to stand trial cannot dismiss his legal representatives, insist on representing himself and then come to this court claiming he should not have been allowed to represent himself.'

In this case the court also considered whether there was an inherent power to appoint representation for a defendant where it is not specifically set out in statute. The court found that (at para 39):

> 'save where statute provides, there is no power to appoint an advocate in these circumstances to perform such a role. Further, there is no need for any such power. The court now has ample powers to ensure a fair trial without resorting to appointing a defence advocate where legal representation has been refused.'

R v Cox[15]

In this case, although the court had found that the defendant would have benefited from the assistance of an intermediary, the fact that one was not available did not make the trial process unfair as the process needed to be adapted to facilitate the needs of the defendant (at para 30):

> 'In the context of a defendant with communication problems, when every sensible step taken to identify an available intermediary has been unsuccessful, the next stage is not for the proceedings to be stayed, which in a case like

14 [2016] EWCA Crim 2175.
15 [2012] EWCA Crim 549.

the present would represent a gross unfairness to the complainant, but for the judge to make an informed assessment of whether the absence of an intermediary would make the proposed trial an unfair trial. It would, in fact, be a most unusual case for a defendant who is fit to plead to be found to be so disadvantaged by his condition that a properly brought prosecution would have to be stayed. That would be an unjust outcome where, on the face of the evidence, a genuine complaint has properly been brought against the defendant. If the question were to arise, this court would have to re-examine whether the principles relating to fitness to plead may require reconsideration.'

R (on the application of OP) v The Secretary of State for Justice[16]

This case found that intermediaries may be needed solely to assist a defendant while giving evidence but not for the duration of the trial. The key reasoning is set out at paras 34–36:

'34. This definition illustrates what lies at the core of this claim, that is that there are likely to be two roles during a trial for which an intermediary is fitted. The first is founded in general support, reassurance and calm interpretation of unfolding events. The second requires skilled support and interpretation with the potential for intervention and on occasion suggestion to the Bench associated with the giving of the defendant's evidence.

35. The first is a task readily achievable by an adult with experience of life and the cast of mind apt to facilitate comprehension by a worried individual on trial. In play are understandable emotions: uncertainty, perhaps a sense of territorial disadvantage, nervousness and agitation.

36. The second requires developed skills of the type contemplated by inclusion in the WIS scheme. The most pressing need for the help of an intermediary self-evidently bites at the point of maximum strain, that is when an accused should he do so elects to give an account of himself by entering the witness box and submitting to cross-examination.'

It is the opinion of the authors of this handbook that this case, although logically set out, does not fully appreciate the need for a defendant to form a professional relationship with the intermediary before their evidence commences so that they feel able to fully access the assistance of the intermediary during their evidence. In the authors' opinion the use of an intermediary is not as simple as, say, the use of an interpreter; the vulnerable person is often dealing with emotionally challenging topics and must not feel more challenged by the introduction of a new person at the stage of them giving evidence.

16 [2014] EWHC 1944 (Admin).

However, *R v Rashid (Yahya)*[17] approved this approach. This case stated that there are two distinct types of assistance which an intermediary can give to a defendant and it will only be very rarely that an intermediary is present throughout a trial. An advocate would be in serious dereliction of their duty to the court if they could not carry out the basic tasks of asking appropriate questions. It is the advocate's duty to do what is needed for the defendant to be able fully to participate in the trial.

Since the cases *R (on the application of OP)* and *R v Rashid (Yahya)* this approach has again been approved in the case of *R v Biddle*.[18]

13.11 Further guidance is available in publications such as Ground Rules Hearings and the Fair Treatment of Vulnerable People in Court (Toolkit 1; The Advocate's Gateway, 2015) and General Principles from Research – Planning to Question a Vulnerable Person or Someone with Communication Needs (Toolkit 2(a); The Advocate's Gateway, 2015). In the absence of an intermediary, these publications include information on planning, how to manage the participation and questioning of the defendant, and the formulation of questions to avert misunderstanding (for example, by avoiding 'long and complicated questions … posed in a leading or 'tagged' manner' (*R v Wills*[19]).

17 [2017] EWCA Crim 2.
18 [2019] EWCA Crim 86.
19 [2012] 1 Cr App R 2, CA.

Chapter 14

JURY DIRECTIONS AND THE JUDGE'S SUMMING UP

INTRODUCTION

14.1 All practitioners are expected to have a up to date knowledge of what jury direction they would both seek and expect in criminal cases. Further, all practitioners are expected to have a clear knowledge of what they would expect from a judge's summing up. Practitioners are expected to know how to respond if the directions are not as they would want them to be or if there is an error/perceived error in the judge's summing up.

Although outside the Crown Court, jury directions and the judge's summing up are not relevant per se, the topics and the basis for the directions are often still as valid and are matters that can very often be properly addressed in a closing speech. Further the CPD set out below contains valuable pointers for applications involving special measures.

In any case which involves a vulnerable witnesses and/or vulnerable defendants there will need to be directions given to the jury as to how they should consider certain matters during their deliberations; which may include what regard they should have to the granting of special measures either for a witness or for a defendant.

THE LEGAL FRAMEWORK

14.2 Criminal Practice Direction Division VI sets out key matters that practitioners should be aware of when acting in cases before a Jury. In particular CPD 26k is entitled 'Juries: Directions, Written material and summing up'. The Practice Direction sets out that its purpose and that of the associated CPR is to give effect to the recommendations made in Sir Brian Leveson's Review of Efficiency in Criminal Proceedings 2015 which contained the following recommendations to improve the efficiency of jury trials:

- Early provision of appropriate directions;
- Provision of a written route to verdict;

- Provisions of a split summing up (a summing up delivered in two parts – the first part prior to the closing speeches and the second part afterwards); and
- Streamlining the summing up to help the jury focus on the issues.

(CPD 26K.1)

The associated rules are found in CPR 2015, Pts 25 (Trial and Sentence in the Crown Court) and 26 (Jurors).

It is important to note that CPD 26 places an obligation on the parties to record the dates and times of submissions, rulings, directions and the summing up (both parts if split) and is clear that these should be provided in the notice of appeal – should there be a subsequent appeal to the Court of Appeal (CPD 26K.7).

14.3 In respect of the early provision of appropriate directions, this is often applicable in cases involving vulnerable witnesses or defendants in particular to ensure that the jury know how to approach any special measures that have been granted by the court. The Practice Direction and associated Criminal Procedure Rules require the court to provide directions about the relevant law *at any time* that will assist the jury to evaluate the evidence (CPD 26K.8 and CPR 2015, r 25.14(2)). The judge may provide an early direction prior to any evidence being called, prior to the evidence to which it relates or shortly thereafter. The test that the judge should apply when deciding if an early direction is required is set out in CPD 26K.9 which states that an early direction is required:

> 'where the judge decides it will assist the jury in:
>
> - Their approach to the evidence; and/or
> - Evaluating the evidence as they hear it.'

The Practice Direction helpfully goes on to give examples of when such an early direction may be required and particularly relevant to vulnerable witnesses or defendants is that one of the examples is:

> 'where special measures are to be used and/or ground rules will restrict the manner and scope of questioning, and early explanation may assist the jury in their approach to the evidence' CPD 26K.10

In the case where special measures are being used either by the defendant or by a witness it is understandable why it may be helpful for the judge to address this early on so that the jury are not left wondering why these measures re being used or what impact they should have on how they consider the evidence.

In respect of the guidance for the judge when providing a route to verdict, CPD 26K.11 states this must be tailored to 'the law to the issues and evidence in the case'.

14.4 Case law further highlights the role of the judge in cases involving vulnerable witnesses.

In *R v Stephen Hamilton*,[1] the following paragraphs highlight the key role of the judge and the importance for the jury to appreciate that any intervention by the judge is not indicative of any views: Para [62]:

> 'it is appropriate to emphasise the vital role that the judge plays in trials of any sexual crime in the pursuit of the interests of justice. He or she must balance, on the one hand, the needs and welfare of the complainant and, on the other, the legitimate interests of the defendant. That is particularly difficult in cases involving children as witnesses, and even more so when considering the evidence of those who are or have been mentally impaired whether as a result of intellectual deficit or by reason of having suffered mental illness.'

The wording used by the judge in the trial addressing the jury with respect to intervention during the witness' evidence is set out below, this was approved by the Court of Appeal: see para [71]:

> 'What I want you to understand in so far as what you have seen, is that there is nothing personal in this, not between me and Miss Griffiths, and there is certainly nothing personal between me and the defendant and I must stress this: that you should not think that by making any interventions or observations about whether questioning is appropriate that I was at the time expressing any view either about the defendant's case that was being put to witnesses or about the honesty or reliability of the witness to whom the case was being put and you should certainly not think that I have a view adverse to the defence case. I was simply doing my job at the time, as best I saw it, to prevent a witness being subjected to any unnecessary or inappropriate question. So I direct you specifically not to hold any of that, which is part of the adversarial court process really, against the defendant.'

As well as jury directions and summing up at the start of every criminal case the judge makes what are referred to as introductory remarks to the jury. This is considered at CPD 26G: Juries: preliminary instructions to Jurors. These preliminary instructions can then be accompanied by the early provision of directions as set out above.

A note about family cases

14.5 Although in family cases the issue of jury directions does not arise, there is still the need for there to be a careful consideration of the issue of vulnerability and there is a need for the judge to properly direct themselves as to the law to be applied and practitioners are required to take an active role in ensuring that the court is properly directed as to the law. *In Re J (A Child)*[2] highlights the impact of a failure to properly address evidence where special measures and protections have been used for a vulnerable witness.

---

1 [2014] EWCA Crim 1555.
2 [2015] EWCA Civ 222.

CROWN COURT COMPENDIUM

14.6 A very useful resource is the Crown Court Compendium which was updated in November 2017 this can be found on the Courts and Tribunals Judiciary website https://www.judiciary.gov.uk/publications/crown-court-bench-book-directing-the-jury-2/.

It should be noted that the trial judge is not required to give the directions set out in this Compendium verbatim, the Compendium is simply guidance. This point was addressed in *Hayes*[3] where the court stated:

> 'They are examples which may be helpful to judges in framing a direction which is tailored to the individual case.'
>
> 'The main aim of this Compendium is to provide guidance on directing the jury in Crown Court trials and when sentencing, though it contains some practical suggestions in other areas …' (Courts and Tribunals Judiciary website)

14.7 The Compendium consists of two separate parts. Part I deals with jury and trial management and summing up. Part II deals with sentencing in the Crown Court. A number of parts of this Compendium are outside the ambit of this handbook the key sections relating to vulnerable witnesses and defendants are set out below.

Key directions from the Crown Court Compendium are found in **Appendix E**.

3 [2010] EWCA Crim 773.

Chapter 15

FAMILY LAW

VULNERABLE WITNESSES/PARTIES DURING A FAMILY CONTESTED HEARING

15.1 The regime applicable to the treatment of vulnerable witnesses and parties in criminal cases has been the subject of both statutory and regulatory provision as set out in detail in **Chapter 13**. There is no comparable special or additional measures regime set out in statute in the Family Courts in England and Wales and until recently there were no specific rules to require consideration of these issues. For this reason practice has tended to vary from court to court and has been heavily dependent upon resources and the discretion of individual judges and court centres. There are no specific statutes or regulations governing the final hearing itself. The work with regard to vulnerable witnesses will have been done prior to trial in the identification of such witnesses and parties and in the provision of participation directions as set out in **Chapter 8**.

15.2 It is then for the judge and practitioners to ensure that the directions are complied with and it may be good practice in more complex cases to hold a pre-trial review to ensure that the directions will have their proper effect and that the hearing will be held in accordance with them. Any deficiencies may then be dealt with in good time.

15.3 It is vital that the identification of a witness or party as vulnerable and any participation directions resulting from that are clearly set out in the order of the court at the ground rules hearing. For the same reason it is important that if a participation direction is refused reasons are given for doing so, preferably in a recital to the order.

15.4 Some specific rules apply in cases where domestic abuse is alleged, and these will be dealt with briefly here. The range of legal principles that apply to cases of domestic abuse is beyond the scope of this handbook and practitioners are directed to other works for more general analysis. However it is possible to set out those matters that go to the provision of and presentation of evidence in those cases where either or both of the participants may also be found to be vulnerable witnesses and may therefore also have to be the subject of assessment under the general provisions dealt with in this book.

Children giving evidence in family cases

15.5 If it is proposed that a child will give evidence within family proceedings it has become standard to conduct what is known by the courts and practitioners as a *Re W* hearing.[1]

Domestic abuse cases

15.6 Although the *Public Law Outline* and FPR 2010, PD12J (Domestic Abuse and Harm) make reference to Special Measures in family proceedings, these are not specifically defined. Special measures are available in the criminal courts for vulnerable and intimidated witnesses (see the *Code of Practice for Victims of Crime)* and these can be used as guidance in family cases. This may include:

- Screening the witness from the accused.
- Giving evidence by live link.
- Giving evidence at a private location.
- Evidence by a pre-recorded interview.
- Evidence via an intermediary or interpreter.
- Using communication aids.

15.7 In addition, The Advocate's Gateway: Vulnerable Witnesses and parties to the family courts Toolkit 13, suggests considering the following:

- Provision of a separate waiting area or reserved conference room.
- Making arrangements for the vulnerable party or witness to arrive and leave court by a different entrance to avoid meeting others in the case.
- Requesting a priority listing to avoid long waiting times at court.
- Allowing representatives from an advocacy service to be present during meeting and conferences and in court.
- Allowing longer periods for a witness or party to file and serve evidence.
- Judges allowing adequate time after handing down judgment for parties to go through it with their advocates.
- Advocates adjusting their style or language when questioning.
- Providing the witness or party with a simple way of communicating the need for a break (a pause card on the table).
- Providing the witness or party with a way of alleviating stress or maintaining concentration whilst giving evidence (eg a stress toy).

---

1 *RE W (Children) (Abuse: Oral Evidence)* [2010] 1 FLR.

15.8 These options should be discussed with the relevant party before they give evidence and relayed to the other parties and court as early as possible so that the necessary arrangements can be made. In addition of course any of the provisions set out in the FPR 2010, Pt 3A may be applicable if either party is also a vulnerable witness or participant according to those regulations. A difficulty may lie in the identification of vulnerability where a party (often the alleged perpetrator of abuse) is not legally represented. It is for all representatives (particularly perhaps those if any representing the children) to co-operate in bringing any relevant matter to the attention of the court under the general duty to assist the court and under the cases which governed the need to identify these issues early that came before the addition of the FPR 2010, Pt 3A.

15.9 Note also that Macfarlane LJ in *Re J (A Child)*[2] stressed that when special measures *are* deployed it is also necessary for the judge evaluating the resulting evidence to assess the degree (if any) to which the process may have affected the ability of the court to rely on the witness's evidence; Gloster LJ went further and considered that the trial procedure in that case had been unfair to the father (the alleged perpetrator in private law fact finding). A balance has to be struck between accommodating the needs of the vulnerable party and ensuring that the trial procedure is still balanced.

15.10 With regard to the arrangements for a fact-finding or composite final hearing and the difficulty of allowing an alleged perpetrator to cross-examine an alleged victim there is no provision for a family court to order that the alleged perpetrator be required to have legal representation for this purpose.

15.11 The FPR 2010, PD 12J sets out a number of considerations for the court when reaching a view as to how a fact finding or final hearing is to be arranged, particularly in para 19 which requires the court to consider

> '(j) what evidence the alleged victim of domestic abuse is able to give and what support the alleged victim may require at the fact-finding hearing in order to give that evidence;
>
> (k) in cases where the alleged victim of domestic abuse is unable for reasons beyond their control to be present at the hearing (for example, abandonment cases where the abandoned spouse remains abroad), what measures should be taken to ensure that that person's best evidence can be put before the court. Where video-link is not available, the court should consider alternative technological or other methods which may be utilised to allow that person to participate in the proceedings;
>
> (l) what support the alleged perpetrator may need in order to have a reasonable opportunity to challenge the evidence; and

---

2 [2014] EWCA Civ 875.

(m) whether a pre-hearing review would be useful prior to the fact-finding hearing to ensure directions have been complied with and all the required evidence is available.'

Paragraph 28 of PD12J also states that

> 'While ensuring that the allegations are properly put and responded to, the fact-finding hearing or other hearing can be an inquisitorial (or investigative) process, which at all times must protect the interests of all involved. At the fact-finding hearing or other hearing –
>
> - each party can be asked to identify what questions they wish to ask of the other party, and to set out or confirm in sworn evidence their version of the disputed key facts; and
> - the judge should be prepared where necessary and appropriate to conduct the questioning of the witnesses on behalf of the parties, focusing on the key issues in the case.'

15.12 However, none of those considerations goes so far as to provide a fully considered mechanism to decide upon or prevent potentially abusive cross-examination as exists in criminal cases. This is a gap in the law that has been the subject of much judicial comment. In *PS v BP*[3] Hayden J gives guidance as to the approach to this question and sets out some proposals as a 'life belt' until the 'rescue craft' of legislation on the matter arrives

'(i) Once it becomes clear to the court that it is required to hear a case 'put' to a key factual witness where the allegations are serious and intimate and where the witnesses are themselves the accused and accuser, a 'Ground Rules Hearing' (GRH) will always be necessary;

(ii) The GRH should, in most cases, be conducted prior to the hearing of the factual dispute;

(iii) Judicial continuity between the GRH and the substantive hearing is to be regarded as essential;

(iv) It must be borne in mind throughout that the accuser bears the burden of establishing the truth of the allegations. The investigative process in the court room, however painful, must ensure fairness to both sides. The Judge must remind himself, at all stages, that this obligation may not be compromised in response to a witnesses' distress;

(v) There is no presumption that the individual facing the accusations will automatically be barred from cross examining the accuser in every case. The Judge must consider whether the evidence would be likely to be diminished if conducted by the accused and would likely to be improved if a prohibition on direct cross-examination was directed.

3 [2018] EWHC 1987 (Fam).

In the context of a fact-finding hearing in the Family Court, where the ethos of the court is investigative, I consider these two factors may be divisible;

(vi) When the court forms the view, from the available evidence, that cross-examination of the alleged victim itself runs the real risk of being abusive, (if the allegations are established) it should bear in mind that the impact of the court process is likely to resonate adversely on the welfare of the subject children. It is axiomatic that acute distress to a carer will have an impact on the children's general well-being. This is an additional factor to those generally in contemplation during a criminal trial;

(vii) Where the factual conclusions are likely to have an impact on the arrangements for and welfare of a child or children, the court should consider joining the child as a party and securing representation. Where that is achieved, the child's advocate may be best placed to undertake the cross-examination. (see M and F & Ors. [2018] EWHC 1720 Fam; Re: S (wardship) (Guidance in cases of stranded spouses) [2011] 1 FLR 319);

(viii) If the court has decided that cross-examination will not be permitted by the accused and there is no other available advocate to undertake it, it should require questions to be reduced to writing. It will assist the process, in most cases, if 'Grounds of Cross-Examination' are identified under specific headings;

(ix) A Judge should never feel constrained to put every question the lay party seeks to ask. In this exercise the Judge will simply have to evaluate relevance and proportionality;

(x) Cross-examination is inherently dynamic. For it to have forensic rigour the Judge will inevitably have to craft and hone questions that respond to the answers given. The process can never become formulaic;

(xi) It must always be borne in mind that in the overarching framework of Children Act proceedings, the central philosophy is investigative. Even though fact finding hearings, of the nature contemplated here, have a highly adversarial complexion to them the same principle applies. Thus, it may be perfectly possible, without compromising fairness to either side, for the Judge to conduct the questioning in an open and less adversarial style than that deployed in a conventional cross-examination undertaken by a party's advocate.'[4]

4 Ibid, at para 34.

APPENDIX A

Edition for use in courts in England

.... Magistrates' Court

Preparation for effective trial

Criminal Procedure Rules Parts 1 & 3

- This form:
  - collects information about the case that the court will need to arrange for an effective trial: CrimPR rules 3.2 and 3.3
  - records the court's directions: CrimPR rule 3.5.
- After the court gives directions for trial, if:
  - information about the case changes, or
  - you think another direction is needed

  you must tell the court at once: CrimPR 1.2(1) & 3.10.

- If the defendant pleads not guilty, and the court requires:
  - the prosecutor must complete Parts 1, 2 and 4
  - the defendant must complete Parts 1, 3 and 4
  - the court will record directions in Parts 4 and 5.

See the separate notes for guidance on the use of this form.

There is extra space on page 4, or attach extra sheets if required. The electronic version of this form will expand.*

A list of standard trial preparation time limits is at page 7.

Court contact details

Address	Phone Fax
Email	

Part 1: to be completed by the prosecutor and the defendant (or defendant's representative)

Defendant		Date of birth: Age: years
	☐ Summons ☐ Requisition ☐ Charge ☐ Bail ☐ Custody Time limit expires:	
Offence(s)		
Police / CPS URN		**Date of first hearing**

1 **Prosecution contact details**

Prosecuting authority		Phone Fax
	Email	

2 **Defendant's contact details**

Defendant	Address	Phone Mobile
	Email	

3 **Defendant's representative** *(if applicable)*

Solicitor		Phone Fax Ref
	Address	
	Email	

Representation is:
Defendant's representative to complete

legal aid granted ☐
legal aid applied for ☐
privately funded ☐

*Forms for use with the Rules are at: http://www.justice.gov.uk/courts/procedure-rules/criminal/formspage.

Part 2: to be completed by the prosecutor

4 Case management information

4.1 Are there any pending enquiries or lines of investigation? ☐ Yes ☐ No
If yes, give brief details:

4.2 Does the prosecutor intend to serve more evidence? ☐ Yes ☐ No
If yes, give brief details:

4.3 Does the prosecutor intend to serve a diagram, sketch map or photos? ☐ Yes ☐ No
If yes, give brief details:

4.4 The prosecution will rely on:
Tick / delete as appropriate

- defendant's admissions in interview ☐
- defendant's failure to mention facts in interview ☐
- [a summary] [a record] of the defendant's interview ☐
- [expert] [hearsay] [bad character] evidence ☐
- [CCTV] [electronically recorded] evidence ☐

4.5 What equipment (live link, DVD or other media player, etc.) will the prosecutor need in the trial courtroom?
The prosecutor must make sure that any DVD or other electronic media can be played in the courtroom.

4.6 Does the prosecutor presently expect the case to involve a complex, novel or unusual point of law and / or fact? *This information will help the court officer to list the case effectively.* ☐ Yes ☐ No
If so what?

4.7 Has the initial duty of disclosure of unused prosecution material been complied with? ☐ Yes ☐ No
If yes, when?

5 Applications for directions

5.1 Does the prosecutor want the court to vary a standard trial preparation time limit? ☐ Yes ☐ No
If yes, give details:

5.2 Does the prosecutor want the court to arrange a discussion of ground rules for questioning? ☐ Yes ☐ No
If an intermediary is appointed, the court must discuss ground rules with the intermediary and advocates. A discussion may be helpful in other cases.

5.3 Does the prosecutor want the court to make any other direction? ☐ Yes ☐ No
If yes, give details:

Part 3: to be completed by the defendant (or defendant's representative)

6 Advice on plea and absence

Does the defendant understand that:

(a) he or she will receive credit for a guilty plea? ☐ Yes ☐ No
A guilty plea may affect the sentence and any order for costs and other financial penalties / charges

(b) the trial can go ahead even if he or she does not attend? ☐ Yes ☐ No
CrimPR rule 24.12

Page 2

7 Partial or different guilty plea

7.1 If more than one offence is alleged, does the defendant want to plead guilty to any of them? ☐ Yes ☐ No ☐ N/A
If yes, which offence(s)?

7.2 Does the defendant want to plead guilty, but not on the facts alleged? ☐ Yes ☐ No
If yes, the court must be given a written note of the facts on which the defendant wants to plead guilty.

7.3 Does the defendant want to plead guilty, but to a different offence? ☐ Yes ☐ No
If yes, what offence?

8 Case management information

8.1 *Initial details of the prosecution case should have been served: CrimPR rule 8.2. The following statements are to help the court find out what is in dispute and give appropriate directions for trial. Tick as appropriate.*

The defendant [carried out] [took part in] the conduct alleged ☐ Yes ☐ No ☐ N/A

The defendant was present at the scene of the offence alleged ☐ Yes ☐ No ☐ N/A

The defendant was correctly identified ☐ Yes ☐ No ☐ N/A

The defendant was arrested lawfully ☐ Yes ☐ No ☐ N/A

[Nature of injury] [extent of loss or damage] ☐ Yes ☐ No ☐ N/A
If not agreed, explain what is in dispute:

[Fingerprint] [DNA] evidence ☐ Yes ☐ No ☐ N/A
If not agreed, explain what is in dispute:

[Medical] [identification of drug] [other scientific] evidence ☐ Yes ☐ No ☐ N/A
If not agreed, explain what is in dispute:

The [alcohol] [drug] testing procedure was carried out correctly ☐ Yes ☐ No ☐ N/A
If not agreed, explain what is in dispute:

Exhibits and samples were collected and delivered as stated (i.e. continuity) ☐ Yes ☐ No ☐ N/A
If not agreed, explain what is in dispute:

Defendant's interview [summary] [record] is accurate ☐ Yes ☐ No ☐ N/A
If not agreed, explain what is in dispute:

The defendant was [disqualified from driving] [subject to the alleged court order] at the time of the offence alleged ☐ Yes ☐ No ☐ N/A

The list of the defendant's previous convictions is accurate ☐ Yes ☐ No ☐ N/A
If not agreed, explain what is in dispute:

8.2 What are the **DISPUTED** issues of fact or law for trial, in addition to any identified in paragraph 8.1? *Give details. This question is to help the court find out what is in dispute and give appropriate directions for trial.* *CrimPR rules 3.2(2)(a), 3.3(1)(a)*

Page 3

8.3 Will the defendant give a defence statement? *Giving a defence statement is voluntary, but if one is given it must include the information collected in paragraphs 8.1 and 8.2 and must include particulars of facts relied on by the defence.* ☐ Yes ☐ No

8.4 Will the defendant need any live link, or DVD or other media player, etc. equipment in the trial courtroom? *The defendant must make sure that any DVD or other electronic media can be played in the courtroom.*

8.5 Does the defendant presently expect the case to involve a complex, novel or unusual point of law and / or fact? *This information will help the court officer to list the case effectively.* ☐ Yes ☐ No
If so what?

9 Admissions

Can any facts which are not in dispute be recorded in a written admission? ☐ Yes ☐ No
Undisputed facts might include any statement accepted in paragraph 8.1.

If yes, a written admission [is set out here] [is attached] [will be served later].
Facts which are admitted are evidence: CrimPR rule 24.6 & Criminal Justice Act 1967, s.10.

If no, explain why:

10 Applications for directions

10.1 Does the defendant want the court to vary a standard trial preparation time limit? ☐ Yes ☐ No
If yes, give details:

10.2 Does the defendant want the court to arrange a ground rules discussion? ☐ Yes ☐ No
If an intermediary is appointed, the court must discuss ground rules with the intermediary and advocates. A discussion may be helpful in other cases.

10.3 Does the defendant want the court to make any other direction? ☐ Yes ☐ No
If yes, give details:

Parts 2 & 3 continued: additional information

Use this space to record any additional information, or to continue an answer started above:

Page 4

Defendant's name:

Part 4: to be completed by the prosecutor, the defendant (or the defendant's representative) and the court

11 Prosecution witnesses. *If this information changes,* ***you must tell the court at once****: CrimPR rule 1.2(1) & 3.10.*

	Prosecutor to complete				*Defendant to complete*	*Both parties to complete*		*For the court*		
	Name of witness	Tick if under 18	Interpreter needed? If so, specify language and dialect.	Special or other measures e.g. live link needed? If so, specify.**	What disputed issue in the case makes it necessary for the witness to give evidence in person?	Tick if attendance proposed		Tick if live link ordered	Evidence to be read ('R') or time required per witness	
						P	D		*EinC*	*X-exam*
1)		☐				☐	☐	☐		
2)		☐				☐	☐	☐		
3)		☐				☐	☐	☐		
4)		☐				☐	☐	☐		
5)		☐				☐	☐	☐		
6)		☐				☐	☐	☐		

12 Expected defence witnesses. *If this information changes,* ***you must tell the court at once****: CrimPR rule 1.2(1) & 3.10.*

	Defendant to complete					*Both parties to complete*		*For the court*		
	Name of witness	Tick if under 18	Interpreter needed? If so, specify language and dialect.	Special or other measures e.g. live link needed? If so, specify.**	Why is it necessary for the witness to give evidence in person?	Tick if attendance proposed		Tick if live link ordered	Evidence to be read ('R') or time required per witness	
						D	P		*EinC*	*X-exam*
1)*		☐				☐	☐	☐		
2)		☐				☐	☐	☐		
3)		☐				☐	☐	☐		

*If the defendant is likely to give evidence, list him or her as the first expected defence witness. **Special or other measures may include screens, evidence by live link or in private, video recorded interview as evidence, intermediary, breaks in examination or other measures to accommodate disability. They may increase the time needed for the witness. In some cases, the defendant may not be allowed to cross-examine a prosecution witness.

Defendant's name:

Part 5: record of court's decisions and directions for effective trial

13 Directions for trial *The court must actively manage the case by giving any direction appropriate to the needs of that case as early as possible: CrimPR rule 3.2(3). Complete or delete the following as appropriate*

13.1 The prosecutor must serve any further evidence by: *(date)*

13.2 If the initial duty of disclosure has not been complied with, the prosecutor must comply by: *(date)*

13.3 A party who wants to use a DVD or other media, etc. must check before the trial that it can be played in the courtroom.

13.4 The court expects only the witnesses listed as attending in Part 4 to give evidence in person and the evidence of other witnesses to be read.

13.5 [Witness summons / warrant] [other steps to secure attendance] for witness(es): *insert name(s)* *CrimPR Part 17; rule 3.9(3)*

13.6 Interpretation in the language(s) specified in Part 4 is required for: To be arranged by:

(defendant) Court staff *CrimPR rule 3.9(5)*

(witness) Prosecutor ☐ Defendant ☐

13.7 Special or other measure, e.g. live link, are directed for: As specified in:

(defendant) Part 4 ☐ paragraph 13.11 ☐

(witness) Part 4 ☐ paragraph 13.11 ☐

(witness) Part 4 ☐ paragraph 13.11 ☐

13.8 The court will discuss ground rules for questioning on: *(date)*
If an intermediary is appointed for a witness or for the defendant, the court must discuss the ground rules for questioning with the intermediary and the advocates before the witness or defendant gives evidence. Sufficient time must be allowed for this.

13.9 The defendant in person may not cross-examine witness(es): *insert name(s)* *CrimPR Part 23*
and the court directs cross-examination for that purpose by: *name representative*

13.10 Standard trial preparation time limits apply [except] [with these variations]:

13.11 Other directions:

14 Arrangements for trial

Date:		
Time:		
Court:		Court category:
Estimated trial length:	.... hours	
including:	Evidence and submissions: .... Deliberations and decision:	
	A detailed trial timetable must be considered and attached if necessary: CrimPR rules 3.9 & 3.11	

After the court gives directions for trial, if information about the case changes, or you think another direction is needed, **you must tell the court at once**: CrimPR rules 1.2(1) & 3.10.

Signatures .... [on the direction of] [court]

Signed: .... for prosecution

Signed: .... [defendant] [defendant's solicitor]

Date: ....

Page 6

Standard trial preparation time limits

The court can vary any of these time limits. Time limits marked * are not prescribed by rules or other legislation.

The total time needed to comply with all these time limits is 6 weeks (9 weeks if paragraph m applies).

Written admissions (Criminal Procedure Rules, r.24.6; Criminal Justice Act 1967, s.10)

a. The parties must serve any written admissions of agreed facts within **14 days.***

Defence statement (Criminal Procedure Rules, r.15.4; Criminal Procedure and Investigations Act 1996, s.6)

b. Any defence statement must be served within **14 days** of the prosecutor complying with the initial duty of disclosure.

Defence witnesses (Criminal Procedure and Investigations Act 1996, s.6C)

c. Defence witness names, etc. must be notified within **14 days** of the prosecutor complying with the initial duty of disclosure.

Application for disclosure (Criminal Procedure Rules, rr.15.2 & 15.5; Criminal Procedure and Investigations Act 1996, s.8)

d. The defendant must serve any application for an order for prosecution disclosure as soon as reasonably practicable after the prosecutor complies with the initial duty of disclosure.* *Under s.8 of the Criminal Procedure and Investigations Act 1996, no such application may be made unless a defence statement has been served.*

e. The prosecutor must serve any representations in response within **14 days after that**.

Witness statements (Criminal Procedure Rules, r.16.4; Criminal Justice Act 1967, s.9)

f. The defendant must serve any defence witness statement to be read at trial at least **14 days before the trial**.*

g. Any objection to a witness statement being read at trial must be made within **7 days of service of the statement.** *This does not apply to the statements listed in Part 4.*

Measures to assist a witness or defendant to give evidence (Criminal Procedure Rules, rr.18.3, 18.13, 18.17, 18.22, 18.26)

h. Any [further] application for special or other measures must be served within **28 days.**

i. Any representations in response must be served within **14 days after that**.

Cross-examination where defendant not represented (Criminal Procedure Rules, rr.23.2, 23.4)

j. The defendant must serve notice of any representative appointed to cross-examine within **7 days**.

k. The prosecutor must serve any application to prohibit cross-examination by the defendant in person as soon as reasonably practicable.

l. Any representations in response must be served within **14 days after that**.

Expert evidence (Criminal Procedure Rules, rr.19.3, 19.4)

m. If either party relies on expert evidence, the directions below apply.
   (i) The expert's report must be served within **28 days**.*
   (ii) A party who wants that expert to attend the trial must give notice within **7 days after (i)**.*
   (iii) A party who relies on expert evidence in response must serve it within **14 days after (ii)**.*
   (iv) There must be a meeting of experts under rule 19.6 within **14 days after (iii)**.*
   (v) The parties must notify the court **immediately after (iv)** if the length of the trial is affected by the outcome of the meeting.*

Hearsay evidence (Criminal Procedure Rules, rr.20.2, 20.3)

n. The prosecutor must serve any notice to introduce hearsay evidence within **28 days**.

o. The defendant must serve any notice to introduce hearsay evidence as soon as reasonably practicable.

p. Any application to determine an objection to hearsay evidence must be served within **14 days of service** of the notice or evidence.

Bad character evidence (Criminal Procedure Rules, rr.21.2, 21.3, 21.4)

q. The prosecutor must serve any notice to introduce evidence of the defendant's bad character within **28 days**.

r. Any application to determine an objection to that notice must be served within **14 days after that**.

s. Any application to introduce evidence of a non-defendant's bad character must be served within **14 days** of prosecution disclosure.

t. Any notice of objection to that evidence must be served within **14 days after that**.

Previous sexual behaviour evidence (Criminal Procedure Rules, rr.22.2, 22.3, 22.4, 22.5)

u. The defendant must serve any application for permission to introduce evidence of a complainant's previous sexual behaviour within **28 days** of prosecution disclosure.

v. The prosecutor must serve any representations in response within **14 days after that**.

Point of law, including abuse of process etc. (Criminal Procedure Rules, rr.3.3, 3.10)

w. Any skeleton argument must be served at least **14 days before the trial**.*

x. Any skeleton argument in reply must be served within **7 days after that**.*

Trial readiness (Criminal Procedure Rules, rr.3.3, 3.10)

y. The parties must certify readiness for trial at least **14 days before the trial**,* confirming which witnesses will give evidence in person and the trial time estimate.

November 2015

Page 7

FORM - PTPH NG 1

PLEA AND TRIAL PREPARATION HEARING FORM

This form must be completed for all cases sent to the Crown Court after ....2015 where a trial is anticipated unless the case is expressly exempted by the CrimPR or CrimPD.
THIS FORM IS TO BE REGARDED AS THE PRIMARY RECORD OF ORDERS MADE.
After the hearing the court will make available copies of the completed form to the parties (whether completed electronically or on paper) and Case Progression Officers and OICs must ensure that they receive and act upon it. Any additional written orders of the court must be attached or incorporated.

PART 1 – PRE-HEARING INFORMATION to be completed by the parties

Crown Court at: T: PTI URN:

	Defendant	*DOB*	*Principal Charge(s)*	*Remand Status*	*Custody Time Limit*	*Elected Trial?*
D1				☐ Unconditional Bail ☐ Conditional Bail ☐ Custody ☐ Youth Det. Remand		☐

	Defence to set out, so far as known, the real issues in the case. CrimPR 3.2;3.3;3.11	*Are the conclusions of any served Streamlined Forensics Report (SFR) admitted as fact. If not identify the disputed issues concerning that conclusion? CrimPR 19.3*
D1		☐YES ☐NO Disputed Issues:

Other Proceedings:		
Are there any associated CRIMINAL proceedings?	☐	Particulars:
Are there any linked FAMILY proceedings?	☐	Particulars:

PLEA AND TRIAL PREPARATION HEARING FORM – DRAFT - 21 October 2015 – Page 1 of 9

FORM - PTPH NG 1

Contact Information and Duties:
The parties must provide the information required below at the PTPH or if not then available it must be provided to the court and other parties in writing within 14 days. The court and other parties must be informed of any change and effective cover must be provided for sickness or absence. The names of individuals must be given but it is acceptable to provide group email addresses provided that they are effectively monitored and acted upon.
If the prosecution or defence have not allocated a trial advocate then the advocate at a hearing or, the prosecution Reviewing Lawyer or the defence solicitor is required to respond to issues in place of the trial advocate.
Parties are reminded that:
All participants have a duty to prepare and conduct the case in accordance with the overriding objective; to comply with the CrimPR, practice directions and directions of the court; and at once to inform the court and all parties of any significant failure - CrimPR1.2.
Prosecution and Defence Case Progression Officers are reminded of their duties to monitor compliance with directions; make sure the court is kept informed of events that may affect the progress of the case; make sure that he or she can be contacted promptly about the case during ordinary business hours; act promptly and reasonably in response to communications about the case and, if he or she will be unavailable appoint a substitute to fulfil his or her duties and inform the other Case Progression Officers - CrimPR3.4.
Parties must actively assist the court to fulfil the overriding objective and engage with other parties to further the overriding objective without or if necessary with a direction - CrimPR3.3. Provided they promptly inform the court Case Progression Officer parties may agree to vary a time limit fixed by a direction if the variation will not affect the date of any hearing that has been fixed or significantly affect the progress of the case in any other way -CrimPR 3.7

Court Case Progression	*Name:*	*Phone:*	*Email:*
Case Progression Officer:			

Prosecution Information	*Name:*	*Phone:*	*Email:*
Advocate at PTPH			
Advocate for trial			
Reviewing Lawyer			
Case Progression Officer (usually Paralegal)			
Officer in the Case (or equivalent)			

Defence Information		*Name and Address for Service:*	*Phone:*	*Email for service:*
D1	Defence Solicitors			☐ Secure ☐ Not Secure
	Case Progression Officer			☐ Secure ☐ Not Secure
	Funding	Private Funding ☐; Legal Rep applied for ☐; OR Legal Rep Order granted ☐		
		Name:	*Phone:*	*Email:*
	Advocate at PTPH			

FORM - PTPH NG 1

	Advocate for trial			

State of Preparation at PTPH

PROSECUTION		*Served*	*If not yet served they can be served by:*
IND	Draft Indictment	☐	
SUM	Summary of circumstances of the offence(s) and of any account given by defendant(s) in interview (this may be in Form MG5).	☐	
EVI	Statements identified by prosecution as being of importance for the purpose of plea and initial case management.	☐	
EVI	Exhibits identified by prosecution as being of importance for the purpose of plea and initial case management.	☐	
TV	Relevant CCTV that would be relied upon by prosecution at trial.	☐	
EXP	Streamlined Forensic Report(s) or indication of scientific evidence that the prosecution is likely to introduce.	☐	
EXP	Indication of medical evidence that the prosecution is likely to introduce.	☐	
EXP	Indication of other expert evidence that the prosecution is likely to introduce.	☐	
BC	Indication of bad character evidence to be relied on.	☐	
HS	Indication of any hearsay evidence to be relied on.	☐	
SM	Indication of special measures to be sought.	☐	
CRO	Defendant's criminal record if any.	☐	
VPS	Victim Personal Statement if any.	☐	

DEFENCE			*Particulars*
ABU FTP	Are there preliminary issues such as Abuse of Process or Fitness to Plead?	☐	
DMS	Is an application for Dismissal anticipated after time for service elapse?	☐	
SEV	Is an application for Severance anticipated? CrimPR 3.21	☐	
ARR	Can the defendant be arraigned at PTPH? If not set out the reason.	☐	
ALT	Is the defendant willing to offer a plea to another offence and/or a plea on a limited basis?	☐	
DS	Is a Defence Statement available at this stage?	☐	

THIRD PARTY DISCLOSURE			*Particulars*
TPD	Is it believed that any third party holds potentially disclosable material?	☐	
TPD	Will the prosecution be making enquiries to review that material?	☐	

FORM - PTPH NG 1

WITNESS REQUIREMENTS KNOWN AT PTPH

List the prosecution witnesses who, at the time of the PTPH, it can be predicted will be required to give live evidence.
You do not need to fill out this part if you are able to fill out the Standard Witness Table at the PTPH

Name of witness	*Page No.*	*Required by:*	*Relevant disputed issue.*	*Mark if availability known?*
				☐
				☐
				☐
				☐
				☐
				☐
				☐
				☐
				☐
				☐

FORM - PTPH NG 1

PART 2 – PLEA AND TRIAL PREPARATION HEARING ORDERS
to be completed by the court.

PLEAS		
1	Pleas entered at PTPH:	
2	Reason if not arraigned at PTPH:	
3	Judicial warnings Given ☑	☐Credit for Plea ☐Warning that failure to provide a sufficiently detailed Defence Statement may count against the Defendant ☐(Bail) Failure to attend is a separate offence ☐(Bail) Trial in absence – advocates may withdraw
	Notes:	

TRIAL		*Date:*		☑ *Facilities required:*	⏱ *Time Estimate*
4			☐ Fixture ☐ Fixed Floater ☐ Warned List commencing.	☐ CCTV ☐ Live Link ☐ Satellite Link from: ☐ Interpreter for defendant(s) (language):	days weeks

FURTHER MANAGEMENT IF REQUIRED		*Date:*		⏱ *Time Estimate*
5	**Pre-Arraignment Further Case Management Hearing to resolve ☑:** ☐ Abuse of Process; ☐ Fitness to Plead; ☐ Dismissal applications; ☐ Joinder/Severance.		☐ Defendant not required ☐ Defendant must attend ☐ Application/skeleton and reports by: ☐ Response by:	Minutes Hours
6	**Further Case Management Hearing** (including Preparatory Hearing or Pre-Trial Hearing).		☐ Defendant not required ☐ Defendant must attend	Minutes Hours
7	**Pre-Trial Review**. The PTR may be vacated on <u>all</u> parties informing the Court CPO in writing that they are fully trial ready and no orders are required.		☐ Defendant not required ☐ Defendant must attend	Minutes Hours
8	**Ground Rules Hearing**		Defendant must attend	Minutes Hours

ORDERS THAT CAN BE MADE AT PTPH WITHOUT FURTHER FORMALITY			
9	**SM**	Special measures orders that can be made at PTPH – CrimPR 18	Special measures granted for the following witnesses: [☐ABE evidence] [☐Live link] [☐Screens] [☐ABE evidence] [☐Live link] [☐Screens] [☐ABE evidence] [☐Live link] [☐Screens]
10	**SAT**	Satellite/Live Link	Live Link order made for the following witnesses (particulars of link to be provided not less than three weeks before trial CrimPD 18.23-4): for Live link from for Live link from for Live link from
11	**WIT**	Young or vulnerable witnesses – CrimPR 18 & 3.9(7)	Young or vulnerable witnesses to which an Advocates' Gateway toolkit applies are to be examined and cross-examined in accordance with that toolkit unless that is superseded by specific ground rules.
12	**EXP**	Expert witnesses – CrimPR 19	Expert witnesses of comparable disciplines must liaise and serve on the parties and the Court a statement of the points on which they agree and disagree with reasons no less than 14 days prior to the trial.
13		Other:	
14		Other:	

STAGE 1 - UNLESS INDIVIDUAL DATES ARE PROVIDED THE PROSECUTION SHALL SERVE THE FOLLOWING BY: Ordinarily 50 days (custody cases) or 70 days (bail cases) after sending.				**Date:**
		ITEM	*Date :*	*Additional requirements/particulars/directions if any:*
15	**EVI**	Service of prosecution case.		As required by Crime and Disorder Act (Service of Prosecution Evidence) Regulations 2005 Regs. 2 & 3 (70 days or 50 days after sending). To include making available ABE transcripts and recordings.
16	**DCL**	Initial disclosure (if not yet served).		
17	**TV**	CCTV relied upon.		To be served in format compatible with systems available at court. Otherwise party to provide system.
18	**IV**	Written record of defendant's taped Interview(s) (ROTI).		The parties are expected to engage pre-trial to agree a summary or editing.
19	**IV**	Audio recording of defendant's tape interviews(s).		
20	**999**	999 call transcript(s) and recording(s).		
21	**TEL**	Telephone records to be relied upon.		
22	**FOR**	Full forensic science statements that can be served by Stage 1.		Full forensic statements will only be ordered if the defendant has identified what conclusion in a Streamlined Report is not admitted and what are the disputed issues concerning that conclusion – CrimPR 19.3.
23	**BC**	Bad character notice(s) CrimPR 21		To include, if to be relied upon, evidence of facts of bad character.
24	**HSY**	Hearsay application(s) CrimPR 20		

FORM - PTPH NG 1

25	**SM**	Special measures application(s) CrimPR 18		
26		Other:		
27		Other:		

THIRD PARTY DISCLOSURE: It is ordered:			*Date:*
28	**TPD**	Prosecution shall either make requests to third party, OR notify defence in writing that it does not intend to make any application for Third Party Disclosure (TPD) by:	
29	**TPD**	If the prosecution is to pursue TPD then the prosecution must serve a report in writing on the outcome of efforts to identify potentially disclosable materials held by third parties and any ongoing enquiries not yet completed by:	
30		Other:	

STAGE 2 - UNLESS INDIVIDUAL DATES ARE PROVIDED IT IS ORDERED THAT THE DEFENCE SHALL SERVE THE FOLLOWING BY: Ordinarily 28 days after Stage 1.				**DATE:**
ITEM			*Date:*	*Additional requirements/particulars/directions:*
31	**DS**	Defence Statement.		To include particulars of alibi; and requests for disclosure.
32	**WIT**	Final list of prosecution witnesses required to give live evidence; defence witnesses and interpreter requirements.		To be submitted in the Standard Witness Table with time estimates.
33	**SM**	Special measures application for defendant or defence witnesses.		Any reply from prosecution or other party to be served within 14 days.
34	**ABE**	List of editing requests or objections to ABE interview recording.		
35	**IV**	List of editing requests for the Defendant's ROTI (if any).		
36	**BC**	Response to prosecution bad character Notice(s) - CrimPR 21.		
37	**HSY**	Response to prosecution hearsay application(s) – CrimPR 20.		
38	**SM**	Response to prosecution special measures application(s) - CrimPR 18.		
39	**EXP**	Defence expert evidence to be relied upon - CrimPR 19.		
40		Other:		
41		Other:		

STAGE 3 – UNLESS INDIVIDUAL DATES ARE PROVIDED IT IS ORDERED THAT THE PROSECUTION SHALL SERVE THE FOLLOWING BY: Ordinarily 14 or 28 days after Stage 2		**DATE:**
ITEM	*Date for Service*	*Additional requirements/particulars/directions:*

42	**DCL**	Further disclosure.		Items required to be disclosed under CPIA resulting from or requested by the Defence Statement.
43	**EVI**	Further evidence to be relied upon that could not be served by Stage 1.		
44	**FOR**	Full forensic science statements that could not be served by Stage 1.		Full statements will only be ordered if the defendant has identified what conclusion in a Streamlined Report is not admitted and what are the disputed issues concerning that conclusion – CrimPR 19.3
45	**EXP**	Expert medical evidence.		
46	**EXP**	Psychiatric evidence.		
47	**EXP**	Other (specify) expert evidence.		
48	**SAT**	Satellite/Live link application(s) CrimPD 18.23-24		
49	**TEL**	Cell site analysis.		
50	**INT**	Intermediary report(s) with draft specific Ground Rules if required. CrimPR 18 & 3.9(7)		For Witness:
51		Other:		
52		Other:		

STAGE 4 – UNLESS INDIVIDUAL DATES ARE GIVEN IT IS ORDERED THAT THE DEFENCE SHALL SERVE THE FOLLOWING BY: Ordinarily 14 or 28 days after Stage 3.				**DATE:**
		ITEM	*Date:*	*Additional requirements/particulars/directions:*
53	**DCL**	Complaint about prosecution non-disclosure		To comply with s.8 CPIA and CrimPR 15.5.
54	**DCL**	Application(s) for witness summons for Third Party Disclosure if the prosecution indicates at PTPH that it will not be pursuing any TPD issues OR any Defendant is dissatisfied with the outcome of prosecution enquiries.		To comply with CrimPR 17.5
55	**EXP**	Defence expert evidence to be relied upon that could not be served by Stage 2 - CrimPR 19		
56	**BC**	s.100 or 101 bad character of non-defendant application - CrimPR 21		Any reply from prosecution or other party to be served within 14 days
57	**SXB**	s.41 Evidence of sexual behaviour application - CrimPR 22		Any reply from prosecution or other party to be served within 14 days
58	**SM**	Response to prosecution intermediary Report(s) - CrimPR 18		
59	**INT**	Intermediary report for defendant or defence witnesses with draft Ground Rules		Any reply from prosecution or other party to be served within 14 days

FORM - PTPH NG 1

60	**SAT**	Satellite/Live link application(s) CrimPD 18.23-24		
61		Other:		
62		Other.		

ADDITIONAL ORDERS:		*Date:*
63		
64		

APPLICATION FOR A SPECIAL MEASURES DIRECTION

(Criminal Procedure Rules, rule 18.3 and 18.10)

Case details

Name of defendant:

Court:

Case reference number:

Charge(s):

<u>**How to use this form**</u>. This form includes notes to help you complete it. They explain when a witness may be eligible for the assistance of special measures.

1. Complete the box above and give the details required in the boxes below. You must complete Parts A and B in all cases, and Parts C to G as appropriate. If you use an electronic version of this form, the boxes will expand. If you use a paper version and need more space, you may attach extra sheets.

2. Sign and date the completed form.

3. Send a copy of the completed form to:

(a) the court, and

(b) each other party to the case.[1]

<u>**Notes**</u>:

1. You must send this form so as to reach the recipients within the time prescribed by Criminal Procedure Rule 18.3. The court may extend that time limit, **but if you are late you must explain why.**

2. A party who wants to make representations about this application must serve those representations under Criminal Procedure Rule 18.13 **not more than 14 days after service of this application.**

PART A: information about this application

A1. Do you want a hearing of this application ?

No ☐ **Yes** ☐ If yes, explain why.

A2. Is this application late ?

No ☐ **Yes** ☐ If yes, explain why.

A3. Have you applied for a special measures direction for this witness in this case before ?

No ☐ **Yes** ☐ If yes, give details and explain what has changed since then.

[1] In some circumstances, an applicant may omit information from the copy of this application that is served on another party: see Criminal Procedure Rule 18.12.

PART B: information about the witness

B1. Witness' details

Name of witness:

Date of birth:

B2. Explain how the witness is eligible for assistance.[2] Tick the category. If the witness is eligible because of **disability**, or **fear or distress**, give details and explain why the quality of the witness' evidence is likely to be diminished because of that.

- Youth ☐
- Disability ☐
- Fear or distress ☐
- Sexual offence ☐
- Weapons offence ☐

B3. Explain why special measures would be likely to improve the quality of the witness' evidence.

B4. Which measure(s) would be likely to maximise so far as practicable the quality of the witness' evidence ? Tick what you propose.

- Screening witness from defendant ☐
- Evidence by live link ☐ complete Part C
- Evidence in private ☐ complete Part D
- Removal of wigs and gowns ☐
- Video recorded interview as evidence in chief ☐ complete Part E
- Intermediary ☐ complete Part F
- Aids to communication ☐ complete Part G

B5. What has been done to help the witness express an informed opinion about special measures ? Care must be taken to explain to the witness (a) what is meant by special measures, (b) what measure(s) may be available, and (c) what they would involve for the witness.[3]

[2] See the notes for guidance at the end of this form.

[3] If the witness does not want a special measure, he or she should be asked to explain why. The witness should also be told that if he or she changes his or her mind as the trial approaches, a further application to the court can be made.

2

B6. What views has the witness expressed about:

(a) his or her eligibility ?

(b) whether special measures would be likely to improve the quality of his or her evidence ?

(c) the measure(s) that you propose ?

The views, concerns and requests expressed by the witness, or on his or her behalf, must be set out in detail.

PART C: evidence by live link[4]

C1. Do you want the witness to give evidence:

using the court's own live link ? ☐ or

from somewhere else ? ☐

Tick which you propose. If you want the witness to give evidence by live link from somewhere else, answer question C2.

C2. Explain why you want the witness to give evidence from somewhere else. Give the address from which you propose the witness should give evidence, unless you want the court to direct that the address need not be revealed.

C3. Who do you propose should accompany the witness while he or she gives evidence ? Give that person's name, if known, and relationship to the witness (if any).

C4. Why would that person be an appropriate companion for the witness ? Include the witness' own views.

[4] See the notes for guidance at the end of this form.

PART D: evidence in private[5]

Explain on what grounds you want the witness to give evidence in private.

PART E: video recorded interview as evidence in chief[6]

E1. When was the interview ? .... (date)

E2. Was the interview conducted through an intermediary ?[7]

No ☐ **Yes** ☐ If yes, complete Part F as well.

E3. Was any aid to communication used in conducting the interview ?

No ☐ **Yes** ☐ If yes, give details.

E4. How long is the full version of the recording ? .... (hours / minutes)

E5. Has an edited version been prepared for use in evidence ?

No ☐ **Yes** ☐

E6. When did you serve[8]**:**

(a) the full version ? .... (date)

(b) the edited version (if any) ? .... (date)

E7. Do you want the court's permission for the witness to give evidence in chief otherwise than by means of the recording ?

No ☐ **Yes** ☐ If yes, explain why.

---

[5] See the notes for guidance at the end of this form.

[6] See the notes for guidance at the end of this form. In some cases, the court must give a direction for this measure. By completing this part, the applicant indicates that the witness will be available to be cross-examined at trial.

[7] The court can give retrospective approval for the use of an intermediary in a video recorded interview. See Part F and the notes for guidance at the end of this form.

[8] A defendant need not serve a recording of defence evidence on the prosecution until the close of the prosecution case at trial.

PART F: intermediary[9]

F1. Describe the witness' communication needs, and the proposed arrangements for questioning the witness. Attach any relevant report, including an intermediary's assessment if available. 'Ground rules' for questioning must be discussed between the court, the advocates and the intermediary before the witness gives evidence, to establish (a) how questions should be put to help the witness understand them, and (b) how the proposed intermediary will alert the court if the witness has not understood, or needs a break.

F2. Is the proposed intermediary registered with the Ministry of Justice Intermediaries Registration Board ?

No ☐ **Yes** ☐

F3. Give the proposed intermediary's (a) name and (b) (if relevant) occupation, skills and professional qualifications.

F4. Is the intermediary known, or related, to the witness ?

No ☐ **Yes** ☐ If yes, give details.

F5. Has the intermediary been used in any other part of the investigation or pre-trial preparation ?

No ☐ **Yes** ☐ If yes, give details.

F6. Where a video recorded interview was conducted through an intermediary:

(a) was that intermediary the person named above ? Yes ☐ **No** ☐
If no, attach an additional Part F in respect of that intermediary, giving the details required by questions F2, F3, F4 and F5.

(b) did that intermediary make a declaration ?[10] **Yes** ☐ **No** ☐

[9] See the notes for guidance at the end of this form.
[10] The declaration required by Criminal Procedure Rule 18.7.

PART G: aids to communication

G1. What device is proposed as a communication aid ?

G2. Might the use of this device affect the conduct of the trial ?

No ☐ **Yes** ☐ If yes, give details.

PART H: supporting material

Have you included with this application any other material ?

No ☐ **Yes** ☐ If yes, list it here.

Signed: .... **[prosecutor]**
[defendant / defendant's solicitor]

Date: ....

Notes for Guidance

Part B: information about the witness
Under section 16 of the Youth Justice and Criminal Evidence Act 1999, a witness is eligible for the assistance of a special measures direction given under section 19 of that Act if—

(a) the witness is under 17 (under 18, when the Coroners and Justice Act 2009 comes into force); or

(b) the witness has—
(i) a mental disorder, or a significant impairment of intelligence and social functioning, or
(ii) a physical disability or disorder
and the court considers that the completeness, coherence and accuracy (the 'quality') of evidence given by the witness is likely to be diminished by reason of those circumstances.

Under section 17 of the 1999 Act, a witness is eligible for such assistance if—

(a) the court is satisfied that the quality of evidence given by the witness is likely to be diminished because of his or her fear or distress in connection with giving evidence, taking account particularly of—
(i) the circumstances of the offence,
(ii) the witness' age, social and cultural background, ethnic origins, domestic and employment circumstances, religious beliefs or political opinions,
(iii) any behaviour towards the witness on the part of the defendant, the defendant's family or associates, or any other potential defendant or witness, and
(iv) the witness' own views;

(b) the witness is the complainant in respect of a sexual offence, and has not declined such assistance; or

(c) (when the Coroners and Justice Act 2009 comes into force) the offence is one of a list of offences involving weapons, and the witness has not declined such assistance.

The statutory special measures are listed in question B4. It is important for the views of the witness to be set out fully. The 1999 Act requires the court to consider any views that he or she has expressed.

Part C: evidence by live link
'Live link' means a live television link or other arrangement by means of which, although the witness is outside the courtroom—

(a) the witness can see and hear the proceedings in the courtroom; and

(b) the judge, the magistrates and jury (as applicable), the parties' legal representatives, and any interpreter or other person appointed to assist the witness can see and hear the witness.

The witness may be in the court building or elsewhere. If elsewhere, the applicant may ask the court to direct that the address need not be revealed.

A live link direction may provide for a specified person to accompany the witness while the witness gives evidence. In deciding who that should be, the court must have regard to the witness' own views. When making the application, the applicant may not know the companion's name. In that case, give such details as are available and inform the court when the companion's name is known.

7

Part D: evidence in private
The court can direct this measure where—

(a) the case concerns a sexual offence; or

(b) there are reasonable grounds for believing that someone other than the defendant has tried, or will try, to intimidate the witness.

The court can exclude from the courtroom anyone except—

(a) the defendant;

(b) the parties' legal representatives; and

(c) any interpreter or other person appointed to assist the witness.

Where the court excludes press representatives, it must still allow one nominated representative to attend.

Part E: video recorded interview as evidence in chief
Under sections 21 and 22 of the Youth Justice and Criminal Evidence Act 1999, a 'child witness' is one who is under 17 (under 18, when the Coroners and Justice Act 2009 comes into force), and a 'qualifying witness' is one who was a child witness when interviewed. Under those sections, the 'primary rule' requires the court to give a special measures direction—

(a) for the evidence of a child witness or of a qualifying witness to be admitted—
(i) by means of a video recording of an interview with the witness, in the place of examination-in-chief, and
(ii) after that, by live link; or

(b) (when the Coroners and Justice Act 2009 comes into force) if one or both of those measures is not taken, for the witness while giving evidence to be screened from seeing the defendant.

The primary rule always applies unless—

(a) (when the Coroners and Justice Act 2009 comes into force) the witness does not want it to apply, and the court is satisfied that to omit a measure usually required by that rule would not diminish the quality of the witness' evidence; or

(b) the court is satisfied that to direct one of the measures usually required by that rule would not be likely to maximise so far as practicable the quality of the witness' evidence. (Until the Coroners and Justice Act 2009 comes into force, this exception does not apply in the case of some sexual and other offences.)

When the Coroners and Justice Act 2009 comes into force, under section 22A of the 1999 Act the Crown Court must, if asked, give a special measures direction for the evidence in chief of a witness who is the complainant of a sexual offence to be admitted by means of a video recording of an interview with the witness.

Part F: intermediary
Under section 29(6) of the Youth Justice and Criminal Evidence Act 1999, the court may approve the admission of a video recorded interview as evidence in chief of a witness who was interviewed through an intermediary. That intermediary must have made the declaration required by section 29(5) of the Act and Criminal Procedure Rule 18.7.

The court may give a special measures direction for the use of an intermediary at trial whether or not one took part in any interview, or in any other part of the investigation or pre-trial preparation.

Judicial Studies Board and Bar Council guidance requires that, before the witness gives evidence, the court, the advocates and the intermediary should discuss 'ground rules' for the conduct of the questioning.

NOTICE OF APPLICATION FOR COURT TO CONSIDER BAIL

(Criminal Procedure Rules, rule 14.7)

Case details

Name of defendant:

Address:

If the defendant is in custody, give prison and prison number, if known.

Court:

Case reference number:

Charge(s):

This is an application by [.... (name of defendant)**]**

[the prosecutor]

for the court to

- ☐ **grant bail**
- ☐ **withdraw bail**
- ☐ **vary a condition or conditions of bail**
  Which condition(s)?:
- ☐ **impose a condition or conditions of bail**

Use this form ONLY for an application about bail to the court dealing with your case, if notice is required under Criminal Procedure Rule 14.7. **Not every bail application need be in writing.** There is a different form for an application or appeal to the Crown Court after a bail decision by a magistrates' court.

If you want the court to grant bail with conditions to be supervised in another European Union member State, you MUST complete (i) this form and (ii) the draft order and draft certificate required by CrimPR 14.16(5). See the notes published with those forms.

1. Complete the boxes above and give the details required in the boxes below. If you use an electronic version of this form, the boxes will expand[1]. If you use a paper version and need more space, you may attach extra sheets.

2. Sign and date the completed form.

3. Send a copy of the completed form to:

(a) the court,

(b) each other party to the case, and

(c) any surety or proposed surety who this application will affect.

A party who opposes this application must let the applicant and the court know at once, and serve on them notice of the reasons for opposing it.

1) Previous bail decision(s). Give brief details of each relevant previous bail decision by the court (including the date), and the reasons which the court gave.

[1] Forms for use with the Rules are at: www.justice.gov.uk/courts/procedure-rules/criminal/formspage.

1

2) Reasons for this application. Explain:

(a) why the court should make the order for which you are applying.

(b) (if this is an application by a defendant) what further information or legal argument, if any, has become available since the most recent previous bail decision was made.

(c) (if this is an application by the prosecutor) what material information has become available since the most recent previous bail decision was made.

3) Proposed condition(s) of bail. If the court decides to impose or vary bail conditions, what condition(s) do you propose ? If the court decides to impose a condition of residence, what should that address be ?

4) I want the court to decide this application:

☐ **at a hearing already fixed.** Give the date:

If there is a court hearing already fixed at which you want the court to consider this application, you must send this form so as to reach the recipients **not less than 2 business days before that hearing.** The court may waive that time limit, **but if you are late you must explain why.**

☐ **at a hearing to be arranged.** If you want a hearing arranged, one will be fixed no later than:

(a) the second business day after this application is served, if it is an application to grant or withdraw bail; or

(b) the fifth business day after this application is served, if it is an application to vary or impose a condition of bail.

If you want an earlier hearing than that, you must explain why.

☐ **without a hearing.** The court can decide an application to vary a bail condition without a hearing if:

(a) the parties to the application agree, or

(b) (on an application by a defendant) there has been no objection to it within 5 business days of service.

Signed[2]: ....**[defendant / defendant's solicitor]**
[prosecutor]

Date: ....

[2] If you use an electronic version of this form, you may instead authenticate it electronically (e.g. by sending it from an email address recognisable to the recipient). See Criminal Procedure Rules, rule 5.3.

2

APPLICATION FOR A WITNESS TO GIVE EVIDENCE BY LIVE LINK

(NOT AS A SPECIAL MEASURES DIRECTION)

(Criminal Procedure Rules, rr. 18.3 and 18.24)

Case details

Name of defendant:

Court:

Case reference number:

Charge(s):

<u>**How to use this form**</u>

This form includes notes to help you complete it. This form is NOT for use where the applicant wants a special measures direction for a young or vulnerable witness under Criminal Procedure Rules 18.3 and 18.10.

1. Complete the box above and give the details required in the boxes below. You must complete Parts A and B in all cases, and Parts C to E as appropriate. If you use an electronic version of this form, the boxes will expand. If you use a paper version and need more space, you may attach extra sheets.

2. Sign and date the completed form.

3. Send a copy of the completed form to:

(a) the court, and

(b) each other party to the case.

<u>**Notes**</u>**:**

1. You must send this form so as to reach the recipients within the time prescribed by Criminal Procedure Rule 18.3. The court may extend that time limit, **but if you are late you must explain why.**

2. A party who wants to make representations about this application must serve those representations under Criminal Procedure Rule 18.26 **not more than 14 days after service of this application.**

PART A: information about this application

A1. Do you want a hearing of this application ?

No ☐ **Yes** ☐ If yes, explain why.

A2. Is this application late ?

No ☐ **Yes** ☐ If yes, explain why.

A3. Have you applied for a live link direction for this witness in this case before ?

No ☐ **Yes** ☐ If yes, give details and explain what has changed since then.

PART B: information about the witness

B1. Witness' details

Name of witness:

B2. Do you want the witness to give evidence by live link:

from outside the United Kingdom ? ☐ **or**

from outside the court building, but inside the UK ? ☐

Tick which you propose. If you want the witness to give evidence from *outside* the UK, answer the questions in Part C. If you want the witness to give evidence from somewhere *inside* the UK (but outside the court building), answer the questions in Part D.

B3. Do you want someone to accompany the witness while he or she gives evidence ?

No ☐ **Yes** ☐ If yes, give that person's name, if possible. Explain why it is appropriate for the witness to be accompanied.

B4. Will the witness need to examine any document or object while giving evidence ?

No ☐ **Yes** ☐ If yes, give details.

PART C: evidence by live link from *outside* the UK

C1. From where do you want the witness to give evidence ? Specify the country. If you do not want to give the address, explain why.

C2. Explain on what grounds you want the court to allow the witness to give evidence by live link[1].

[1] There are no statutory grounds. Applicants may find it helpful to consider the grounds relevant to Part D. See the notes for guidance at the end of this form.

2

PART D: evidence by live link from *inside* the UK

D1. From where do you want the witness to give evidence ? Specify the area. If you do not want to give the address, explain why.

D2. Explain why it would be in the interests of the efficient or effective administration of justice for the witness to give evidence by live link[2].

PART E: supporting material

Have you included with this application any other material ?

No ☐ **Yes** ☐ If yes, list it here.

Signed: .... **[prosecutor]**
[defendant / defendant's solicitor]

Date: ....

[2] See the notes for guidance at the end of this form.

3

Notes for Guidance

Evidence by live link

This form is NOT for use where the applicant wants a special measures direction for a young or vulnerable witness under Criminal Procedure Rules 18.3 and 18.10. See the form for use with those rules.

'Live link' means a live television link or other arrangement by means of which, although the witness is outside the courtroom—

(a) the witness can see and hear the proceedings in the courtroom; and

(b) the judge, the magistrates and jury (as applicable), the defendant, the parties' legal representatives, and any interpreter or other person appointed to assist the witness can see and hear the witness.

Under section 32 of the Criminal Justice Act 1988, the court can allow a witness who is *outside* the United Kingdom to give evidence by live link—

(a) in proceedings in a youth court, or on appeal from such proceedings; or

(b) at a trial in the Crown Court, or on appeal from such a trial.

The Act specifies no other criteria.

Under section 51 of the Criminal Justice Act 2003, the court can allow a witness who is *in* the United Kingdom, but outside the building in which the proceedings are held, to give evidence by live link if the court is satisfied that that is in the interests of the efficient or effective administration of justice.

The court must consider all the circumstances of the case and in particular—

(a) the availability of the witness;

(b) the need for the witness to attend in person;

(c) the importance of the witness' evidence to the proceedings;

(d) the views of the witness;

(e) the suitability of the facilities at the place where the witness would give evidence through a live link;

(f) whether a direction might tend to inhibit any party to the proceedings from effectively testing the witness' evidence.

If the court thinks it appropriate, a live link direction may provide for a specified person to accompany the witness while the witness gives evidence. In deciding whether to make such a direction, and who the companion should be, the court will have regard to the witness' own views. When making the application, the applicant may not know the proposed companion's name (for example, because it will be a member of the witness service not yet identified). In that case, give such details as are available and inform the court when the companion's name is known.

The applicant should give the address from which the witness will give evidence, unless there are reasons for asking the court to allow it to be withheld.

Arrangements for establishing a live link

Guidance produced by Her Majesty's Courts Service is available from the court.

APPLICATION FOR A WITNESS SUMMONS

(Criminal Procedure Rules, rr. 17.3 and 17.4.
This form is NOT for use where rule 17.5 (confidential information) applies.)

Case details

Name of defendant:

Court:

Court office address:

Court phone number:

Case reference number:

Charge(s):

THIS IS AN APPLICATION FOR AN ORDER THAT

.. (name of proposed witness)

must attend court to [give the evidence] [produce the documents or objects] described in this application.

<u>**How to use this form**</u>

This form is NOT for use where the applicant wants the witness to produce in evidence documents recording **confidential information about another person**.

The form includes notes to help you complete it. There are notes for guidance for the applicant **and for the witness** at the end of the form.

1. Complete the boxes above and Parts A, B, C and D below. If you use an electronic version of this form, the boxes will expand. If you use a paper version and need more space, you may attach extra sheets.

2. Sign and date the completed form.

3. Send a copy of the completed form to the court.
Unless the court otherwise directs, you do not need to send a copy to the proposed witness. But a witness who receives a copy of this application and who wants to make representations to the court must do so **as soon as possible after receiving it.** See the notes for guidance.

PART A: information about the applicant *(tick and delete as applicable)*

[I am] [I represent] the prosecutor ☐
the defendant ☐

Name: ....

Address: ....

Phone: ....

Fax: ....

Email: ....

1

PART B: information about the application

The witness can [give the following evidence] [produce the following documents or objects]:

The evidence is likely to be material to what is in issue in the case because:
(Explain why you think the evidence would be material. The court CANNOT order the witness to give or produce evidence unless you can show that it is likely to be material evidence.)

I have taken the following steps to obtain the witness' attendance, but the witness will not attend without a summons:
(Explain why it is in the interests of justice to issue a summons.)

I have made this application as soon as reasonably practicable because:
(Explain any delay.)

I have served this application on the proposed witness **No** ☐ **Yes** ☐

PART C: supporting material

Have you included with this application any other information ?
No ☐ **Yes** ☐ If yes, list it here.

PART D: declaration

The statements contained in this application are true to the best of my knowledge and belief. I make them knowing that if I have wilfully stated anything which I know to be false or do not believe to be true I may be liable to prosecution.

Signed: ....

[[for] prosecutor]
[defendant / defendant's solicitor]

Date: ....

2

Notes for Guidance

A. If you are the applicant

1. When to use this form

Unless the court otherwise directs, you do not have to use this form but it may help you to do so. See Criminal Procedure Rule 17.3(3).

If you want the court to issue a witness summons for the proposed witness to produce in evidence, or to give evidence about information contained in, a document that records **confidential information relating to another person** - for example, information recorded in notes kept by a social services authority, in a patient's health records, or in a pupil's school records – do NOT use this form. You **MUST** instead use the form of Application for a Witness Summons (Confidential Information Relating to Another Person). See Criminal Procedure Rule 17.5.

2. Letting the witness know about the application

Unless the court otherwise directs, you need only serve a copy of this application on the proposed witness if you wish. See Criminal Procedure Rule 17.4(2).

B. If you are the witness

This is an application for the court to order you to attend to give evidence in person in the case described at the beginning of the form. The applicant thinks you can give the material evidence described in Part B of this application. **You are encouraged to take legal advice.**

If a witness summons is issued, you can be arrested, and fined, imprisoned or both, for failure to obey.

1. Objecting to an application

You can ask the court not to issue a witness summons if

- you cannot give the evidence the applicant thinks you can
- you do not think it would be material evidence
- you think your duties or rights, or those of any other person (including that person's rights of confidentiality), outweigh the reasons for the application.

If any of these apply to you, you must contact the court office **as soon as possible**. You should explain your objection in writing and send copies to the court office and to the person who applied for the witness summons.

2. Applying to the court to withdraw a summons

If the court has already issued a witness summons and you did not know about the application, you can ask the court to withdraw the summons if

- you cannot give the evidence required of you
- you do not think it would be material evidence
- you think your duties or rights, or those of any other person (including that person's rights of confidentiality), outweigh the reasons for the application.

If any of these apply to you, you must apply to the court at once. Contact the court office **urgently**. See Criminal Procedure Rule 17.7.

In a Crown Court case, if the court withdraws the summons it may order the person who applied for it to pay your legal costs. See Criminal Procedure Rule 45.7.

APPENDIX B

IN THE CROWN COURT SITTING...... Indictment No: ....

BETWEEN:

REGINA

-v-

[Name of defendant]

TEMPLATE ADVICE ON THE INSTRUCTION OF A FORENSIC PSYCHOLOGIST AND INTERMEDIARY

1 I am instructed to advise on the merits of instructing a forensic psychologist to examine and prepare a report on XXXXX with respect to his intellectual ability/cognitive function and the impact that his functioning has on his ability to stand trial and to engage with the trial process. For the reasons set out below, I advise that an expert should be instructed forthwith to prepare such a report, and that the representation order ought properly to be extended for this to be done. Furthermore, I advise that the psychologist should consider whether an assessment by an intermediary is necessary in this case and if the psychologist advises that this is necessary in my opinion funding also should properly be extended for this assessment and report. In my opinion it is very likely that both the assessment of the psychologist and the assessment of the intermediary will be necessary in this case.

2 XXXXX has been sent for trial to the Crown Court on XXXXX; at this hearing the Judge permitted the defendant not to be arranged having heard submissions from his counsel that a report was going to be sort from a psychologist to address the defendant's cognitive function. The fact that the Judge approved this course of action is supportive of the need for the report and the funding to be extended.

3 This defendant faces a serious allegation and it is important that the defendant is properly and fully able to engage with the proceedings he faces so that he is fairly tried. These types of proceedings ....

4 [Details of the defendant where relevant: eg age, known diagnoses, inability to read and write]

5 Opinions of legal representatives: eg both the defendant's instructing solicitors and counsel have now both met with XXXXX and there is a consensus that there is a real need to have his cognitive functioning assessed fully and reported upon by the appropriate expert.

6 There is evidence in the papers to assist those representing XXXXX, eg intermediary at the police station, unable to understand questions etc.

7 The assessment of the defendant's cognitive function is something that can only be done by an appropriate expert, that being a forensic psychologist. This assessment is not something that the defendant's legal team can do on his behalf and, further, it is in my opinion fundamental to the interests of justice and the defendant being fairly tried, if he is able to be tried, that such an assessment is completed and the appropriate assistance is given for him to be able to appropriately engage in the proceedings.

8 Therefore, in my opinion a forensic psychologist should be instructed to assess the defendant's cognitive function. The psychologist should do a full assessment of the defendant's ability to engage with proceedings and what, if any, assistance he should be provided with/is required for him to engage in proceedings including addressing whether an assessment of an intermediary is necessary. As stated above in my opinion if the psychologist is of the view that the assessment of an intermediary is necessary then in my opinion funding should be extended to cover this without the need for a further advice from counsel.

9 In summary, in my opinion:

- A forensic psychologist should be instructed to fully assess the defendant;
- The first question for the psychologist will be whether the defendant, given his cognitive function, is fit to stand trial.
- If the defendant is fit to stand trial the psychologist is asked to address what assistance the defendant would require and explain the difficulties he will face at the trial when engaging in the trial process and what steps can assist with this.
- The assessment should include advising on the need for an intermediary to assess the defendant.
- If the psychologist advises that the defendant should be assessed by an intermediary then legal aid should be extended to cover this.

10 Any other relevant matters.

11 If I can be of any further assistance, do not hesitate to contact me.

IN THE CROWN COURT SITTING AT..... Indictment number

BETWEEN:

REGINA

-V-

[Defendant's name]

---

s. 41 Application

---

1 This is an application on behalf of the defence under s. 41 YJCEA to adduce evidence of and ask the complainant XXXXX about sexual behaviour other than that in the offences alleged.

2 This application will be expanded upon orally – in summary the defence apply to adduce the matters set out below. The questions the defence seek to ask are set out also.

1) General sexual behaviour:

a) Topic areas

Set out the matters sought to be adduced

b) The questions

The defence would seek to ask the following questions of XXXXX

Set out the questions

c) Issue in the case this goes to

Set out the issues these matters go to

Eg

- The date when the sexual activity with the defendant commenced
- Credibility of the defendant's account

2) Specific sexual behaviour not relating to the defendant:

a) Topic areas

Set out the matters sought to be adduced

b) The questions

The defence would seek to ask the following questions of XXXXX

Set out the questions

c) Issue in the case this goes to

Set out the issues these matters go to

3) Other/relevant intercourse/sexual activity between the complainant and the defendant

a) Topic areas

Set out the matters sought to be adduced

b) The questions

The defence would seek to ask the following questions of XXXXX

Set out the questions

c) Issue in the case this goes to

Set out the issues this goes to

General submissions

1 It is submitted that the matters sought to be relied upon have been limited to only the essential matters and the defence are not seeking to go into unnecessary detail.

2 It is submitted that under s. 41 (2)(b) *refusal to permit the defence to adduce the above maters might have the result of rendering unsafe a conclusion of the jury on any relevant issue in the case.* In particular it is submitted that it is essential for the Jury to have all the relevant information that assists in identifying....................

3 It is submitted that under s. 41(3) the evidence and the questions as set out above relate to relevant issues in the case, as set out under each section and that these do not solely relate to consent. [Where relevant..... Although the matters do have an impact upon the issue of consent, they in the main go to the defendant's belief that the complainant was consenting in a sexual relationship with him and therefore as defined under s. 42 are not excluded re s. 41(3) which does not include any issue as to the belief of the accused that the complainant so consented.]

APPENDIX C

YOUTH JUSTICE AND CRIMINAL EVIDENCE ACT 1999

(1999 Chapter 23)

Part II
Giving of evidence or information for purposes of criminal proceedings

Chapter I
Special measures directions in case of vulnerable and intimidated witnesses

Preliminary

16 Witnesses eligible for assistance on grounds of age or incapacity.

(1) For the purposes of this Chapter a witness in criminal proceedings (other than the accused) is eligible for assistance by virtue of this section—

(a) if under the age of [18][1] at the time of the hearing; or

(b) if the court considers that the quality of evidence given by the witness is likely to be diminished by reason of any circumstances falling within subsection (2).

(2) The circumstances falling within this subsection are—

(a) that the witness—

(i) suffers from mental disorder within the meaning of the Mental Health Act 1983, or

(ii) otherwise has a significant impairment of intelligence and social functioning;

(b) that the witness has a physical disability or is suffering from a physical disorder.

(3) In subsection (1)(a) 'the time of the hearing', in relation to a witness, means the time when it falls to the court to make a determination for the purposes of section 19(2) in relation to the witness.

(4) In determining whether a witness falls within subsection (1)(b) the court must consider any views expressed by the witness.

(5) In this Chapter references to the quality of a witness's evidence are to its quality in terms of completeness, coherence and accuracy; and for this purpose

'coherence' refers to a witness's ability in giving evidence to give answers which address the questions put to the witness and can be understood both individually and collectively.

Amendment

1 Substituted by the Coroners and Justice Act 2009, s 98(1), (2).

17 Witnesses eligible for assistance on grounds of fear or distress about testifying.

(1) For the purposes of this Chapter a witness in criminal proceedings (other than the accused) is eligible for assistance by virtue of this subsection if the court is satisfied that the quality of evidence given by the witness is likely to be diminished by reason of fear or distress on the part of the witness in connection with testifying in the proceedings.

(2) In determining whether a witness falls within subsection (1) the court must take into account, in particular—

(a) the nature and alleged circumstances of the offence to which the proceedings relate;

(b) the age of the witness;

(c) such of the following matters as appear to the court to be relevant, namely—

(i) the social and cultural background and ethnic origins of the witness,

(ii) the domestic and employment circumstances of the witness, and

(iii) any religious beliefs or political opinions of the witness;

(d) any behaviour towards the witness on the part of—

(i) the accused,

(ii) members of the family or associates of the accused, or

(iii) any other person who is likely to be an accused or a witness in the proceedings.

(3) In determining that question the court must in addition consider any views expressed by the witness.

(4) Where the complainant in respect of a sexual offence [or an offence under [section 1 or 2 of the Modern Slavery Act 2015][1]][2] is a witness in proceedings relating to that offence (or to that offence and any other offences), the witness is eligible for assistance in relation to those proceedings by virtue of this subsection unless the witness has informed the court of the witness' wish not to be so eligible by virtue of this subsection.

[(5) A witness in proceedings relating to a relevant offence (or to a relevant offence and any other offences) is eligible for assistance in relation to those proceedings by virtue of this subsection unless the witness has informed the court of the witness's wish not to be so eligible by virtue of this subsection.

(6) For the purposes of subsection (5) an offence is a relevant offence if it is an offence described in Schedule 1A.

(7) The Secretary of State may by order amend Schedule 1A.][3]

Amendments

1 Substituted by the Modern Slavery Act 2015, s 46(1), (2).

2 Inserted by the Trafficking People for Exploitation Regulations 2013, SI 2013/554, reg 5, Schedule, paras 1, 2.

3 Inserted by the Coroners and Justice Act 2009, s 99(1), (2).

18 Special measures available to eligible witnesses

(1) For the purposes of this Chapter—

(a) the provision which may be made by a special measures direction by virtue of each of sections 23 to 30 is a special measure available in relation to a witness eligible for assistance by virtue of section 16; and

(b) the provision which may be made by such a direction by virtue of each of sections 23 to 28 is a special measure available in relation to a witness eligible for assistance by virtue of section 17;

but this subsection has effect subject to subsection (2).

(2) Where (apart from this subsection) a special measure would, in accordance with subsection (1)(a) or (b), be available in relation to a witness in any proceedings, it shall not be taken by a court to be available in relation to the witness unless—

(a) the court has been notified by the Secretary of State that relevant arrangements may be made available in the area in which it appears to the court that the proceedings will take place, and

(b) the notice has not been withdrawn.

(3) In subsection (2) 'relevant arrangements' means arrangements for implementing the measure in question which cover the witness and the proceedings in question.

(4) The withdrawal of a notice under that subsection relating to a special measure shall not affect the availability of that measure in relation to a witness if a special measures direction providing for that measure to apply to the witness's evidence has been made by the court before the notice is withdrawn.

(5) The Secretary of State may by order make such amendments of this Chapter as he considers appropriate for altering the special measures which, in accordance with subsection (1)(a) or (b), are available in relation to a witness eligible for assistance by virtue of section 16 or (as the case may be) section 17, whether—

(a) by modifying the provisions relating to any measure for the time being available in relation to such a witness,

(b) by the addition—

  (i) (with or without modifications) of any measure which is for the time being available in relation to a witness eligible for assistance by virtue of the other of those sections, or

  (ii) of any new measure, or

(c) by the removal of any measure.

Special measures directions

19 Special measures direction relating to eligible witness.

(1) This section applies where in any criminal proceedings—

(a) a party to the proceedings makes an application for the court to give a direction under this section in relation to a witness in the proceedings other than the accused, or

(b) the court of its own motion raises the issue whether such a direction should be given.

(2) Where the court determines that the witness is eligible for assistance by virtue of section 16 or 17, the court must then—

(a) determine whether any of the special measures available in relation to the witness (or any combination of them) would, in its opinion, be likely to improve the quality of evidence given by the witness; and

(b) if so—

  (i) determine which of those measures (or combination of them) would, in its opinion, be likely to maximise so far as practicable the quality of such evidence; and

  (ii) give a direction under this section providing for the measure or measures so determined to apply to evidence given by the witness.

(3) In determining for the purposes of this Chapter whether any special measure or measures would or would not be likely to improve, or to maximise so far as practicable, the quality of evidence given by the witness, the court must consider all the circumstances of the case, including in particular—

(a) any views expressed by the witness; and

(b) whether the measure or measures might tend to inhibit such evidence being effectively tested by a party to the proceedings.

(4) A special measures direction must specify particulars of the provision made by the direction in respect of each special measure which is to apply to the witness's evidence.

(5) In this Chapter 'special measures direction' means a direction under this section.

(6) Nothing in this Chapter is to be regarded as affecting any power of a court to make an order or give leave of any description (in the exercise of its inherent jurisdiction or otherwise)—

(a) in relation to a witness who is not an eligible witness, or

(b) in relation to an eligible witness where (as, for example, in a case where a foreign language interpreter is to be provided) the order is made or the leave is given otherwise than by reason of the fact that the witness is an eligible witness.

20 Further provisions about directions: general.

(1) Subject to subsection (2) and section 21(8), a special measures direction has binding effect from the time it is made until the proceedings for the purposes of which it is made are either—

(a) determined (by acquittal, conviction or otherwise), or

(b) abandoned,

in relation to the accused or (if there is more than one) in relation to each of the accused.

(2) The court may discharge or vary (or further vary) a special measures direction if it appears to the court to be in the interests of justice to do so, and may do so either—

(a) on an application made by a party to the proceedings, if there has been a material change of circumstances since the relevant time, or

(b) of its own motion.

(3) In subsection (2) 'the relevant time' means —

(a) the time when the direction was given, or

(b) if a previous application has been made under that subsection, the time when the application (or last application) was made.

(4) Nothing in section 24(2) and (3), 27(4) to (7) or 28(4) to (6) is to be regarded as affecting the power of the court to vary or discharge a special measures direction under subsection (2).

(5) The court must state in open court its reasons for—

(a) giving or varying,

(b) refusing an application for, or for the variation or discharge of, or

(c) discharging,

a special measures direction and, if it is a magistrates' court, must cause them to be entered in the register of its proceedings.

(6) [Criminal Procedure Rules][1] may make provision—

(a) for uncontested applications to be determined by the court without a hearing;

(b) for preventing the renewal of an unsuccessful application for a special measures direction except where there has been a material change of circumstances;

(c) for expert evidence to be given in connection with an application for, or for varying or discharging, such a direction;

(d) for the manner in which confidential or sensitive information is to be treated in connection with such an application and in particular as to its being disclosed to, or withheld from, a party to the proceedings.

Amendment

1 Substituted by the Courts Act 2003, s 109(1), Sch 8, para 384(a).

21 Special provisions relating to child witnesses.

(1) For the purposes of this section—

(a) a witness in criminal proceedings is a 'child witness' if he is an eligible witness by reason of section 16(1)(a) (whether or not he is an eligible witness by reason of any other provision of section 16 or 17);

(b) ...[1]; and

(c) a 'relevant recording', in relation to a child witness, is a video recording of an interview of the witness made with a view to its admission as evidence in chief of the witness.

(2) Where the court, in making a determination for the purposes of section 19(2), determines that a witness in criminal proceedings is a child witness, the court must—

(a) first have regard to subsections (3) to [(4C)][2] below; and

(b) then have regard to section 19(2);

and for the purposes of section 19(2), as it then applies to the witness, any special measures required to be applied in relation to him by virtue of this section shall be treated as if they were measures determined by the court, pursuant to section 19(2)(a) and (b)(i), to be ones that (whether on their own or with any other special measures) would be likely to maximise, so far as practicable, the quality of his evidence.

(3) The primary rule in the case of a child witness is that the court must give a special measures direction in relation to the witness which complies with the following requirements—

(a) it must provide for any relevant recording to be admitted under section 27 (video recorded evidence in chief); and

(b) it must provide for any evidence given by the witness in the proceedings which is not given by means of a video recording (whether in chief or otherwise) to be given by means of a live link in accordance with section 24.

(4) The primary rule is subject to the following limitations—

(a) the requirement contained in subsection (3)(a) or (b) has effect subject to the availability (within the meaning of section 18(2)) of the special measure in question in relation to the witness;

(b) the requirement contained in subsection (3)(a) also has effect subject to section 27(2); ...[1]

[(ba) if the witness informs the court of the witness's wish that the rule should not apply or should apply only in part, the rule does not apply to the extent that the court is satisfied that not complying with the rule would not diminish the quality of the witness's evidence; and][3]

(c) the rule does not apply to the extent that the court is satisfied that compliance with it would not be likely to maximise the quality of the witness's evidence so far as practicable (whether because the application to that evidence of one or more other special measures available in relation to the witness would have that result or for any other reason).

[(4A) Where as a consequence of all or part of the primary rule being disapplied under subsection (4)(ba) a witness's evidence or any part of it would fall to be given as testimony in court, the court must give a special measures direction making such provision as is described in section 23 for the evidence or that part of it.

(4B) The requirement in subsection (4A) is subject to the following limitations—

(a) if the witness informs the court of the witness's wish that the requirement in subsection (4A) should not apply, the requirement does not apply to the extent that the court is satisfied that not complying with it would not diminish the quality of the witness's evidence; and

(b) the requirement does not apply to the extent that the court is satisfied that making such a provision would not be likely to maximise the quality of the witness's evidence so far as practicable (whether because the application to that evidence of one or more other special measures available in relation to the witness would have that result or for any other reason).][3]

[(4C) In making a decision under subsection (4)(ba) or (4B)(a), the court must take into account the following factors (and any others it considers relevant)—

(a) the age and maturity of the witness;

(b) the ability of the witness to understand the consequences of giving evidence otherwise than in accordance with the requirements in subsection (3) or (as the case may be) in accordance with the requirement in subsection (4A);

(c) the relationship (if any) between the witness and the accused;

(d) the witness's social and cultural background and ethnic origins;

(e) the nature and alleged circumstances of the offence to which the proceedings relate.][3]

(5) ...[1]

(6) ...[1]

(7) ...[1]

(8) Where a special measures direction is given in relation to a child witness who is an eligible witness by reason only of section 16(1)(a), then—

(a) subject to subsection (9) below, and

(b) except where the witness has already begun to give evidence in the proceedings,

the direction shall cease to have effect at the time when the witness attains the age of [18][4].

(9) Where a special measures direction is given in relation to a child witness who is an eligible witness by reason only of section 16(1)(a) and—

(a) the direction provides—

(i) for any relevant recording to be admitted under section 27 as evidence in chief of the witness, or

(ii) for the special measure available under section 28 to apply in relation to the witness, and

(b) if it provides for that special measure to so apply, the witness is still under the age of [18][4] when the video recording is made for the purposes of section 28,

then, so far as it provides as mentioned in paragraph (a)(i) or (ii) above, the direction shall continue to have effect in accordance with section 20(1) even though the witness subsequently attains that age.

Amendments

1 Repealed by the Coroners and Justice Act 2009, ss 100(1), (2), (4)(a), (7), 178, Sch 23, Pt 3.

2 Substituted by the Coroners and Justice Act 2009, s 100(1), (3).

3 Inserted by the Coroners and Justice Act 2009, s 100(1), (4)(b), (5), (6).

4 Substituted by the Coroners and Justice Act 2009, s 98(1), (3).

22 Extension of provisions of section 21 to certain witnesses over [18][1].

(1) For the purposes of this section—

(a) a witness in criminal proceedings (other than the accused) is a 'qualifying witness' if he—

(i) is not an eligible witness at the time of the hearing (as defined by section 16(3)), but

(ii) was under the age of [18][1] when a relevant recording was made;

(b) …[2]; [and]

(c) a 'relevant recording', in relation to a witness, is a video recording of an interview of the witness made with a view to its admission as evidence in chief of the witness.

[(2) Subsections (2) to (4) and (4C) of section 21, so far as relating to the giving of a direction complying with the requirement contained in section 21(3)(a), apply to a qualifying witness in respect of the relevant recording as they apply to a child witness (within the meaning of that section).][3]

Amendments

1 Substituted by the Coroners and Justice Act 2009, s 98(1), (4).

2 Repealed by the Coroners and Justice Act 2009, ss 100(1), (8)(a), 178, Sch 23, Pt 3.

3 Substituted by the Coroners and Justice Act 2009, s 100(1), (8)(b).

[22A Special provisions relating to sexual offences

(1) This section applies where in criminal proceedings relating to a sexual offence (or to a sexual offence and other offences) the complainant in respect of that offence is a witness in the proceedings.

(2) This section does not apply if the place of trial is a magistrates' court.

(3) This section does not apply if the complainant is an eligible witness by reason of section 16(1)(a) (whether or not the complainant is an eligible witness by reason of any other provision of section 16 or 17).

(4) If a party to the proceedings makes an application under section 19(1)(a) for a special measures direction in relation to the complainant, the party may request that the direction provide for any relevant recording to be admitted under section 27 (video recorded evidence in chief).

(5) Subsection (6) applies if—

(a) a party to the proceedings makes a request under subsection (4) with respect to the complainant, and

(b) the court determines for the purposes of section 19(2) that the complainant is eligible for assistance by virtue of section 16(1)(b) or 17.

(6) The court must—

(a) first have regard to subsections (7) to (9); and

(b) then have regard to section 19(2);

and for the purposes of section 19(2), as it then applies to the complainant, any special measure required to be applied in relation to the complainant by virtue of this section is to be treated as if it were a measure determined by the court, pursuant to section 19(2)(a) and (b)(i), to be one that (whether on its own or with any other special measures) would be likely to maximise, so far as practicable, the quality of the complainant's evidence.

(7) The court must give a special measures direction in relation to the complainant that provides for any relevant recording to be admitted under section 27.

(8) The requirement in subsection (7) has effect subject to section 27(2).

(9) The requirement in subsection (7) does not apply to the extent that the court is satisfied that compliance with it would not be likely to maximise the quality of the complainant's evidence so far as practicable (whether because the application to that evidence of one or more other special measures available in relation to the complainant would have that result or for any other reason).

(10) In this section 'relevant recording', in relation to a complainant, is a video recording of an interview of the complainant made with a view to its admission as the evidence in chief of the complainant.][1]

Amendment

1 Inserted by the Coroners and Justice Act 2009, s 101.

Special measures

23 Screening witness from accused.

(1) A special measures direction may provide for the witness, while giving testimony or being sworn in court, to be prevented by means of a screen or other arrangement from seeing the accused.

(2) But the screen or other arrangement must not prevent the witness from being able to see, and to be seen by—

(a) the judge or justices (or both) and the jury (if there is one);

(b) legal representatives acting in the proceedings; and

(c) any interpreter or other person appointed (in pursuance of the direction or otherwise) to assist the witness.

(3) Where two or more legal representatives are acting for a party to the proceedings, subsection (2)(b) is to be regarded as satisfied in relation to those representatives if the witness is able at all material times to see and be seen by at least one of them.

24 Evidence by live link.

(1) A special measures direction may provide for the witness to give evidence by means of a live link.

[(1A) Such a direction may also provide for a specified person to accompany the witness while the witness is giving evidence by live link.

(1B) In determining who may accompany the witness, the court must have regard to the wishes of the witness.][1]

(2) Where a direction provides for the witness to give evidence by means of a live link, the witness may not give evidence in any other way without the permission of the court.

(3) The court may give permission for the purposes of subsection (2) if it appears to the court to be in the interests of justice to do so, and may do so either—

(a) on an application by a party to the proceedings, if there has been a material change of circumstances since the relevant time, or

(b) of its own motion.

(4) In subsection (3) 'the relevant time' means —

(a) the time when the direction was given, or

(b) if a previous application has been made under that subsection, the time when the application (or last application) was made.

(5) ...[2]

(6) ...[2]

(7) ...[2]

(8) In this Chapter 'live link' means a live television link or other arrangement whereby a witness, while absent from the courtroom or other place where the proceedings are being held, is able to see and hear a person there and to be seen and heard by the persons specified in section 23(2)(a) to (c).

Amendments

1 Inserted by the Coroners and Justice Act 2009, s 102(1).

2 Repealed by the Courts Act 2003, s 109(3), Sch 10.

25 Evidence given in private.

(1) A special measures direction may provide for the exclusion from the court, during the giving of the witness's evidence, of persons of any description specified in the direction.

(2) The persons who may be so excluded do not include—

(a) the accused,

(b) legal representatives acting in the proceedings, or

(c) any interpreter or other person appointed (in pursuance of the direction or otherwise) to assist the witness.

(3) A special measures direction providing for representatives of news gathering or reporting organisations to be so excluded shall be expressed not to apply to one named person who—

(a) is a representative of such an organisation, and

(b) has been nominated for the purpose by one or more such organisations,

unless it appears to the court that no such nomination has been made.

(4) A special measures direction may only provide for the exclusion of persons under this section where—

(a) the proceedings relate to a sexual offence [or an offence under [section 1 or 2 of the Modern Slavery Act 2015][1]][2]; or

(b) it appears to the court that there are reasonable grounds for believing that any person other than the accused has sought, or will seek, to intimidate the witness in connection with testifying in the proceedings.

(5) Any proceedings from which persons are excluded under this section (whether or not those persons include representatives of news gathering or reporting organisations) shall nevertheless be taken to be held in public for the purposes of any privilege or exemption from liability available in respect of fair, accurate and contemporaneous reports of legal proceedings held in public.

Amendments

1 Substituted by the Modern Slavery Act 2015, s 46(1), (3).

2 Inserted by the Trafficking People for Exploitation Regulations 2013, SI 2013/554, reg 5, Schedule, paras 1, 3.

26 Removal of wigs and gowns.

A special measures direction may provide for the wearing of wigs or gowns to be dispensed with during the giving of the witness's evidence.

27 Video recorded evidence in chief.

(1) A special measures direction may provide for a video recording of an interview of the witness to be admitted as evidence in chief of the witness.

(2) A special measures direction may, however, not provide for a video recording, or a part of such a recording, to be admitted under this section if the court is of the opinion, having regard to all the circumstances of the case, that in the interests of justice the recording, or that part of it, should not be so admitted.

(3) In considering for the purposes of subsection (2) whether any part of a recording should not be admitted under this section, the court must consider whether any prejudice to the accused which might result from that part being so admitted is outweighed by the desirability of showing the whole, or substantially the whole, of the recorded interview.

(4) Where a special measures direction provides for a recording to be admitted under this section, the court may nevertheless subsequently direct that it is not to be so admitted if—

(a) it appears to the court that—

(i) the witness will not be available for cross-examination (whether conducted in the ordinary way or in accordance with any such direction), and

(ii) the parties to the proceedings have not agreed that there is no need for the witness to be so available; or

(b) any [Criminal Procedure Rules][1] requiring disclosure of the circumstances in which the recording was made have not been complied with to the satisfaction of the court.

(5) Where a recording is admitted under this section—

(a) the witness must be called by the party tendering it in evidence, unless—

(i) a special measures direction provides for the witness's evidence on cross-examination to be given [in any recording admissible under section 28][2], or

(ii) the parties to the proceedings have agreed as mentioned in subsection (4)(a)(ii); and

[(b) the witness may not without the permission of the court give evidence in chief otherwise than by means of the recording as to any matter which, in the opinion of the court, is dealt with in the witness's recorded testimony.][3]

(6) Where in accordance with subsection (2) a special measures direction provides for part only of a recording to be admitted under this section, references in subsections (4) and (5) to the recording or to the witness's recorded testimony are references to the part of the recording or testimony which is to be so admitted.

(7) The court may give permission for the purposes of [subsection (5)(b)][3] if it appears to the court to be in the interests of justice to do so, and may do so either—

(a) on an application by a party to the proceedings, …[4] or

(b) of its own motion.

(8) …[4]

(9) The court may, in giving permission for the purposes of [subsection (5)(b)][3], direct that the evidence in question is to be given by the witness by means of a live link …[5].

[(9A) If the court directs under subsection (9) that evidence is to be given by live link, it may also make such provision in that direction as it could make under section 24(1A) in a special measures direction.][6]

(10) ...[7]

(11) Nothing in this section affects the admissibility of any video recording which would be admissible apart from this section.

Amendments

1 Substituted by the Courts Act 2003, s 109(1), Sch 8, para 384(b).

2 Substituted by the Coroners and Justice Act 2009, s 177(1), Sch 21, para 73.

3 Substituted by the Coroners and Justice Act 2009, s 103(1), (2), (3)(a), (5).

4 Repealed by the Coroners and Justice Act 2009, ss 103(1), (3)(b), (4), 178, Sch 23, Pt 3.

5 Repealed by the Coroners and Justice Act 2009, s 178, Sch 23, Pt 3.

6 Inserted by the Coroners and Justice Act 2009, s 102(2).

7 Repealed by the Criminal Justice Act 2003, s 332, Sch 37, Pt 4.

28 Video recorded cross-examination or re-examination.

(1) Where a special measures direction provides for a video recording to be admitted under section 27 as evidence in chief of the witness, the direction may also provide—

(a) for any cross-examination of the witness, and any re-examination, to be recorded by means of a video recording; and

(b) for such a recording to be admitted, so far as it relates to any such cross-examination or re-examination, as evidence of the witness under cross-examination or on re-examination, as the case may be.

(2) Such a recording must be made in the presence of such persons as [Criminal Procedure Rules][1] or the direction may provide and in the absence of the accused, but in circumstances in which—

(a) the judge or justices (or both) and legal representatives acting in the proceedings are able to see and hear the examination of the witness and to communicate with the persons in whose presence the recording is being made, and

(b) the accused is able to see and hear any such examination and to communicate with any legal representative acting for him.

(3) Where two or more legal representatives are acting for a party to the proceedings, subsection (2)(a) and (b) are to be regarded as satisfied in relation to those representatives if at all material times they are satisfied in relation to at least one of them.

(4) Where a special measures direction provides for a recording to be admitted under this section, the court may nevertheless subsequently direct that it is not to be so admitted if any requirement of subsection (2) or [Criminal Procedure Rules][1] or the direction has not been complied with to the satisfaction of the court.

(5) Where in pursuance of subsection (1) a recording has been made of any examination of the witness, the witness may not be subsequently cross-examined or re-examined in respect of any evidence given by the witness in the proceedings (whether in any recording admissible under section 27 or this section or otherwise than in such a recording) unless the court gives a further special measures direction making such provision as is mentioned in subsection (1)(a) and (b) in relation to any subsequent cross-examination, and re-examination, of the witness.

(6) The court may only give such a further direction if it appears to the court—

(a) that the proposed cross-examination is sought by a party to the proceedings as a result of that party having become aware, since the time when the original recording was made in pursuance of subsection (1), of a matter which that party could not with reasonable diligence have ascertained by then, or

(b) that for any other reason it is in the interests of justice to give the further direction.

(7) Nothing in this section shall be read as applying in relation to any cross-examination of the witness by the accused in person (in a case where the accused is to be able to conduct any such cross-examination).

Amendments

1 Substituted by the Courts Act 2003, s 109(1), Sch 8, para 384(c).

29 Examination of witness through intermediary.

(1) A special measures direction may provide for any examination of the witness (however and wherever conducted) to be conducted through an interpreter or other person approved by the court for the purposes of this section ('an intermediary').

(2) The function of an intermediary is to communicate—

(a) to the witness, questions put to the witness, and

(b) to any person asking such questions, the answers given by the witness in reply to them,

and to explain such questions or answers so far as necessary to enable them to be understood by the witness or person in question.

(3) Any examination of the witness in pursuance of subsection (1) must take place in the presence of such persons as [Criminal Procedure Rules][1] or the direction may provide, but in circumstances in which—

(a) the judge or justices (or both) and legal representatives acting in the proceedings are able to see and hear the examination of the witness and to communicate with the intermediary, and

(b) (except in the case of a video recorded examination) the jury (if there is one) are able to see and hear the examination of the witness.

(4) Where two or more legal representatives are acting for a party to the proceedings, subsection (3)(a) is to be regarded as satisfied in relation to those representatives if at all material times it is satisfied in relation to at least one of them.

(5) A person may not act as an intermediary in a particular case except after making a declaration, in such form as may be prescribed by [Criminal Procedure Rules][1], that he will faithfully perform his function as intermediary.

(6) Subsection (1) does not apply to an interview of the witness which is recorded by means of a video recording with a view to its admission as evidence in chief of the witness; but a special measures direction may provide for such a recording to be admitted under section 27 if the interview was conducted through an intermediary and—

(a) that person complied with subsection (5) before the interview began, and

(b) the court's approval for the purposes of this section is given before the direction is given.

(7) Section 1 of the Perjury Act 1911 (perjury) shall apply in relation to a person acting as an intermediary as it applies in relation to a person lawfully sworn as an interpreter in a judicial proceeding; and for this purpose, where a person acts as an intermediary in any proceeding which is not a judicial proceeding for the purposes of that section, that proceeding shall be taken to be part of the judicial proceeding in which the witness's evidence is given.

Amendments

1 Substituted by the Courts Act 2003, s 109(1), Sch 8, para 384(d).

30 Aids to communication.

A special measures direction may provide for the witness, while giving evidence (whether by testimony in court or otherwise), to be provided with such device as the court considers appropriate with a view to enabling questions or answers to be communicated to or by the witness despite any disability or disorder or other impairment which the witness has or suffers from.

Supplementary

31 Status of evidence given under Chapter I.

(1) Subsections (2) to (4) apply to a statement made by a witness in criminal proceedings which, in accordance with a special measures direction, is not made by the witness in direct oral testimony in court but forms part of the witness's evidence in those proceedings.

(2) The statement shall be treated as if made by the witness in direct oral testimony in court; and accordingly—

(a) it is admissible evidence of any fact of which such testimony from the witness would be admissible;

(b) it is not capable of corroborating any other evidence given by the witness.

(3) Subsection (2) applies to a statement admitted under section 27 or 28 which is not made by the witness on oath even though it would have been required to be made on oath if made by the witness in direct oral testimony in court.

(4) In estimating the weight (if any) to be attached to the statement, the court must have regard to all the circumstances from which an inference can reasonably be drawn (as to the accuracy of the statement or otherwise).

(5) Nothing in this Chapter (apart from subsection (3)) affects the operation of any rule of law relating to evidence in criminal proceedings.

(6) Where any statement made by a person on oath in any proceeding which is not a judicial proceeding for the purposes of section 1 of the Perjury Act 1911 (perjury) is received in evidence in pursuance of a special measures direction, that proceeding shall be taken for the purposes of that section to be part of the judicial proceeding in which the statement is so received in evidence.

(7) Where in any proceeding which is not a judicial proceeding for the purposes of that Act—

(a) a person wilfully makes a false statement otherwise than on oath which is subsequently received in evidence in pursuance of a special measures direction, and

(b) the statement is made in such circumstances that had it been given on oath in any such judicial proceeding that person would have been guilty of perjury,

he shall be guilty of an offence and liable to any punishment which might be imposed on conviction of an offence under section 57(2) (giving of false unsworn evidence in criminal proceedings).

(8) In this section 'statement' includes any representation of fact, whether made in words or otherwise.

32 Warning to jury.

Where on a trial on indictment [with a jury][1] evidence has been given in accordance with a special measures direction, the judge must give the jury such warning (if any) as the judge considers necessary to ensure that the fact that the direction was given in relation to the witness does not prejudice the accused.

Amendment

1 Inserted by the Criminal Justice Act 2003, s 331, Sch 36, paras 74, 75.

33 Interpretation etc. of Chapter I.

(1) In this Chapter—

'eligible witness' means a witness eligible for assistance by virtue of section 16 or 17;

'live link' has the meaning given by section 24(8);

'quality', in relation to the evidence of a witness, shall be construed in accordance with section 16(5);

'special measures direction' means (in accordance with section 19(5)) a direction under section 19.

(2) In this Chapter references to the special measures available in relation to a witness shall be construed in accordance with section 18.

(3) In this Chapter references to a person being able to see or hear, or be seen or heard by, another person are to be read as not applying to the extent that either of them is unable to see or hear by reason of any impairment of eyesight or hearing.

(4) In the case of any proceedings in which there is more than one accused—

(a) any reference to the accused in sections 23 to 28 may be taken by a court, in connection with the giving of a special measures direction, as a reference to all or any of the accused, as the court may determine, and

(b) any such direction may be given on the basis of any such determination.

[(5) For the purposes of this Chapter as it applies in relation to a witness who is the complainant in respect of [a relevant offence][1], where the age of the witness is uncertain and there are reasons to believe that the witness is under the age of 18, that witness is presumed to be under the age of 18.

[(6) In subsection (5) 'relevant offence' means—

(a) a sexual offence;

(b) an offence under section 1 of the Protection of Children Act 1978;

(c) an offence under section 160 of the Criminal Justice Act 1988;

(d) an offence under [section 1 or 2 of the Modern Slavery Act 2015][2].][1]][3]

Amendments

1 Substituted by the Special Measures for Child Witnesses (Sexual Offences) Regulations 2013, SI 2013/2971, reg 2.

2 Substituted by the Modern Slavery Act 2015, s 46(1), (4).

3 Inserted by the Trafficking People for Exploitation Regulations 2013, SI 2013/554, reg 5, Schedule, paras 1, 4.

APPENDIX D

CRIMINAL PROVISIONS ON COSTS AND FUNDING SPECIFICALLY RELATING TO VULNERABLE PEOPLE

A full and detailed consideration of legal aid, costs, compensation etc is outside the scope of this handbook. However, set out below are some key areas with respect to costs and funding when considering vulnerable witnesses and defendants within the court system:

Criminal Costs and Funding

The Criminal Legal Aid Manual is a key source of information.

Applicants with mental health problems

With the exception of applicants with severe mental health problems, the applicant for legal aid must sign the form CRM14 eForm (which amalgamates the CRM14, CRM15 & CRM15C).

Criminal Legal Aid Manual, paras 3.5.6 and 3.5.7

> '3.5.6 Signing the form
> For audit purposes and with the exception of applicants with severe mental health problems, the applicant must sign the applicant declaration form in all cases.
> Even though there are some circumstances where a solicitor interviews a client via video link or from behind a screen, the applicant must still sign the applicant declaration form. For clients appearing via video link the applicant declaration form can be faxed to the applicant to sign.'

Para 3.5.7 provides details of who can sign the form in the alternative:

> 'The applicant declaration form may be signed by
> - The applicant's attorney or deputy appointed under the Mental Capacity Act 2005
> - The applicant's nearest relative or guardian

- A person acting as a Litigation friend
- Any other person who is acting in the applicant's best interest and who has sufficient knowledge of the applicant's financial affairs to be able to sign the declaration on the applicant's behalf'

It should be noted that the solicitor or any other member, employee or associate of the solicitor's firm cannot sign the form.

Expenses for witnesses attending court

The Prosecution of Offences Act 1985, s 19(3) permits the Lord Chancellor to make regulations authorising the payment out of central funds for a number of possible areas that may occur in a criminal case. These include witness expenses and also funding for the cross-examination of a witness where the defendant is not so permitted (see below). The full provision is set out below as it is relevant to a number of areas that may be relevant to vulnerable defendants and witnesses:

> **19** (3) The Lord Chancellor may by regulations make provision for the payment out of central funds, in such circumstances and in relation to such criminal proceedings as may be specified, of such sums as appear to the court to be reasonably necessary—
>
> (a) to compensate any witness in the proceedings and any other person who in the opinion of the court necessarily attends for the purpose of the proceedings otherwise than to give evidence, for the expense, trouble or loss of time properly incurred in or incidental to his attendance;
>
> (b) to cover the proper expenses of an interpreter who is required because of the accused's lack of English;
>
> (c) to compensate a duly qualified medical practitioner who—
>
> (i) makes a report otherwise than in writing for the purpose of section 11 of the Powers of Criminal Courts (Sentencing) Act 2000 (remand for medical examination); or
>
> (ii) makes a written report to a court in pursuance of a request within subsection (3B) below;
>
> for the expenses properly incurred in or incidental to his reporting to the court.
>
> (d) to cover the proper fee or costs of a person appointed by the Crown Court under section 4A of the Criminal Procedure (Insanity) Act 1964 to put the case for the defence.
>
> (e) to cover the proper fee or costs of a legal representative appointed under section 38(4) of the Youth Justice and Criminal Evidence Act 1999 (defence representation for purposes of cross-examination) and any expenses properly incurred in providing such a person with evidence or other material in connection with his appointment.

The Regulation of the Costs in Criminal Cases (General) Regulations 1986, SI 1986/1335 provide for the witnesses expenses to be paid out of central funds – Part V is entitled allowances to witnesses and regulation 16 states:

General

16 (1) Where, in any proceedings in a criminal cause or matter in a magistrates' court, the Crown Court, a Divisional Court of the Queen's Bench Division, the Court of Appeal or the House of Lords—

(a) a witness attends at the instance of the accused, a private prosecutor or the court; or

(b) an interpreter is required because of the accused's lack of English; or

(c) a medical practitioner makes a report otherwise than in writing,

the expenses properly incurred by that witness, interpreter or medical practitioner shall be allowed out of central funds in accordance with this Part of these Regulations, unless the court directs that the expenses are not to be allowed out of central funds.

Prosecution witnesses

Further, in relation to prosecution witnesses there are two key websites which assist practitioners with the in details asto expenses for prosecution witnesses these are:

https://www.cps.gov.uk/victims-witnesses
https://www.cps.gov.uk/legal-guidance/witness-expenses-and-allowances

Allowances and expenses payable to prosecution witnesses attending court are governed by Regulations made by the Attorney General (the Regulations) (The Crown Prosecution Service (Witnesses' etc. Allowances) Regulations 1985). There are four classes of witnesses:

(i) *ordinary* (defined as a witness to fact - a witness who is neither a professional nor expert and who gives evidence based on their first-hand knowledge of events relevant to the case);

(ii) *professional* (defined by The Crown Prosecution Service (Witnesses' etc Allowances) Regulations 1988 at section 3 as 'a witness practising as a member of the legal or medical profession or as an accountant, dentist or veterinary surgeon');

(iii) *expert* (defined as a witness whose level of specialised knowledge or skill in a particular field qualifies them to present their opinion about the facts of a case. An expert may give an opinion by virtue of education, training, certification, skills or experience); and

(iv) *interpreter*.

The CPS's website states that it is responsible for paying allowances and expenses to witnesses who are called to give evidence in prosecutions conducted by the CPS. This can include costs towards travel expenses, loss of earnings, meals and refreshments, and the cost of child care. The amount a witness can claim is set by the Attorney General and further information is available at https://www.cps.gov.uk/legal-guidance/witness-expenses-and-allowances. The CPS's website states that all correctly completed witness expense claims are paid within ten working days of receipt and that witnesses will be given a copy of the expenses form at court.

Post-trial

Compensation

Post-trial if there is a conviction then the court has the power to make a compensation order under the Powers of Criminal Courts (Sentencing) Act 2000, ss 130–134.

> **130 Compensation orders against convicted persons.**
>
> (1) A court by or before which a person is convicted of an offence, instead of or in addition to dealing with him in any other way, may, on application or otherwise, make an order (in this Act referred to as a "compensation order") requiring him—
>
> (a) to pay compensation for any personal injury, loss or damage resulting from that offence or any other offence which is taken into consideration by the court in determining sentence; or
>
> (b) to make payments for funeral expenses or bereavement in respect of a death resulting from any such offence, other than a death due to an accident arising out of the presence of a motor vehicle on a road;
>
> but this is subject to the following provisions of this section and to section 131 below.

(NB see the full statutory provisions for exceptions to the making of compensation orders.)

The general provision re compensation orders are:

- A compensation order is part of a sentence of the court.
- A victim does not have to apply for compensation for an order to be made.
- Save for child defendants, there is no statutory limit on the amount of compensation a court can order. For child defendants the maximum amount is £5,000.
- Compensation orders are not able to be used to 'buy' a person's way out of a sentence: *R v Inwood (Roland Joseph)* (1974) 60 Cr App R 70.

- They were introduced as a convenient and rapid means of avoiding the expense of resort to civil litigation when the criminal clearly has means which would enable compensation to be paid *R v Inwood (Roland Joseph)* (1974) 60 Cr App R 70
- Priority is given to compensation over a fine: Powers of Criminal Courts (Sentencing) Act 2000, s 130(12)

Restitution order

Criminal Courts also have the power to make restitution orders under the Powers of Criminal Courts (Sentencing) Act 2000, s 148.

APPENDIX E

KEY EXAMPLE DIRECTIONS FROM THE CROWN COURT COMPENDIUM

Defendant unfit to plead and/or stand trial

Directions from the Crown Court compendium

If the judge rules that D is unfit:

- Jury selection proceeds in the usual way save that D has no right of challenge.
- The jurors take an oath or affirm in a form requiring them to determine whether D did the act or made the omission charged as the offence, or is not guilty.
- As part of his introductory remarks, the judge should explain to the jury the nature of the proceedings, and that although D is not fit to be tried for the offence there is an important public interest in ascertaining whether or not he did the act or made the omission: see the Example below. 10. If, as is likely, D does not give evidence the judge should discuss with the advocates in the absence of the jury before closing speeches whether the jury should be directed that they may or must not draw an adverse inference: see Chapter 17–5.
- The summing up will be in the conventional form save that the jury is concerned only with whether D did the act or made the omission, and not with his state of mind. Care will be needed to identify those elements of the offence of which they jury must be sure: see paragraph 6 above.
- If D is being tried jointly with other defendants who are being tried conventionally, the differences between the issues arising and the verdicts available should be explained clearly to the jury.
- The verdict will be: (1) 'D did the act charged'; or (2) 'D made the omission charged'; or (3) 'Not Guilty'.

3–6 Special Measures

The YJCEA 1999, s 32 states:

Directions *from the* Crown Court compendium

- In respect of any special measures for witnesses the purpose of a direction is to explain what is to happen or has happened and to ensure that there is no prejudice to the defendant. This should be done before the evidence is presented and a short reminder of this should be given in the summing up.

- In all special measures cases an explanation should be given about the purpose of presenting evidence with special measures: to permit a witness who may be nervous about giving evidence in open court to give evidence without having to see/be seen by anyone other than those who need to see the witness give evidence (jury, advocates, judge) and to put the witness, so far as is possible, at ease.
- A transcript of an ABE interview should only be provided to the jury to enable them better to follow the evidence of the witness. If the interview is inaudible, the transcript must not be used as a substitute and the witness may have to give oral evidence at the trial.
- If the jury are provided with a transcript of an ABE interview, they should be told: (1) This is only so that they can more easily follow the interview. However, it is what they see and hear on the recording which is the evidence not what they read on the transcript. For this reason they must take care to watch the video as it is shown, so that they can assess the manner/demeanour of the witness when giving evidence. (2) [If appropriate:] The transcript will be/has been withdrawn after the playing of the recording because there is no transcript of the cross examination of the witness or any of the evidence of other witnesses and to avoid the danger of concentrating on the transcript, rather than on the evidence as a whole. (3) The transcript cannot be revisited and should not be requested during retirement.
- The transcript should never normally be retained by the jury after the witness has completed their evidence in chief. If, in an exceptional case it is suggested by one or more of the advocates or by the jury themselves that the jury should retain a transcript after the evidence in chief and/or that the recording should be re-played, the judge must hear submissions of the advocates and decide on the appropriate course. Should he permit either course, the judge must always ensure that the cross-examination and re-examination of the witness concerned are fully summed up, and direct the jury that they must base their verdict(s) on the evidence as a whole and must not be over-reliant on the transcript/recording. The case of R68 highlights how much care is called for if a jury are to be given access to transcripts. It is a decision that should never be made without very careful consideration of the relevant authorities and after discussion with the parties.

3–7 Intermediaries

Procedure and Directions

- At the PTPH/FCMH, orders should have been given concerning the involvement of an intermediary. These should include (1) the order appointing the intermediary; (2) the instructions to be given to the intermediary; (3) the date for filing the intermediary's report; (4) the date by which the advocates must file their questions with the intermediary and the Court; (5) arrangements for the advocates and intermediary to discuss the questions before the day of the GRH; (6) the date and time of the GRH; (7) an order that the intermediary must attend the GRH.

- If the intermediary is for the benefit of D: (1) If the intermediary is for D, the stage/s of the trial during which the intermediary should be present. (2) An agreed form of words will be required in which the jury are told about the difficulties D has and his need for an intermediary. (3) Care must be taken not to give to the jury any information which might later be relied on if D elects not to give evidence; and consideration must be given to a direction on the inferences that might be drawn in that event. (4) A neutral phrase, such as "communication difficulties", is appropriate if it is not possible to give any other detail of D's difficulties. (5) The presence of the intermediary sitting next to D in the dock should be explained to the jury as part of the "Introductory words": see Chapter 3–1 above.
- At the trial, before W/D gives evidence, the judge should explain to the jury the following: (1) The need for an intermediary: e.g. by identifying the problems arising from the age or other difficulties of W/D (2) The purpose of an intermediary: which is to assist in communication, among other things by helping advocates to ask questions in a way W/D can understand and/or assisting W/D to communicate his answers to the jury. (3) The intermediary is independent of the parties, is present only to assist communication and is not a witness and so is not permitted to give evidence. (4) The use of the intermediary must not affect the jury's assessment of the evidence of W/D and is no reflection on D or W. (5) If D elects to give evidence it may be appropriate at this point to give more detail of any difficulties D has, if those difficulties may affect the perception of the jury of his evidence. Before W/D gives evidence, the intermediary should be sworn or affirm in the presence of the jury.

3–8 Anonymous witnesses

- The jury will need careful direction to ensure that: (1) no unfair prejudice to the defendant is drawn from the use of such measures; and (2) the disadvantages faced by the defendant because of the inability to know the identity of the witness are highlighted. In Ellis v UK the European Court relied on the judge's careful directions to the jury as a counterbalancing factor to safeguard against an unfair trial when a witness gave evidence anonymously.

7–1 Child defendants including doli incapax

Directions

- The need for, and form of, any directions to the jury relating to D's age should be discussed with the advocates in the absence of the jury before closing speeches.
- Should a direction be thought appropriate, its exact terms will have to be tailored to the circumstances of the individual case. It will have to include an identification of the issue to which D's age is relevant and a direction that the jury.

10–5 Evidence of children and vulnerable witnesses

Directions at trial

- Any special measures, including the use of an intermediary, should be explained.
- Depending on the age of the child or the vulnerability of W, it may help the jury to explain how his level of understanding, regardless of intelligence, may be limited. This may be done before W gives evidence.
- It may also help the jury and fair to all parties to explain to the jury, before such a witness is cross examined, that the cross examination will not be conducted in the same way as it would have been if the witness had been an adult/ non–vulnerable adult.
- Any particular difficulties which have arisen in the course of the case should be addressed in a manner which is fair to both/all parties.
- Where offences are said to have occurred within the home, the jury should be alerted to the potential difficulties which a child may have perceived in reporting matters:
- Where grooming is alleged to have occurred, the concept of grooming and the potential difficulties of a witness' realisation and/or recollection of innocent attention becoming sexual should be explained.

INDEX

[*All references are to paragraph numbers.*]